# REVELATION
# AND THE CHURCH

## Vatican II in the Twenty-first Century

# REVELATION AND THE CHURCH

## Vatican II in the Twenty-first Century

Edited by Raymond A. Lucker
and William C. McDonough

ORBIS BOOKS

Maryknoll, New York 10545

Founded in 1970, Orbis Books endeavors to publish works that enlighten the mind, nourish the spirit, and challenge the conscience. The publishing arm of the Maryknoll Fathers and Brothers, Orbis seeks to explore the global dimensions of the Christian faith and mission, to invite dialogue with diverse cultures and religious traditions, and to serve the cause of reconciliation and peace. The books published reflect the views of their authors and do not represent the official position of the Maryknoll Society. To learn more about Maryknoll and Orbis Books, please visit our website at www.maryknoll.org.

Library of Congress Cataloging-in-Publication Data

Revelation and the Church : Vatican II in the twenty-first century /
edited by Raymond A. Lucker and William C. McDonough.
    p. cm.
Includes bibliographical references.
  ISBN 1-57075-479-9 (pbk.)
  1. Revelation. 2. Catholic Church—Doctrines. 3. Vatican Council
(2nd : 1962-1965) I. Lucker, Raymond A. II. McDonough, William C.
  BT127.3 .R48 2003
  230'.2—dc21
                         2002152128

# Contents

# Abbreviations used in this volume

This book cites sources parenthetically within the text of each article, and gives a full reference for those sources at the end of each article. That is true except in the case of biblical citations, which follow the English language *New Revised Standard Version,* except when an author makes her or his own translation from the biblical languages. Also, the following church texts will be referred to by abbreviation.

**Texts from Vatican II** (Except where specifically noted, English language citations from conciliar texts are from Austin Flannery, O.P., ed., *Vatican II: Constitutions, Decrees, Declarations*, a completely revised translation in inclusive language. Northport, N.Y.: Costello Publishing Company, 1996.)

*AG*  *Ad Gentes,* Decree on the Church's Missionary Activity, December 7, 1965

*CD*  *Christus Dominus,* Decree on the Pastoral Office of Bishops in the Church, October 28, 1965

*DH*  *Dignitatis Humanae,* Declaration on Religious Liberty, December 7, 1965

*DV*  *Dei Verbum,* Dogmatic Constitution on Divine Revelation, November 18, 1965

*GS*  *Gaudium et Spes,* Pastoral Constitution on the Church in the Modern World, December 7, 1965

*LG*  *Lumen Gentium,* Dogmatic Constitution on the Church, November 21, 1964

*NA*  *Nostra Aetate,* Declaration on the Relation of the Church to Non-Christian Religions, October 28, 1965

*OE*  *Orientalium Ecclesiarum,* Decree on the Catholic Eastern Churches, November 21, 1965

*SC*  *Sacrosanctum Concilium,* Constitution on the Sacred Liturgy, December 4, 1963

*UR*  *Unitatis Redintegratio,* Decree on Ecumenism, November 21, 1964

**Papal Encyclicals** (Unless specifically noted, English language citations from papal encyclicals are taken from Claudia Carlen, I.H.M., *The Papal Encyclicals,* volume three (1903–1939), volume four (1939–1958), and volume five (1958–1981). Raleigh, North Carolina: Mc-Grath Publishing Company, 1981. Citations of papal encyclicals issued since 1981 are taken from *The Encyclicals of John Paul II.* Ed. J. Michael Miller, C.S.B. Huntington, Ind.: Our Sunday Visitor Publishing Division, 1996.)

*CA*      John Paul II, *Centesimus Annus,* On the Hundreth Anniversary of *Rerum Novarum,* May 1, 1991

*CC*      Pius XI, *Casti Connubii,* On Christian Marriage, December 31, 1930

*DAS*     Pius XII, *Divino Afflante Spiritu,* On the Promotion of Biblical Studies, September 30, 1943

*EV*      John Paul II, *Evangelium Vitae,* On the Value and Inviolability of Human Life, March 25, 1995

*HV*      Paul VI, *Humanae Vitae,* On the Regulation of Birth, July 25, 1968

*MM*      John XXIII, *Mater et Magistra,* On Christianity and Social Progress, May 15, 1961

*OA*      Paul VI, *Octogesima Adveniens,* A Call to Action, May 14, 1971

*PP*      Paul VI, *Populorum Progressio,* On the Development of Peoples, March 27, 1967

*PT*      John XXIII, *Pacem in Terris,* On Establishing Universal Peace in Truth, Justice, Charity, and Liberty, April 11, 1963

*QA*      Pius XI, *Quadragesimo Anno,* On the Reconstruction of the Social Order, May 15, 1931

*RH*      John Paul II, *Redemptor Hominis,* On Redemption and the Dignity of the Human Race, March 4, 1979

*RN*      Leo XIII, *Rerum Novarum,* On the Condition of the Working Classes, May 15, 1891

*SRS*     John Paul II, *Sollicitudo Rei Socialis,* On Social Concern, December 30, 1987

*UUS*     John Paul II, *Ut Unum Sint,* On Commitment to Ecumenism, May 25, 1995

*VS*      John Paul II, *Veritatis Splendor,* Regarding Certain Fundamental Questions of the Christian Moral Life, August 6, 1993

## Bishop Raymond Lucker's Pastoral Letters

Lucker    Raymond A. Lucker, Bishop of the Diocese of New Ulm, Minnesota. *Prairie Views: Twenty-Five Years of Pastoral Letters.* Waite Park, Minn.: Park Press, Inc., 2000.

# Preface

Bishop Raymond Lucker died peacefully at Our Lady of Good Counsel Cancer Home in St. Paul, Minnesota, on September 19, 2001. He had moved into this hospice facility in early July of the same year, at the invitation of the Dominican Sisters who run it. Bishop Lucker had served as bishop of the Diocese of New Ulm, Minnesota, for twenty-five years, retiring only at the end of 2000. After moving into the priests' retirement residence in St. Paul, he started to plan a project. He wanted to write a book about faith. This present book is an attempt to bring Bishop Lucker's plan to fruition.

Here is how the present book came about. For four or five summers during the 1990s, Bishop Lucker taught a course on "Faith" at the College of St. Catherine. He was scheduled to teach that course again in the summer of 1999, but was diagnosed with the return of malignant melanoma late that spring. I was invited to teach the course in his place, though Bishop Lucker was well enough to come into one session of the course. He brought with him two informal lists he had been working on over the years: one list contained sixty-four particular church teachings that have changed through history, and the other contained twenty-two more teachings that might some day change. (Portions of both lists form an appendix to this volume.) Bishop Lucker planned to turn these lists—along with files and files of articles and his notes on them from magazines like *America* and *Commonweal* and *The Tablet* as well as from journals such as *Theological Studies*—into his book.

During that time Bishop Lucker told his friend and publisher Michael Leach about his dream. They had collaborated on *The People's Catechism: Catholic Faith for Adults* and often shared their enthusiasm for their faith in telephone conversations and at dinners with other friends at conferences (see Lucker, Brennan, and Leach, 1995). When Bishop Lucker's health began to fail, he asked Mike to recommend a writer to complete the book for him. Mike suggested that it would be best for the bishop to collaborate with a theologian of his choice nearby, and assured him that he would oversee the publication of the book just as the bishop wished.

In June, 2001, and knowing that he was dying, Bishop Lucker invited me to work with him on his book project. We met at least once weekly through the summer, mostly talking about the articles and his vision for the book. We taped the conversations, excerpts of which now form this book's introduction.

He asked me to take the files and annotated articles home and start reading them. One of the last articles he glossed is from the July 16-23, 2001 issue of *America* magazine. It is a brief essay by Monika Hellwig on Catholic higher education. Bishop Lucker circled and starred the following text:

> Did we lose some of the integrity and sharp definition of the 1950s? I think so . . . But it had to happen sooner or later; the sleepers had to wake up and deal as responsible people with the real world. They had to realize that risk and change are essential to growth and thus to human and Christian life . . . They were awakening to what the German theologian Romano Guardini (1885–1968), far in advance of his time, had called "prophetic obedience." (Hellwig, 24)

He liked the term "prophetic obedience," and wrote in the margins of Hellwig's article: "This is a good quote on the development of doctrine." Bishop Lucker stopped reading and annotating new articles sometime in the middle of August. In late August, he handed the project over to me "and to whoever wants to work with you on it." We stopped our book planning, but continued talking about faith and the church until a week before he died.

Before we stopped our collaboration, we decided to organize the book around the four great constitutions of the Council. He showed me a text he loved from Cardinal Suenens saying the documents of Vatican II are "like unopened buds awaiting the sun" (Suenens, cited by McBrien, 254). He told me: "The book should say that the Constitution on Divine Revelation is the most forgotten text of the Council. It says that God has been communicating to us 'in words and deeds' since the beginning of history (*DV* 2). It says that God has been reaching out in love toward all of us from the beginning, and that God wants some response from us."

This book attempts to communicate Bishop Lucker's faith in this understanding of revelation. Two events that have dominated the last year were unknown to Bishop Lucker at the end of his life. First, he did not know about the terrorist attacks of September 11, 2001, and responses to them. The attacks occurred a week before his death, but he was close enough to death to be spared knowing of their horror. He knew something of, and held strong beliefs about, war and peace. Pax Christi USA, the national Catholic peace movement, came to the cancer home late in the summer of 2001 to confer on Bishop Lucker its highest award, the "Ambassador of Peace" Award. Though he and I never discussed it, an essay on "peace and justifiable war" in Catholic thinking concludes this book.

The second dominant event of the last year is the crisis of authority in the church around sexual abuse by priests and responses to such abuse by bishops. No essay in this book focuses directly on the scandal, and I wish now I had known last year and talked with Bishop Lucker about his 1993 pastoral letter on sexual abuse. Almost ten years before the current crisis, he wrote in that letter:

> I would like to focus on one issue: public scandals by the clergy and others in the church, especially over the issue of sexual abuse of minors . . . I believe we are being forced to our knees, forced to recognize that we are not in charge, but rather God is in charge of the church . . . I believe this applies especially to bishops, who for so long have carried the trappings of feudal lords . . . It seems to me that we are being forced to recognize that we do not have much power, and that is all right. We are called to be ministers of the word, of the worship of God, and the service of others . . . I hope and pray that through the grace of God we will be able to respond to the present scandals in the church, reach out in love and healing to victims, reach out in forgiveness and reconciliation to perpetrators, and come before the Lord as a community of believers to recognize our need. (Lucker, 398–399)

In the year since Bishop Lucker died, we have encountered much that could make us "recognize our need." He believed that deeper awareness of Vatican II could help us all live with integrity in the face of our need, and he wanted to write a book demonstrating that. We have called this book *Revelation and the Church: Vatican II in the Twenty-first Cen-*

*tury.* The book might also have been subtitled *The Legacy of Raymond A. Lucker.* This man went off to Rome as a priest-graduate student in 1964, the year of the promulgation of the Council's Dogmatic Constitution on the Church (*Lumen Gentium*). Coincidentally, he lived exactly half his life (1927–2001) before the promulgation of that document and exactly half his life after it. May we who live on in this life continue to live the legacy of the Council, and of Bishop Lucker.

This is the book that Bishop Lucker began to write. Fifteen of us— all teaching at Catholic colleges, universities, or seminaries in Minnesota—have finished the book. Though I am sure this is not exactly the book he would have written, I hope and trust he would like what we have done.

William McDonough
College of St. Catherine
September, 2002

## References

Hellwig, Monika. "The Survival of Catholic Higher Education." *America* 185/2 (July 16-23, 2001): 23–24.

Lucker, Raymond, Patrick Brennan, and Michael Leach, eds. *The People's Catechism: Catholic Faith for Adults.* New York: Crossroad, 1995.

McBrien, Richard. *Report on the Church.* San Francisco, Calif.: HarperCollins, 1992.

# Introduction:
# The beauty and challenge of divine revelation

BISHOP RAYMOND A. LUCKER

For a long time, I have wanted to write a book about two ideas and their connection with each other. First, I have wanted to express something of the beauty and attraction of divine revelation. Students in theology classes helped lead me here. Some have had negative experiences. They would come to class and say: "I defy you to show me that this faith stuff means anything." They have had these experiences, and I tried never to deny that. I tried to listen to what they said, and often it was hard stuff. Often enough, after hearing them, I would add something like this: "That surely is a real part of your life experience. Have you had other experiences?" And then I would listen again.

In the last few years of my teaching, I grew bold enough to ask the students a more direct question. Often at the beginning of class, I would ask the whole group: "Was there a time when you felt closer to God recently?" It would take some time for students to begin, but they would answer with statements like "when I held my baby," or "when I was out walking and noticed how beautiful the world is." When this happened I thought we were starting to do theology. I'd say, "Well, maybe there are things and statements in our history as a church that will help us think about these and other moments in all of our lives."

Then I would bring out the text of the Second Vatican Council on revelation. I would tell them that theology seeks to investigate the God who, "from the fullness of His love, speaks to men and women as friends." It seeks to investigate the "deeds and words" by which "God provides constant evidence of himself in created realities" (*DV* 2, 3).

---

From recorded conversations with Bishop Raymond Lucker, with some transitions and textual references added by William McDonough.

I talked about revelation recently with Tom Roberts of the *National Catholic Reporter*. That article was, for some reason, one of those things that hit it right (Roberts, 6–7). It picks up as well as anything what I have to say about revelation, about how it is God's self-communication. I emphasized there the text from *Dei Verbum* that "God, from the fullness of his love (his, I am going to have to use 'his' here and it is very diffi- cult; no matter what you do, you have a problem in this context) ad- dresses men and women as friends." God wanted to communicate be- cause God is a community. God is a communion, Father, Son, and Holy Spirit, in their very essence. Their very essence is loving mercy. The very essence of God is faithful love, everlasting love. And so from all eternity God is communicating with Son and Spirit, and loving and showing how to love. From that communication God calls forth love. This is how Vatican II understands creation: an act of love by God. We try to explain it humanly and we can't do it. The very love that God calls forth is the Spirit of God. The very love of God is the Word of God. God is love, and God wants us to love in return.

God revealed himself to us, and wants us to love him. And what does God reveal? "I love you; I love you and want to be one with you." And I say, "Yes, Lord, how do I show my love for you? Just tell me." But then we can't do it without being moved by God, which is itself a gift. Moved by the grace of God, we are able to say, "Yes, Lord, I love you and turn my life over to you. I want to live the way you want me to live." How do we do that? By loving one another, and by loving God with all our heart, all our mind, all our strength, and all our soul. And we do that by using the gifts that God gives us.

Our own official teaching says that God is a person, not primarily an idea. Studying theology with students has helped me see that what we are trying to do as the church is help each other understand more deeply the communication that God has always wanted to share with us. So, this book is about the beauty of divine revelation.

The second idea I have wanted to write about is the challenge that divine revelation is to all of us. The idea is expressed in another text from *Dei Verbum* that also got quoted in my interview in the *National Catholic Reporter*:

> The tradition that comes from the apostles makes progress in
> the church, with the help of the holy Spirit. There is a growth in
> insight into the realities and words that are being passed on. This
> comes about through the contemplation and study of believers

who ponder these things in their hearts (see Luke 2:19 and 51). It comes from the intimate sense of spiritual realities which they experience. And it comes from the preaching of those who, on succeeding to the office of bishop, have received the sure charism of truth. Thus, as the centuries go by, the church is always advancing towards the plenitude of divine truth, until eventually the words of God are fulfilled in it. (*DV* 8)

We are always advancing toward the full truth. We do not yet have the fullness of truth. None of us does. I personally had a deep experience of this. It happened sometime around Pentecost, 2000, while I was celebrating the Eucharist. During the preparation of the gifts I was saying the words "By the mystery of this water and wine, may we share in the divinity of Christ who humbled himself to share in our humanity..." and something happened. The words evoked something in me I had never experienced before. I was already sick and thinking about my illness, and after I recited those words I added to myself: "Yes, Lord, this is what I want, to share in the divinity of Christ. And I want to bring my whole life here, now, just as it is." After forty-eight years of celebrating Eucharist I felt I was understanding something for the first time.

Where the beauty and challenge of revelation come together is in the church. After Mass, on that same day, a young woman whom I know well—a spiritually active person who, I would say, has a deep sense of practical faith—walked up to me and said: "Something happened to you during the presentation of the gifts. I could see it in your face." I said, "Yes, it did." She said "Thanks." She was able to break through and see something. This is what we need to be for each other, support for growth in our understanding of and response to God's revelation. This is not something I understood when I was first ordained; I have learned it in the church, from people.

It is that way with revelation: the beauty of God comes first, but we only experience it in the church. The four constitutions of the Second Vatican Council are usually listed in this order: first comes the document on the church (*Lumen Gentium*), then the one on revelation (*Dei Verbum*), then the one on liturgy (*Sacrosanctum Concilium*), and last the one on the church in the modern world (*Gaudium et Spes*). First, the church; then revelation. *Lumen Gentium* explains why this is:

The holy people of God shares also in Christ's prophetic office: it spreads abroad a living witness to him, especially by a life of faith and love and by offering to God a sacrifice of praise, the fruit of lips confessing his name. The whole body of the faithful who have received an anointing which comes from the holy one cannot be mistaken in belief. (*LG* 12)

This means it is the church's prophetic charism of truth that allows God's deeds and words to be understood in the world. We carry on Jesus' mission as God's prophet, and we become the way for God's revelation to continue to be understood and lived in the world. The beauty of revelation is that it enlightens our whole lives; its challenge is that we bear responsibility for communicating it to the world.

And so our book about the beauty and challenge of revelation is about church teaching and changing formulations of church teaching. This is the way it has always been, since the beginning. Through the centuries the church has been able to formulate its teachings and apply them in such a way that we are all able to come up with a consensus, and are able to say: "Ah, yes, of course... Of course, we are against slavery..." But that was the consensus of the church over finally free discussion, after a long time, in some cases kicking and screaming, with weeping and gnashing of teeth, in some cases a more gradual development over a period of time.

This was the case even in the development of the Gospels, that they first were remembered sayings of Jesus and the basic faith of the church, the *kerygma* (Greek for "preaching"). Then there was the collection of the infancy and passion narratives, and then the parables or whatever else came in. And then finally these were written down in stages, by more than one evangelist. After almost a hundred years people could say, "Well this is what Jesus did and said." And there were further developments later.

No expression of faith may contradict Jesus, or the basic meaning of Jesus as Son of God, as beloved. If you come up with something that does, why then there is something wrong. Revelation has been going on since the beginning. I suppose in the early church the fathers and doctors of the church had to deal with the most fundamental issues. They were dealing with controversies about Jesus as Christ, about the Trinity, about things of that scope. They had to deal with "things of the essence." The challenge of coming up with language had to be dealt with, and we still have to deal with that, but not as much. We have come to accept words that originated in a Greek philosophical tradition. We have come to accept those as somehow participating in revelation. This language has almost been taken over in the language of faith. I don't know exactly how to deal with this fully; maybe it will come to us someday or maybe we will simply have to accept that we will not fully know this until the Last Day.

Still, you can take anything the church teaches and have the attitude that I want us to go into our book with. It is an attitude of reverence for the "deeds and words" of God. The development of doctrine is the life of the church. The development of doctrine is ongoing because the ever-given charism of the church as prophet (which is given to the whole church) is ongoing.

God gave the gifts of prophecy to Jesus first. God gave this gift of the Spirit of wisdom to Jesus, first. And God shares with us the gift of prophecy. The prophet is God's mouth-piece, but action-piece, too. That is why revelation is always "words and deeds." It is words and deeds through which God communicates himself to us in his everlasting love. So we are called to share that.

God gives that gift of prophetic ministry to every member of the church. Bishops are given it by their very ordination. Priests, too. But the special charism of priests is not prophecy, but holiness, as it says in the ordination prayer for priests. The special sign-gift of deacons is service. All have special charisms, but God shares the gift of prophecy with every single member of the church. Therefore it is not only priests and bishops, and the Holy See, and the curia and the pope who share in the gifts of prophecy by having special roles in the church. All people, everybody, shares in the gift of infallibility. *Lumen Gentium* is based on the notion that God reveals himself to us and shares the gift of prophecy with us, and we are called to be part of that.

There is much to do here. The practical part of our book could begin with revelation, with the beauty of revelation. I think it is fair to do this as long as we do not imply that revelation is separate from the life of the church. Only in our shared prophetic charism can we receive revelation. To speak of the church is in a sense to talk about the essence of who we are. And then in *Dei Verbum* we are talking about communication of who we are. In this way, *Lumen Gentium* comes first and then *Dei Verbum* comes next. This goes along with the adage that what we do flows from who we are: *agere sequitur esse*. That is, the church *is* the prophetic presence of God on earth and what it *does* is enable people to experience God's revelation. So, there is a doubling up between these two documents: what the church is and what it does.

By the way, this doubling up happens again between the Constitution on the Sacred Liturgy and the Dogmatic Constitution on the Church. *Sacrosanctum Concilium* doubles up with *Lumen Gentium*, which talks about the essence of the church as sharing in the very being of God, the very divine nature of God. *Sacrosanctum Concilium*, on liturgy, deals with how we proclaim and express that mystery by sharing in the divine life through the sacraments, the sacraments of initiation (Baptism, Confirmation, Eucharist), the sacraments of reconciliation, the sacraments of social order. So we have the church; we have the liturgy; and then we have the church in the modern world.

All of this comes together in the Eucharist: we have the proclamation of the word and the offering of the gifts—taking the bread, breaking it, blessing it, and giving it to the disciples. We are being told: "Take this . . . this is my body . . . and then bring this with you, bring my body into the world." We have here all the action of human life wrapped up into the divine liturgy, the divine action. We don't usually see our life this way, though, since we are so word-oriented and rational.

My own approach is to understand the other three major constitutions as related to the one on revelation. They are reflections on Christ's threefold way of revealing God. Christ reveals as prophet (*Lumen Gentium*), as priest (*Sacrosanctum Concilium*), and as king (*Gaudium et Spes*).

So, you may surely begin the book by looking at our understanding of revelation. I think it would be good to talk about our church's changed understanding of its relationship with science. Notice that *Dei Verbum* speaks of revelation even before it speaks of the creation of human beings. This has real implications for our need for a greater appreciation of science. The document says: "God, who creates and conserves all things by His Word, provides constant evidence of himself in created realities. Furthermore . . . he manifested himself to our first parents from the very beginning" (*DV* 3).

In this part of the book, you could also look at how the church's own approach to the Bible has changed. When we talk about the Bible, it is more than a debate about Bible translations. I think this includes thinking through what is in the Bible, just as the Bible itself is a process of thinking through God's revelation. For example, the Bible itself records the prophets re-thinking some of the stories of the conquest of the promised land. How do we use the Bible in the same way for our own life as a church?

Then, next, take up the whole question of the church. Look at the church and how our understanding of what it is to be a church has grown and changed. In the chapter on the church, on *Lumen Gentium*, we are looking at Christ as prophet. I think we can discuss the issue of the relation between the local and universal church. I was on a panel for the Catholic Theological Society of America in the mid-1990s on this (see Wood, 1993, 148). I was just one member of the panel. This is not too controversial for us to address in our book. Right now, this summer, we are in the midst of that issue. It has been opened up by the conversation between Cardinal Ratzinger and Cardinal Kasper. Once an issue gets to this level, it is out. There may be some people who would say we have to stop it for a while, but there is really no way of stopping it in a true and real sense. Cardinals are involved. The debate about the synod is going on. So, there is very much there right now that we can say on this topic.

In this section on the church, why not look more at how we come to differentiate what is definitive from what is authoritative teaching in the church? I have worked on understanding six levels of teaching in the church (see Susan Wood's essay in this book). I have also prepared some informal lists of changes in church teaching (see Appendix).

*Lumen Gentium* 25 is where the Council makes the distinction between definitive and authentic teaching. In the thirty-five years since the Council we have had further reflection on the secondary object, on those things not revealed in scripture but necessary in support of what is revealed there. Now we are trying to figure out what belongs in that secondary object. There was never a debate about changing definitive teaching. We are asking how one knows what goes in the secondary object and so is definitive.

We want to look at another question, namely the difficulty in coming to know what is a definitive (unchangeable) teaching and what is an authoritative (not unchangeable) teaching. I think this is how we should address the whole issue of the ordination of women, not as a doctrinal issue itself but as an issue relating to how we determine what definitive teaching is. I wrote my own position down in the margins of a recent article in *The Tablet*. Let's add those words in here: "My own position is to call for a free and open discussion . . . Let *all* bishops, all theologians, all members participate, if it is a free discussion. Then one (I) could discuss favoring a dissenting position. If after open, free discussion over *a period of years,* the church came down on the side of non-ordination, I would bow to the collegial discussion. I would not go against the church. Nor would I today" (marginal notes of Bishop Lucker on the essay "Women raise their voices," July 7, 2001).

Earlier, I had thought all this was getting pretty clear for me, until the pope came out with the teaching that we can't talk about ordination of women. The new instruction then started moving toward saying this teaching is definitive, so closely connected with revelation that you cannot change it.

In light of all this, I want us to look from a different perspective. Our book should not address women's ordination as a doctrinal issue to be critiqued. Instead, we are interested in how the church knows what is a definitive teaching. Maybe ultimately it is going to come down as a definitive teaching. If that is the way it is, and if I don't accept it as a definitive teaching, then I am about to start my own church. And then we have a problem! I don't want to do that; we don't want to do that; you don't want to do that. So, if the discussion turns out—after free and full discussion—that we have come to the conclusion that this is definitive, then we get to a point of saying: "In the end, we bow in the face of definitive teaching."

There is a lot of conversation we need to have about this secondary object, about its meaning. And that might give us an opening to my second list, my list of teachings that have not yet changed, but perhaps could change (see Appendix).

I think it would be excellent to handle the recent papal apologies— for torture, for the Crusades, for anti-Semitism, for discrimination against women, and for many other things. This is an ecclesiological matter, and it is about poorly handling our task of being the church.

The third section of the book, the section that takes up questions about liturgy, reflects on Vatican II's *Sacrosanctum Concilium*. Again, I read this constitution as reflecting on Christ as priest. We need to think so much more about the Eucharist. Pope Pius X's decree on frequent communion was certainly a good thing, but so centered us on first communion that we forgot about life. The text I spoke about earlier— "Through the mystery of this water and wine"—is about the holiness of daily life. We need to think more deeply about the relationship between the Eucharist and our social life together as human beings.

There is also the issue that we say the Eucharist is the primary sacrament of healing. Godfrey Diekmann has identified those prayers in the Sacramentary that thank God for forgiving our sins through the Eucharist. Godfrey has identified about one hundred of them. Just read the prayers after communion, especially during Lent. I don't have the words memorized, but the themes are all like this: "We thank you, God, for taking away our sins in this Eucharist." "We thank you for this source of healing." So, the Eucharist is the sacrament of healing, which has changed the way we celebrate penance.

In the fourth part of the book, you could take up changes in our understanding of the church's way of being in the world. In *Gaudium et Spes* we are reflecting on Christ as king, on Christ as ruler of the world.

There is so much there. One group of issues could surely be those related to the pope's idea of "a culture of life" and Cardinal Bernardin's idea of a "consistent ethic of life."

The challenge here is that the pope has so far identified only abortion as definitive; not capital punishment and not nuclear war. So, there are different levels of teaching operating here. On the other hand, John Paul II's recent acknowledgment (in his 1995 encyclical "On the Value and Inviolability of Human Life") that the church itself must do more to model respect for life could help us all think more deeply: "We need to begin with the *renewal of a culture of life within Christian communities themselves"(EV* 95; emphasis is in the original text). The pope is asking us all to develop a "culture of life." He is asking us to think about how the church affects public life.

Our whole changing understanding of marriage is also a good issue to look at here. I like Ann Wilson Shaef's book about *Women's Reality.* She says women tend to see love as an infinite cycle (Shaef, 124–125). I accept that; I also think this is a wonderful image for God. It is a description of the giving and receiving of love in the Trinity, in a very human way. You see, we get nervous about speaking of God in sexual terms. Maybe that is why we have such a tough time with *Humanae Vitae*; we have such a hard time accepting that sexual love is sacred, in accepting that married couples in expressing their love are expressing the worship of God.

This is what *Gaudium et Spes* said in claiming that married love is "assumed" into God (*GS* 48). This is what we said, but we haven't followed through on it. So the beauty, the sacredness, and the holiness of all God's teachings do not get fully understood by any of us. If teaching is expressed in heavy-handed ways it comes off as though we do not believe it; it does not come off right. We need to look at our understanding of marriage.

In the end, we must not undermine our own understanding of revelation. God started all of this, and just wants us to return it. God just wants us to respond. And think of that! Wow! It is amazing, that God has first loved us, that we are the beloved, that God has called us into being. . . Oh boy. Or, as Godfrey Diekmann says, we start at the top. He is quoting that gruff Western church father who wasn't canonized . . . Tertullian. Quote Tertullian!

Be flexible in putting all this together. You may end up dealing with different issues. We are just trying to figure out how to be a church. I am not trying to start my own church; we are just trying to figure out together how to be a church. How to be a good church. How to be a renewed church, and how to touch the hearts of people.

Talking about the beauty and challenge of revelation is not only something for the beginning of the book, but something that should be in every chapter. We need to return to this in every chapter to integrate the book. Anything we do as a church has meaning only as it helps us be attentive and responsive to revelation. The only point for the church is to lead us to respond in faith and love to the love of God for us. "Yes, Lord, I believe." Revelation is always going to lead to, or can lead under the grace of God to a deeper response to God. The question is always: *How can this lead us to a deeper experience of God and God's love and presence?*

OK, that is enough for now.

Our Lady of Good Counsel Home
St. Paul, Minnesota
July and August, 2001

## References

Roberts, Tom. "Lucker's Final Certainty: God Is Here." *National Catholic Reporter* 37 (May 25, 2001): 6–7.

Shaef, Ann Wilson. *Women's Reality: An Emerging Female System in a White Male Society,* 3rd edition. San Francisco, Calif.: HarperSanFrancisco, 1992.

"Women Raise Their Voices." *The Tablet* 255 (July 7, 2001): 1001.

Wood, Susan. "Seminar on Ecclesiology." *The Catholic Theological Society of America: Proceedings of the Forty-Eighth Annual Conference* 48 (1993): 146–148.

# I

# On Revelation

## Re-reading *Dei Verbum*
## for what it is asking of the church in our day

*Vatican II: "It pleased God, in his goodness and wisdom, to reveal him-self and to make known the mystery of his will, which was that people can draw near to the Father, through Christ, the Word made flesh, in the holy Spirit, and thus become sharers in the divine nature . . . The 'obedience of faith' must be our response to the God who reveals. By faith one freely commits oneself entirely to God." (DV 2, 5)*

*Bishop Lucker: "Quote Tertullian!" (from this book's introduction)*

*Tertullian: Caro est cardo salutis (The flesh is the hinge of salvation).*

The opening essay of this first section is the book's most intellectually challenging. In "Revelation and Evolution: The Journey of Creation into God," Terence Nichols calls for a rapprochement between religion and science. Development and change characterize both science and theology. Without science, theology and religion are in danger of skipping over the intricacy, interconnectedness, and (at times terrifying) beauty of God's creation. And without theology, science is in danger of turning its observations into an ideology that denies the existence of anything that cannot be measured. In Nichols's view, science can push theology to remember that the life of the soul is *in the body*. Theology adds this: it is the destiny *of the soul* that gets worked out in our life in the body. Tertullian is right: our human flesh is the hinge of God's salvation.

Catherine Cory and Corrine Patton follow with an essay entitled "Toward a Scriptural Understanding of Revelation: God Inserts God's Self in History." They pick up where Nichols leaves off and develop a threefold understanding of God's entry into history in Christ: as law, as prophet, and as wisdom. Their theology leaves no room for easy or other-worldly moralizing about "finding God." Our path to God will be Christ's, a courageous journey of love: "When we come finally to abide in love, we are utterly transformed, because God is love."

Last, two other Bible scholars, Chris Franke and Vincent T. M. Skemp, write on "A Growing Understanding of the Bible in the Life of the Church." They show the almost head-spinning progress that the official Catholic Church has made in the last hundred years in its understanding of the Bible. They say the church is coming to understand the truth of the Bible in a biblical way! The Hebrew word for truth, *emet,* means trustworthiness, constancy, faithfulness. The kind of truth we can find in the Bible is one "for the sake of our salvation," they say, highlighting Vatican II's words. Until salvation itself is complete, the church will not come to the end of understanding God's word in scripture.

These essays on revelation and our response to it offer a fitting reflection on the last lines of Bishop Lucker's last pastoral letter, written in November 2000: "I look back on twenty-five good years. Throughout all of this I have felt the support of the community I live with in New Ulm, of my numerous family, and above all, the love and care of the Lord Jesus. The motto I chose when I was appointed a bishop was: 'I believe, help my lack of trust (Mark 9.24).' That has guided all of my ministry in these years" (Lucker, 569).

# 1
# Revelation and evolution:
# The journey of creation into God*

TERENCE NICHOLS

I n his introduction to this book, Bishop Lucker highlights "the beauty and
the challenge of revelation." I follow him here in both ideas, though in
recent conversations between faith and science, challenge has perhaps
been more apparent than beauty. As it was in Bishop Lucker's introduction, so my starting point here is a specific text from Vatican II's Dogmatic
Constitution on Divine Revelation. Surely one of the great insights of the
Council was its recognition that our understanding of revelation develops:

> The tradition that comes from the apostles makes progress in
> the church, with the help of the holy Spirit. There is a growth
> in insight into the realities and words that are being passed
> on. This comes about through the contemplation and study of
> believers . . . and . . . from the preaching of those who, on suc-
> ceeding to the office of bishop, have received the sure charism
> of truth. Thus, as the centuries go by, the church is always ad-
> vancing towards the plenitude of divine truth, until eventually
> the words of God are fulfilled in it. (*DV* 8)

For Bishop Lucker this text was an invitation to lifelong openness to
change in his pastoral and spiritual life. I will suggest here that the same
might be true of the church itself. For much of Catholic history, Christian revelation was understood as a static "deposit of faith" to be passed
on by the church without adding or subtracting anything. But in open-

---

*This essay is based on an earlier essay by the same author: Nichols, "Evolution: Jour-
ney or Random Walk?" *Zygon* 37/1 (March, 2002): 193–210.

ing the church to an evolutionary view of history, Vatican II also made it possible for the church to fully engage the theory of evolution itself and its implications for Christian revelation.

This essay will explore how the church might reconcile evolutionary theory with its theology of revelation. I will proceed in four steps, and then offer a brief conclusion. The first step considers the question: Are the Christian and scientific stories necessarily at odds? The second section traces the development since Darwin of the various scientific interpretations of evolution. The third develops a theology of evolution based on Catholicism's understanding of revelation. The fourth addresses a theological understanding of human evolution. In the conclusion, I return to my (and Bishop Lucker's) starting point: how development characterizes both science and theology.

## I. The Christian and scientific stories about us: Are they at odds?

As the text quoted above from *Dei Verbum* indicates, one of the ways that the understanding of revelation develops is by the "contemplation and study of believers." This certainly includes the study of the natural sciences. As we learn more about the natural world, we come to a more nuanced understanding of Christian revelation. We realize, for instance, that God's creation of the world and humanity was not as simple as it is described in Genesis, but occurred through a long process of evolution. Now many Christians see the theory of evolution as in conflict with Christian revelation. But it is fundamental to Catholic doctrine that God made the world and God revealed the scriptures, and that since God does not contradict himself, the book of nature and the book of scripture, rightly understood, cannot contradict each other. Rather, both point to the same author. If there appears to be a conflict, it is because one or the other is misunderstood.

I shall argue that there is no necessary conflict between evolutionary theory and Christian revelation. The real conflict is due to the philosophical interpretation that has been placed on evolutionary theory by many of its academic expositors. That interpretation is *philosophical naturalism,* that is, the doctrine that only matter and nature exist, and that science, which alone gives us a true understanding of nature, can therefore explain everything, with no need of revelation. (Philosophical naturalism must be distinguished from methodological naturalism. It is intrinsic to the method of the natural sciences to explain phenomena by natural causes. The natural sciences are therefore committed to methodological naturalism. But natural scientists need not be committed to naturalism as a metaphysical philosophy. It is possible to do first-rate scientific work and believe in God, or even in miracles.) Evolution, however, does not need to be interpreted as a purely natural process; it can be understood as a theistically guided process. But even if it is so understood, it will still force us to reconsider what is essential and what is culturally conditioned in Christian revelation.

For at least fourteen hundred years, the biblical account of the origins and destiny of humanity was thought in the West to be the basic outline of the history of the world. St. Augustine, writing *The City of God,* would have had little disagreement with John Milton, writing *Paradise Lost*, on the central events of world history: the creation and fall of humanity, the revelation to the Jewish prophets, the atonement and resurrection of Jesus, and the eventual parousia, in which all humanity would be resurrected, judged, and consigned to heaven or hell. This traditional narrative, which set both nature and humanity within a supernatural context, formed the fundamental worldview of Christian civilization until about 1800.

But in the West this account has been largely displaced by that of naturalistic evolution. In this story, matter/energy comes into being through the big bang and develops on its own, without God, into a vast array of galaxies, stars, and planets. One planet, through natural processes, developed living beings, higher animals, and humanity. But natural science, which gives us this account, can discern no original human pair or originating sin, no atonement or resurrection, nor any ultimate purpose or goal for human life. The whole process of evolution, understood naturalistically, is undirected; complex creatures, including humanity, are simply the products of random mutation and the blind forces of natural selection. As paleontologist Stephen Gould writes: "The origin of *Homo Sapiens*, as a tiny twig on an improbable branch of a contingent limb of a fortunate tree, lies well below the boundary [of law and contingency]. In Darwin's scheme, we are a detail, not a purpose or embodiment of the whole—'with the details, whether good or bad, left to the workings of what we call chance'" (Gould, 291). Thus, as Nobel Laureate biochemist Jacques Monod wrote: "The ancient covenant is in pieces; man knows at last that he is alone in the universe's unfeeling immensity, out of which he emerged only by chance" (Monod, 180).

These two stories could hardly be more different. In the first, the ultimate framework of reality and history is supernatural and personal; humanity is the central actor in a story pervaded by the providence of

God, and nature reflects the design and transcendent beauty of its creator. In the second, the ultimate framework of reality is nature and impersonal forces; humanity is an accidental spin-off of a blind, indifferent process, and nature, though beautiful, will end in a universal death as the stars burn out and the galaxies collapse into black holes. The worldview presupposed by the second story is naturalism. In this view, there is no God, there are no angels or immortal souls, there is no transcendent destiny or possibility of afterlife. Increasingly, this view dominates academic culture, though the traditional Christian story still prevails among sections of popular culture, especially in the United States.

Of course, Christian thinkers from the time of Darwin have argued for a Christianized and theistic version of evolution, in which God is understood as creating the world and humanity through the evolutionary process. But this is not the interpretation of evolution that has gained hegemony in academic culture or in the media. Furthermore, attempts to reconcile Christianity and evolution usually succeed only by sacrificing many elements of traditional Christian revelation, such as the historical reality of an original pair, an originating sin, an immortal human soul, and often (as in process theology) the omnipotence and omniscience of God. Even a theistic interpretation of evolution, then, challenges the traditional understanding of revelation.

## II. Darwin and his followers: Various theories of evolution

Charles Darwin did not invent the idea of evolution; what he contributed was a naturalistic explanation of the evolution of species. (By evolution Darwin meant "descent [from a common ancestor] with modification.") He noted that the members of any species exhibit a range of variations, for example, strength and speed among horses. Furthermore, every species produces far more progeny than the environment can sustain. Therefore, large numbers of every generation die young and leave no progeny. Darwin proposed that those that die young are those less adapted to the environment, or less "fit." Just as animal breeders select only certain animals for breeding, in order to enhance particular characteristics such as strength or speed, so nature unconsciously also selects those members who are best adapted for survival. In this way, any variant characteristic that confers even a slight degree of survival value would be enhanced by what Darwin called "natural selection," and those characteristics that put individuals at a disadvantage in the struggle for survival would be diminished. A simple example is protective coloration. Animals that, because of random mutations, blend in with their surroundings will be more likely to survive predation than animals that stand out. And so protective coloration gradually develops.

In his *On the Origin of Species* (originally published in 1859), Darwin applied this notion of natural selection to a particularly hard case: the eye (Darwin, 85–87). The eye of a mammal, like a camera, is an enormously complex instrument, which would seem to have been designed. William Paley, in his famous book *Natural Theology* (1802), argued that if one were to find a watch on a heath, one would certainly conclude that it had been designed by an intelligent designer. So with the eye, which is more intricate and complex than any watch; it must have been designed by God, who made each organ and species perfectly adapted to its environment. But Darwin argued that the eye could have emerged through natural variation and natural selection. He pointed out that it is possible to find animals that exhibit all stages of a continuum, from simple light sensitive spots, to light sensitive nerves, to primitive "eyes" with crude lenses, to fully developed eyes in insects and vertebrates.

Thus at a stroke Darwin apparently removed one of the strongest arguments for God: the argument from design. Instead, he showed how even the most complex organs and creatures could have emerged from simple beginnings, through cumulative variations across eons of time, by a purely natural process. Eventually (in *The Descent of Man*) Darwin applied this idea to the emergence of humanity as well, arguing that human beings could have emerged gradually from ape-like ancestors. This undermined the traditional Judeo-Christian (and Muslim) idea that human beings had been created directly by God and were essentially different from the animals.

Darwin's ideas also changed the way people looked at nature. Before Darwin, nature had been thought of as exhibiting the harmony and beauty of its creator. This was a prominent feature of Romantic literature (e.g., Wordsworth, Emerson, and others) and painting (e.g., Thomas Cole, Frederick Church, and the Hudson River School). But by the mid nineteenth century, the view of nature had changed. Nature was not a tableau manifesting the harmony and beauty of God, but was a perennial struggle for survival, "red in tooth and claw" in Tennyson's famous phrase. Darwin himself lost his Christian faith (and ended as an agnostic) partly because of his realization of the enormous amount of suffering in nature. He could not understand, he wrote, how a good God could design creatures like certain wasps that lay their eggs in living worms so that the developing wasp larvae can eat the worms alive.

The development of modern genetics gave Darwinian theory a precise way to explain the origin of variations in populations of plants and animals, and a mechanism explaining how these variations are passed on. The modern synthesis of Darwin's theory with genetics, called Neo-Darwinism, is the standard theory taught today in courses across the country. But if there is a consensus within biology as to the fact of evolution, there is no consensus as to the mechanism of evolution: What factors actually cause evolutionary change, so that new species emerge from old?

One group, represented by Oxford zoologist Richard Dawkins, holds that the only mechanisms are random genetic variation and natural selection. Genes mutate naturally, and natural selection (which according to Dawkins acts primarily at the level of the gene) sifts these mutations so that only those conferring some advantage survive in a population. Evolution thus proceeds gradually by minute changes, and over time slight variations within a single species become magnified until the original variants have become separate species.

Across the Atlantic and *contra* Dawkins, Stephen Gould argues that evolution is characterized by long periods of stasis, in which a species may not change at all, followed by an extinction and the rapid emergence of new species. Natural selection is only one factor of several responsible for evolution. Chance is a major factor: vast numbers of fit species may be wiped out by a single catastrophe, as happened to the dinosaurs at the end of the Mesozoic period, 65 million years ago. "The history of life is a story of massive removal followed by differentiation within a few surviving stocks, not the conventional tale of steadily increasing excellence, complexity, and diversity" (Gould, 25). Further, organisms are not just passively shaped by natural selection; they also actively modify their environment, thus increasing their own "fitness." Finally, natural selection does not just operate at the level of the gene; it operates at many levels: the gene, the individual, groups, clades, and species.

Other writers also question the centrality of natural selection in evolution. Stuart Kauffman, of the Santa Fe Institute, holds that besides mutation and natural selection, a principal source of order in biological processes is self-organization. Complex systems, from computer-modeled networks to biological systems, exhibit a surprising degree of spontaneously generated, emergent order (simple examples of this, in physics, are the hexagonal structure of snowflakes, or the emergent order of a star). The idea that self-organizing processes are the origin of much of the order in living systems seems to be gaining ground among biologists.

Another and older idea, represented by biologists such as Mae-Wan Ho and Peter Saunders, is that the development of species is an inner-driven process, like the development of an embryo. David Depew and Bruce Weber (authors of *Darwinism Evolving*) comment on this theory:

> By contrast to Darwinism's stress on random variation and se-lection by external, environmental forces, an older and surpris-ingly persistent developmentalist tradition has consistently maintained that the evolution of kinds (phylogeny) should be viewed as an inner driven process like the unfolding of an em-bryo (ontogeny)...Latter day developmentalists have been as-serting of late that natural selection, and so Darwinism, will not survive the transition from the "sciences of simplicity" to the "sciences of complexity." (Depew and Weber, 18)

The application of the science of chaos and complexity to biology has also been emphasized by Robert Wesson. Evolution, he says, is the story of the development of complex systems, exactly the kind of sys-tems described by chaos and complexity theory. Wesson sees the emer-gence of stable genomes and stable biological patterns as examples of what are called in complexity theory "attractors." Wesson thinks that "Evolution is the result of at least four major factors—environment, se-lection, random-chaotic development, and inner direction—and one might no more expect to find any law to govern it than to find a law of the mind" (Wesson, 291).

Finally, and far out on the spectrum of modern biologists, is Michael Denton, a molecular biologist at the University of Otago in New Zealand. Denton argues (in *Nature's Destiny*) that the environment of the earth seems to have been designed so as to bring forth life. Evo-lution, he holds, is not a random, undirected process, but a process di-rected by some form of higher intelligence, be it a world soul or God.

From this I conclude that though there is agreement in the biologi-cal and scientific community on the fact of evolution, there is not agreement on the mechanism of evolution. There are therefore many theories of evolution, not just one. And this indicates that the theory of evolution is not a finished or complete theory; it is a theory in the mak-ing, or, as Depew and Weber put it, a theory "evolving."

There are other reasons to emphasize the tentativeness of the the-ory of evolution. The history of science over the last few centuries teaches us that scientific theories are provisional, and may be subject to drastic reformulation even after having commanded a consensus for decades or for centuries (as in the case of Newton's theory). A striking example of this is the fate of the theory concerning the ether. The existence of the ether, as a necessary medium to transmit light waves, was unquestioned by physicists for most of the nineteenth century (Jaki, 79–86). Indeed, James Clerk Maxwell, one of the giants in the history of physics, wrote the article on the ether for the ninth edition of the *Encyclopaedia Britannica* (1878), in which he calculates the coefficient of rigidity and density of the ether to two decimal places. He concludes the article with these words:

> Whatever difficulties we may have of forming a consistent idea of the constitution of the ether, there can be no doubt that the interplanetary and interstellar spaces are not empty, but are occupied by a material substance or body which is certainly the largest, and probably the most uniform body of which we have any knowledge. (Maxwell, 572)

This was written about 124 years ago. And yet, today no one believes that space is filled with ether. The theory of the ether has gone the way of the phlogiston theory and the geocentric universe. A similar change has taken place, more recently, in geology. In the 1930s, a German meteorologist named Alfred Wegener formulated the continental drift theory. But Wegener's arguments were ridiculed and ignored by geologists until about the 1960s, when the actual mechanism for the movement of continents became known. Now the continental drift theory is one of the foundational theories of geology.

Thus it is risky to speculate on what the theory of evolution might look like one hundred years from now, especially with potentially revolutionary developments on the horizon. This in turn means that we can give only a very tentative account of how evolutionary theory might fit with Christian revelation, for any account we give now may have to be drastically reformulated fifty or one hundred years hence. My proposal, then, is that a theology of evolution should be based only on the most general features of the evolution. It would be a mistake to tailor one's theology, that is, one's interpretation of revelation, to whatever theory of evolution is now in vogue. Thus, in the following pages, I will attempt to present a theological interpretation of evolution that is scientifically responsible, while also being faithful to what is indispensable in Christian revelation.

## III.  A theology of evolution: The "journey to see God" (*DV* 7)

Evolution in its general character is the development of complex entities from simpler and earlier entities. One theological approach to evolution is to hold that God does not direct the process of evolution, but created and maintains the physical laws that allow the universe to evolve by a process of self-organization. We know that the balance of the physical laws and constants has to be almost perfect in order for a universe which will produce life to exist (Ellis). Thus, God may have designed a universe that would bring forth life after billions of years of self-organizing evolution, without guiding or directing the process. This is appealing scientifically, because it posits a universe governed only by natural and scientifically knowable forces. But it is problematic theologically, for it assumes the absentee God of Deism, rather than the biblical God who responds to prayer and acts in history. Not only theologians, but also some scientists, find this idea inadequate.

Another interpretation, more in keeping with the Christian belief that God is active in history, is that God in some way directs the course of evolution so that intelligent life might emerge and eventually reach union with God. This is the vision etched out by Teilhard de Chardin. Christ, as the goal of creation, draws the process of evolution toward him. As the universe becomes more complex, consciousness and conscious beings increase. Eventually, evolution jumps to the sphere of mind and culture, where it progresses more rapidly. The culmination of the whole process is the union of creation with God.

Teilhard's work has been seminal in Catholic thought, but it has some limitations. For one thing, Teilhard did not emphasize genetics or natural selection, but, influenced by philosopher Henri Bergson, thought of evolution as moved by a kind of inner energy. Consequently, his views have had little influence in the biological sciences. Another limitation is that the role of evil generally, and original sin in particular, was poorly developed in his theology.

While affirming the general lines of Teilhard's thought, we have to acknowledge that chance and evil play a large role in evolution. After Darwin, it is difficult to view the natural world in the idealized perspective of the Romantics. We now know that few creatures in any generation, or any species, survive to reach maturity, and that 99 percent of the species that have existed have become extinct. How can we reconcile this reality with the Christian God of love?

One way is to severely limit God's power. This is the route taken by those theologians influenced by process theology, such as Ian Barbour and John Haught. In this view, each event is influenced by God, but is also influenced by the past events that impinge upon it. God does not and cannot control events, but can only gently steer them in the appropriate direction. God never coerces, but only persuades. This, according to Haught, is entirely consistent with the Christian view of God as self-sacrificing love. The evil in creation then is not God's fault; God loves and suffers as we do, and does not will the evil that occurs. This view is able to acknowledge the presence of a great deal of chance and evil in the evolutionary process, but at the price of sacrificing God's omnipotence. However, this is a steep theological price to pay. It is questionable if God, conceived along process lines, has the power to create the universe from nothing, or to accomplish miracles, including the resurrection.

We can still acknowledge the presence of evil and chance in the process of creation and preserve God's omnipotence if we hold that God limits his power for the sake of a greater good. According to John Polkinghorne and others, that good is the freedom of the created process to make itself. God wishes to create, but also wishes to give his creatures the gift of freedom, which is the gift of love. In humanity, this takes the form of free will: humans are given the freedom to follow God's will or not to. If this gift were lacking, humanity could not freely return to God in love. We would be like robots or animals, driven by genetic drives. Similarly, the gift of freedom to the evolutionary process allows the world to make itself, to develop along its own lines, guided by but not controlled by God.

Think, for example, about snowflakes, each of them hexagonal, a consequence of the molecular structure of water. But every snowflake is different, a consequence of its unique journey from the clouds to earth. Does God stipulate every detail of every snowflake? It seems more likely that physical laws determine the general pattern, while the details of each flake are left to chance. So also with the turning of the leaves in autumn, or the colors of a sunset. The laws of physics and chemistry govern the changing of colors in autumn leaves and in sunsets, but the details of each leaf and each sunset are left to contingency. In this way, a marvelous and beautiful diversity emerges from within the created order, which is ever changing and ever new. But the price of this changing contingency is death and suffering, for new life could not emerge if old life did not die, and the same processes that bring the gold to the sunset or scarlet to the leaf also cause genetic disorders and natural disasters.

Providence, in this view, does not entail God's controlling each event. If this were the case, God would be directly responsible for evil, rather than allowing it for the sake of a greater good. God wishes creation to develop in the direction of complexity, and to bring forth intelligent, moral beings who can freely return to him in love. But God structures creation so it develops through a long, evolutionary process, with the risks entailed by the presence of free will and chance. There is a story of a Persian master carpet weaver who weaves a carpet from one end and allows his young son to begin weaving from the other. The master has a design in mind. But his son makes occasional mistakes. Yet so great is the skill of the master that he modifies his design as he weaves to incorporate the mistakes of his son. So also does God, in allowing for our human freedom and the effects of physical chance. In this process there is design, for the evolution of life could not occur at all if the physical laws and constants were not precisely what they are to allow evolution to happen. And, further, God has a design for the end of creation: to bring all into union with him. But he does not determine all the intermediate steps. Thus, we can hold that self-organization and natural selection might account for many features of evolution, such as protective coloration and finches' beaks, while holding that God gradually draws the whole process in the direction of increasing complexity and consciousness.

If we assume that evolution is directed by a higher intelligence, rather than being a random, undirected process, then it has the character of a journey, rather than of a random walk. And this, I would argue, is the interpretation of evolution that fits best with Christian revelation. But it also coheres with the scientific data. One feature that characterizes most of the course of evolution is that the evolutionary process results in the build-up of complexity, and therefore of information. Dawkins and others argue that this can be done through random variation and natural selection. But this is a hard case to make, for random processes normally produce disorder, not order. Natural selection, it is true, is a non-random factor, in that it winnows out all random variations which do not contribute to survival. But it is not clear that this can account for the build-up of highly complex organisms over the course of evolution. Simple bacteria are as well adapted to the environment as, and survive as well as (or better than) any species on earth. Why, then, do more complex organisms develop at all?

Many biologists, such as Kenneth Miller, argue that increasing complexity (and therefore information) by means of random mutation and natural selection has been demonstrated in the laboratory. The basis for this claim is that colonies of bacteria that have been artificially deprived of the genes that allow them to metabolize lactose, when placed on a lactose medium, change so that they can metabolize lactose. This occurs by mutation of two genes simultaneously (Miller, 145–147). But when one examines the original scientific article which was the basis for this claim, one finds that the mutations were in fact *not* random, a fact that the author of the article acknowledges: "We can only conclude that under some conditions spontaneous mutations are not independent events—heresy, I am aware" (Hall, 143). Physicist Lee Spetner, a specialist in information theory, argues that in cases of bacteria acquiring a resistance to antibiotics, the adaption results in a loss of information on the part of the bacteria— they become less complex, not more complex (Spetner, 139–141). Spetner thus argues that the increasing complexity of evolution is best explained by *nonrandom evolution*, that is, by directed evolution.

Finally, if evolution is the result of a random, undirected, and purposeless process, as Dawkins, Gould, and many others propose, then to be consistent we should hold that humanity is also a result of this same process. But this gives us a picture of humanity as simply a material, complex organism, which emerged as a result of adaptation to its environment. The only real value in such a process is survivability. Human freedom, moral values, and spirituality are hard to account for in this explanation, and are usually explained away as illusory by naturalists like Dawkins. But human beings are part of the world of evolution also, and any satisfactory theory of evolution should be able to give us a complete account of human nature, not the truncated version that we get from naturalist thinkers. It is precisely on this ground that many scientists themselves, such as John Polkinghorne and George Ellis, argue for a God who is active in natural processes and in human life.

If evolution is a journey, then, like any journey, it can be fully understood only when one knows its end. If one observes a car traveling east from Los Angeles, it would be foolish to speculate what the end of its journey is until it reached its destination. So it is with evolution. Now, the end of the journey is something that Christians claim to know: it is the union of humanity and the restored creation with God (Rom 8; see *DV* 7). This end, however, is known only through revelation, and is not discernible by science, which, because of its method, cannot know what the end of the evolutionary journey is.

Thus I think it likely that, when viewed within the context of a Christian worldview, evolution will be perceived as a kind of journey, which has, after all, a goal. We can see evolution in the most general sense as a movement from simple systems to complex systems, both at the cosmic level and at the level of organic evolution, and we can also see this in the Christian view of history. For the end and culmination of history is, according to Christianity, the gathering of all the blessed into fellowship with God, through Christ and the Holy Spirit. And that is not all: Paul prophesies that the whole cosmos as well will "be set free from its bondage to decay and obtain the glorious freedom of the children of God" (Rom 8:21). Certainly this would be the most complex system of all, containing maximal diversity but also maximal unity.

But to say that evolution, perceived within the context of Christian theology, is a journey, is not to say that the sole aim of the evolutionary process is to produce human beings, or even intelligent life. Genesis 1 declares that all of creation is good in its own right, quite apart from the goodness of humanity. This point is also brought home by the doctrine of the resurrection, especially if that involves the cosmos, as Paul and the book of Revelation proclaim. As John Polkinghorne has written (Polkinghorne, 105) and as traditional Christian doctrine affirms, in the eschaton, nothing that is good will be lost.

But if evolution can be seen as a kind of journey, culminating in the reconciliation of all things in Christ, it is a journey fraught with tragedy. In nature, the price of life is the death of another, both to make room for new life and to provide resources for new life. There is no better example of this than the extinction of the dinosaurs, which had flourished for more than a hundred million years; their sudden extinction opened the way for the flourishing of the mammals, by the process biologists call adaptive radiation.

More than most religions, Christianity has resources to make sense of this tragic and paradoxical evolutionary history, for theologically the suffering, death, and subsequent creative transcendence of evolutionary history is the same pattern that is manifested in the life and death of Jesus: cross, death, and resurrection. So too in organic evolution there is a pattern of cross, death, and subsequent transcendence.

## IV. The evolution of humanity:
## On the "mystery of humanity enlightened by Revelation" (GS 22)

Finally, evolution poses a challenge to the traditional account of the origin and nature of humanity. Catholic doctrine affirms that although the body might emerge from physical evolution, the soul is created directly by God. But what can this mean? Almost no one in the biological or psychological sciences today defends the reality of a soul that can survive the death of the body. Instead, two positions dominate the field. One is so-called "eliminative materialism," which holds that human beings are nothing but atoms and molecules. Biologist Francis Crick espouses this position: "The Astonishing Hypothesis is that 'You,' your joys and your sorrows, your memories and your ambitions, your sense of personal identity and free will, are in fact no more than the behavior of a vast assembly of nerve cells and their associated molecules" (Crick, 3). Such a position, however, reducing consciousness to neural networks and eliminating as it does human freedom, spirituality, and God, is hardly compatible with Christian revelation.

Among Christians involved in the sciences, a more common position is so-called "non-reductive physicalism" (see Brown, Murphy, and Malony). This idea is that human consciousness emerges from and is always dependent on the activity of the human brain. But consciousness cannot be reduced to the physical activity of the brain. Though dependent on that activity, consciousness can affect the processes of the brain, as when a person makes a free decision. There is thus causality in both directions: physical brain states affect consciousness, but consciousness also affects physical brain states. This position is consonant with the scientific data, which show that the physical processes and states of the brain do affect consciousness; but it attempts also to preserve the Christian belief in human freedom and spirituality: humans can respond to God and make free decisions. In this view, the human person is a psycho-physical unity, not an immaterial soul in a body. The "soul," therefore, does not survive the death of the body; the only possibility for afterlife would be if the whole person is resurrected. Furthermore, there is no sharp discontinuity between persons and animals in this view; persons emerge by degrees from animal ancestors, who display simpler forms of consciousness.

However, Jaegwon Kim, a prominent thinker in the area of philosophy of mind, argues that non-reductive physicalism is not cogent. If a given state of consciousness, M, is entirely dependent on a given physical state of the brain, P, as non-reductive physicalism affirms, then M cannot also exercise a causal influence on P. To claim that it does is like claiming that the shadow of an object, say an auto, somehow causes changes in the auto itself. Non-reductive physicalism, therefore, cannot cogently claim that its theory of the mind allows for free decisions that can affect the brain (for example, by causing it to send a nerve impulse down the arms causing me to move my arm).

The alternative to eliminative materialism and non-reductive physicalism is the belief (called in philosophy "dualism") that the mind/soul can function independently of and apart from the body. This is the traditional Christian belief in an immortal and immaterial soul. However, in philosophical circles this position is almost always equated with that of Descartes, who held that the body and the soul are two completely independent substances. The problem with Descartes's belief is that there seems to be, by definition, no way the body could influence the soul or vice versa. But this cannot be correct. We know that brain states influence mental states. This has been known at least since the discovery of alcohol, but recent psychological research has greatly strengthened the point (Jeeves). Strokes, Alzheimer's disease, and drugs all markedly affect our mental states. Therefore, Descartes's position is almost universally rejected.

The problem is that most thinkers in the area of philosophy of mind seldom consider any intermediate positions, such as that of Aquinas, which bridges the physicalist and the dualist positions. Aquinas held that the soul, as the form or organizing principle of the body, influences the body, but that the matter of the body also influences the soul. The soul and body always interact, so that in this life the person is a psychophysical unity. Yet Aquinas also held that the soul can survive the death of the body.

Now, it is longstanding Christian (and especially Catholic) doctrine that the human soul is immortal and survives the death of the body (though the body will be recovered in the resurrection). The usual arguments have been philosophical: the act of knowing and of free choice transcend materiality, and must be the actions of a non-material soul. Jaegwon Kim's criticism of non-reductive physicalism can be used in support of this idea, for if free will is a reality, then the mind must in some sense be independent of the brain and body, and able to act on its own. If it cannot, then we cannot defend free choice.

Can we affirm both the fact that the brain/body influences the mind (and hence the soul), but also that the soul can survive the death of the body? I think we can. Aquinas's position helps us here. If the soul is the organizing principle of the body, so that it and the matter of the body interact, then certainly brain states will affect consciousness. Indeed, the soul in this life develops and shapes its eternal destiny through the choices it makes in and through the body. So, to repeat, in this life the person is a psychophysical unity. How then can we explain the immortality of the soul? The soul is not naturally immortal (as in Platonism), but becomes immortal through its relationship with God. God, freely and graciously, establishes a relationship, or a covenant, with the nascent person. There are two results of this relationship. First, the capacities of the person are elevated, so that free choice and abstract reasoning become possible when the brain and the personality have developed sufficiently to exercise these gifts. Second, because of this relationship, God holds the soul in being after the death of the body. God, through his relationship, gives the person a potentiality very early in life (perhaps at conception, perhaps after). This potentiality confers the capacity for free choice and abstract reasoning, as well as an awareness of a transcendent spiritual reality. What is unique about the human soul then is not the quality of subjectivity—higher animals can experience sensations and emotions; it is the capacity for free choice and spiritual awareness of a transcendent reality. And these capacities are a result of divine grace, which enhances and elevates the natural abilities of humanity, raising them to an awareness of spiritual reality.

This is evident in the course of human evolution. One behavior which seems to be uniquely human, and which emerges at the dawn of human history, is the burial of the dead with food and grave goods. This practice can be documented back to Cro-Magnon times, some twenty-eight thousand years ago. And it is striking evidence for a belief in after-life among early humans, and therefore for a sense of a transcendent reality. Anthropologist Ian Tattersall writes: "It is here that we have the most ancient incontrovertible evidence for the existence of religious experience" (Tattersall, 11). I would argue that religious experience, which at its core is an awareness of a transcendent reality, is one of the distinctive marks of humanity and of a human soul, a mark that distinguishes humans from their close biological cousins, the great apes.

It is impossible to tell, at this distance in time, if this gift originally came only to a few, or to many human beings. Most biologists and anthropologists argue that humanity never consisted only of one pair and was never less than a few thousand individuals (Ayala, 36). But of course they are not in a position to assess the spiritual state of early humans. It is possible that, at some point in human evolution, God granted to two or to many individuals an enlarged spiritual horizon, so that they were aware of transcendent realities and were capable of abstract reason and of free choices. Such a change would probably not have been immediately discernable to an external observer. And of course it could only have happened once the human brain had reached

sufficient complexity so that self-consciousness and foresight were possible. But, I would maintain that the spiritual gift—the awareness of
God and of freedom—did not and could not simply emerge from a
complex material matrix; it was and is a gift of God that constitutes us
as human. In this sense, then, the human soul comes from God. It is not
a foreign "thing" which is injected into the human body; it is an eleva-
tion of natural capacities already present, for grace, theology tells us,
builds on nature; it does not contradict it. As *Gaudium et Spes* affirms:
"All men and women are endowed with a rational soul and are created
in God's image…There is a basic equality between all and it must be accorded ever greater recognition" (*GS* 29).

All this has implications for the doctrine of original sin. We can
hardly hold that death came into the world as a result of human sin (as
Genesis asserts). After all, animals had been present, and dying, for mil-
lions of years before humanity appeared. But we can hold that the interior union with God, which in unfallen humanity would be unbroken
(as in Jesus' consciousness, and Mary's also, for Catholics), was partly
disrupted as a result of the first act of turning from God. Instead of
being turned outward to God, human beings became curved in upon
themselves, selfish and self-centered, and so suffered a kind of spiritual
death, an alienation from God, who is the source of eternal life. From
this stems all the violence and distortion which is then passed on in
human society.

It is this radical self-centeredness which must be reversed if we are
to be at one with God. And Jesus' life, sacrificial death, and resurrection opens to us the possibility of a radical conversion and new life. The
resurrection, in turn, is a promise and an image of what Christians believe will be the end of the evolutionary process. Yet, in all likelihood
we will not peacefully evolve into the resurrection. Jesus' resurrection
was preceded by a terrible death. We have seen that this pattern seems
to be part of the story of evolution: cross, death, then transcendence.
Probably the same will be true in the case of the resurrection: the new
creation would follow upon the death of the old (Polkinghorne, 107).

Christians see the resurrection as the reconciliation of humanity
and creation, with Christ, the incarnate Logos, through whom creation
was formed. As Teilhard wrote, it is Christ, working through the Spirit,
who draws the process toward a goal which, like any journey, cannot be
fully understood except from the perspective of the end, which can be
known only through revelation.

## Conclusion: The journey of creation into God

*Dei Verbum* affirms that God "provides constant evidence of himself in created realities" (*DV* 3). This, indeed, is one of the principal ways that God is revealed to us. And perhaps the greatest gift of science to religion is that science helps to show us the marvelous intricacy, beauty, and interconnectedness of God's creation. Indeed, wonder and curiosity concerning the created order are primary motives for doing science. But, left to itself, science, because of the limitations of its method, cannot tell us anything about ultimate purpose or value, or about the spiritual order, including God. Scientists therefore often too easily conclude that the natural order is all that exists, and that science is the only valid means of knowledge. In other words, they assent to the ideology of philosophical naturalism. To balance this tendency, and for a knowledge of purpose, value, and spiritual reality, including the soul and God, we need revelation.

It is not inappropriate to return here to some words of Bishop Lucker. In his homily at the February, 2001 Mass that marked both his twenty-fifth anniversary as bishop and his retirement as bishop of New Ulm, he preached a very short sermon. "Well," he said, "after twenty-five years one thing stands out as the most important. More than anything else, I have learned this one truth. And the truth is simply, 'God is here'" (Unsworth, 21).

For the dialogue of faith and science, Bishop Lucker's words imply this: evolution can be understood within a framework of faith and personalism. It does not necessarily entail a naturalistic framework of impersonal forces, an interpretation that ends by debasing human beings to accidental spin-offs of a blind mechanical process. But to bring evolutionary theory within a theistic framework, we must conjoin it with revelation; the book of nature must be complemented by the book of scripture. This will entail modifications both for our understanding of science and for our understanding of revelation. In the end, the evolution of creation and the church's developing understanding of revelation are aspects of the same journey: the journey of creation into God.

## References

Ayala, Francisco. "Human Nature: One Evolutionist's View." In *Whatever Happened to the Soul?* Ed. W. Brown, N. Murphy, and H. N. Malony. Minneapolis: Fortress Press, 1998. Pp. 31–48.

Brown, Warren, Nancey Murphy, and H. N. Malony, eds. *Whatever Happened to the Soul?* Minneapolis: Fortress Press, 1998.

Crick, Francis. *Life Itself: Its Origin and True Nature.* New York: Simon & Schuster, 1981.

Darwin, Charles. *On the Origin of Species,* 6th ed. Chicago: Encyclopaedia Britannica, Great Books, 1859, 1952.

Dawkins, Richard. *The Blind Watchmaker.* New York: W. W. Norton, 1987.

Denton, Michael. *Nature's Destiny.* New York: The Free Press, 1998.

Depew, David, and Bruce Weber. *Darwinism Evolving.* Cambridge, Mass.: MIT Press, 1995.

Ellis, George. *Before the Beginning.* London/New York: Boyars/Bowerdean, 1993.

Gould, Stephen Jay. *Wonderful Life.* New York: Norton, 1989.

Hall, Barry. "Evolution in a Petri Dish." *Evolutionary Biology* 15 (1982): 85–150.

Haught, John. *God After Darwin.* Boulder, Colo.: Westview Press, 2000.

Ho, Mae-Wan, and Peter Saunders, eds. *Beyond Neo-Darwinism: An Introduction to the New Evolutionary Paradigm.* London: The Academic Press, 1984.

Jaki, Stanley. *The Relevance of Physics.* Chicago: University of Chicago Press, 1966.

Jeeves, Malcolm. "Brain, Mind, and Behavior." In *Whatever Happened to the Soul?.* Ed. W. Brown, N. Murphy, and H. N. Malony. Minneapolis: Fortress Press, 1998. Pp. 73–97.

Kauffman, Stuart. *At Home in the Universe.* New York: Oxford, 1995.

Kim, Jaegwon. *Mind in a Physical World.* Cambridge, Mass.: MIT Press, 1998.

Maxwell, James Clerk. "Ether." *Encyclopaedia Britannica,* 9th edition, vol. 7 (1878).

Miller, Kenneth. *Finding Darwin's God.* New York: HarperCollins, 1999.

Monod, Jacques. *Chance and Necessity.* New York: Random House, 1972.

Polkinghorne, John. *Serious Talk.* Valley Forge, Pa.: Trinity Press International, 1995.

Spetner, Lee. *Not By Chance!* Brooklyn: Judaica Press, 1998.

Tattersall, Ian. *Becoming Human: Evolution and Human Uniqueness.* New York: Harcourt Brace, 1998.

Teilhard de Chardin, Pierre. *The Phenomenon of Man.* New York: Harper, 1959.

Unsworth, Tim. "A Man Who Was 'Filled with God.'" *National Catholic Reporter* 37/42 (October 5, 2001): 21.

Wesson, Robert. *Beyond Natural Selection.* Cambridge, Mass.: MIT Press, 1991.

## 2
## Toward a scriptural understanding of revelation: God inserts God's self into history

CATHERINE CORY AND CORRINE PATTON

In its preface to *Dei Verbum,* the Dogmatic Constitution on Divine Revelation, the Second Vatican Council set forth a most lofty goal. The
Council said that it wanted to articulate a teaching about revelation
and how it is passed on, for it wanted "the whole world to hear the
summons to salvation, so that through hearing it may believe, through
belief it may hope, through hope it may come to love" (*DV* 1). In other
words, the goal of its teaching on revelation was to invite not only
church members, but also all of humanity to be possessed by the revelatory experience and to enter into a transformative journey, which manifests itself and comes to fruition finally in *agape* (love). Bishop Lucker
knew from his own life experiences and in his daily meditation on
scripture the transformative character of revelation. To him we dedicate
this essay on scriptural understandings of revelation.

In a rather dramatic turn from the scholastic theology of times past,
*Dei Verbum* gave priority to the Bible as the source and foundation for
Christian theology. Thus it asserted that "sacred theology relies on the
written word of God, taken together with sacred tradition, as its permanent foundation . . . Therefore, the study of the sacred page should
be the very soul of sacred theology" (*DV* 24). What then does sacred
scripture have to tell us about a Christian theology of revelation? Our
essay proceeds in three parts. In part one, we summarize the understanding of revelation in the Old Testament scriptures. In part two, we
do the same in the New Testament scriptures. In our essay's conclusion,
we outline the implications of the scriptural material for an understanding of revelation in our day.

## I. Revelation in the Old Testament

While the ancient Israelite authors did not use the same categories to describe the modes of God's revelation as Catholic teaching does today, the Old Testament witnesses to the variety of ways by which Israel came to know God. Probably the three most prominent ways in which the canon describes God's revelation are through prophetic revelation, through the revelation embedded in the Torah, and through the views of God's revelation contained in the wisdom traditions. A closer examination of these three broad categories clarifies the Old Testament roots of a Christian theology of revelation.

### Prophetic revelation

When people hear the word "revelation," the image that is conjured up is often that of the prophet who has access to a direct experience of God and God's message. Like the image of the thrown book in Flannery O'Connor's short story, "Revelation," God's revelation is supposed to hit us like a ton of bricks, an experience that is both uncomfortable and life changing. Although Old Testament texts do not often describe the exact mechanisms by which prophets received their messages, the canon does speak about the unique quality of prophetic revelation. For instance, in many Pentateuchal texts, Moses is presented as the perfect prophet: he hears God's voice clearly (Ex 20:22), speaks to God face to face (Ex 33:11), or at least has an unmediated experience of "God's back" (Ex 33:23). In the closing verses of the Pentateuch, the text states, "Never since has there arisen a prophet in Israel like Moses, whom the LORD knew face to face" (Deut 34:10).

The Old Testament canon reinforces the distinction between prophet and people. God reveals God's self to Moses in front of the people so that they will recognize that he is a true prophet and that they need his mediation (Ex 19:9). In the law of the prophet in the book of Deuteronomy, God affirms that the people are in danger if they listen to God face to face; they need a prophet to mediate God's message to them (Deut 18:16-18). Two lengthy passages in Ezekiel (3:17-21 and 33:1-9) examine the burden of culpability placed on the prophet. Because the prophet has special, clear, and direct knowledge of God's judgment against the people for their sins, the prophet becomes guilty of their death if he or she does not warn them.

Prophets are more than just passive recipients of God's revelation. They enter into conversations with God, seen most clearly when prophets intercede with God on behalf of the people. But even when prophets receive non-negotiable messages of doom, they can converse with God about the reasons or the effects of the pronouncements. For instance, when Isaiah asks God how long the destruction will last in Isaiah 6:11, God provides an answer, even though it is not comforting. In 1 Kings 22:19-23, Micaiah ben Imlah explains his prophecy of doom after the king has objected to his message; this passage shows that he has more information about God's revelation than his first oracle revealed. Similarly in the book of Jonah, the prophet simply declares, "Forty days more, and Nineveh shall be overthrown!" (3:4), even though the reader knows he has lengthier conversations with God both before and after the city's salvation. These texts tell us that revelation at its clearest and most direct results in a conversation, not just in pronouncements.

Lastly, the Old Testament continuously witnesses to the life-changing aspect of prophetic revelation. In fact, it is this last feature of revelation that makes revelation seem so unattractive. We read of prophet after prophet who was called to a life of thankless responsibility and personal peril. Many prophets were accused of being criminals or traitors by governments which did not like their messages: Moses, Elijah, Amos, and Jeremiah, to name a few. Even those who seemed to have the ear of those in power hardly led a carefree life; Isaiah, for example, had the terrible burden of knowing the punishment God was poised to enact. Ezekiel's sentinel passages remind us that God stands waiting to accuse the prophet who fails in his or her duties. With more direct revelation comes awesome responsibility.

The goal of prophetic revelation is the transformation of the community. Recent anthropological studies of prophecy have served to remind scholars of the communal context and goal of prophetic revelation. Prophets are mediators, not solely recipients: they receive a message that must be delivered to a community. The goal of prophetic speech is usually to change behavior. Even when the prophet seems only to be providing information, this information or knowledge should result in a changed community, one that will then act differently because it has a better understanding of the implications of being in covenant with this God.

### Torah as revelation

Prophetic revelation, that is, God's direct revelation mediated through a specific individual, is not the only means by which the Israelites knew the will of God. Within the biblical canon, the Torah holds a premier place as the locus of God's revelation. While the book of Genesis certainly describes important revelatory moments, the revelation at Sinai remains a paradigmatic instance of Yahweh's revelation. Even so, how often do Christians forget or ignore the fact that God revealed a wide variety of laws on Sinai?

The legal texts are at the heart of God's revelation at Sinai. These legal texts direct the social, religious, and personal lives of the ancient Israelites. The laws are set within a clear framework of revelatory speech. God calls all the people to the foot of the mountain for the revelation of the law (Ex 19:10-11, 17). The people assemble and hear from Moses the revelation of the Decalogue, but then beg to be released from having to hear the terrifying voice of God (Ex 20). As Moses alone approaches the "thick darkness," prepared to receive the legal prescriptions that follow, God's first statement links revelation with human response. "You [plural] have seen for yourselves that I spoke with you from heaven" (Ex 20:22), that is, you have experienced revelation directly. Therefore, "you shall not make gods of silver alongside me, nor shall you make for yourselves gods of gold" (Ex 20:23), that is, the people will not make idols, which represent false, or silent gods. From an authentic experience of revelation, specific actions in all aspects of life follow.

The book of Deuteronomy expresses a basic teaching about revelation. When Moses speaks to the Israelites who surround him as he is about to die, he repeatedly asserts that "you were there" when the Torah was revealed. Yet, the reality is that the generation to whom he speaks was not physically present at Sinai. That generation had died out because they had sinned, and the majority of the crowd that Moses addresses had not yet been born at the time when God revealed the law at Sinai. This literary device allows the character, Moses, to speak directly to every generation that reads this book. Just as Moses declares to the crowd, "You were there," so too he declares this same thing to us, speaking directly to anybody who hears this speech. "The LORD spoke with *you* face to face on the mountain from the midst of the fire" (Deut 5:4; emphasis added).

The laws represent God's gift outlining how the Israelites are called to respond to God's life-changing revelation. The book of Deuteronomy expresses the lasting quality of this revelatory experience most clearly. Deuteronomy 6:5 states, "You shall love the LORD your God with all your heart, and with all your soul, and with all your might." This passage seeks more than a passing emotive response to God. It commands the Israelites to be so bound to God that it is part of their very nature, part of their very being. The Deuteronomist calls them to a life that cannot possibly be lived apart from their relationship with God. For the Deuteronomic redactor, the legal texts should remind the reader of one very important thing: a relationship with God is life-changing. It is not enough to hear God's voice, or to study God objectively, if such an encounter does not lead to fundamental changes in how a person leads her or his life. The laws remind us that these changes are more than just changing our habits, more than just "acting" differently. These are *fundamental changes.*

### Revelation in the wisdom literature

In the twentieth century, theological discussions of revelation have turned more to questions of God's general revelation, that is, the way in which all humans know something true and good about God. This particular framing of the question certainly reflects modern concerns, but the notion that God is revealed to all is an integral part of the Old Testament. The wisdom literature, most evident in the proverbial texts, works off of the notion that all people, not just priests and prophets, can know God. Modern discussions of general revelation can benefit from a deeper look into the theological structure that underlies the wisdom literature's assumptions about God's revelation.

Wisdom theology works on what might be called "creation theology." This is the principle that God's primary act, and therefore a fundamental way by which God is known, is through creation. The Israelites explicitly believed that creation is not the result of haphazard circumstances, but reflects careful design by the creator. In texts that deal with creation specifically, this is expressed by the fact that what stands opposed to creation is not "nothingness," but chaos. Creation, by this very definition, is an act of order and purpose. This order, coming from God, reveals God.

The proverbial texts contain hymns to Lady Wisdom. Although biblical scholars disagree as to her precise origin and relationship to God, the poems make clear that wisdom is the principle by which God created the world. Wisdom is built into the world, and humans have access to that wisdom by observing creation. In Proverbs 8, Lady Wisdom declares that she worked beside God as the world was created; as a result, she calls all to heed her "instruction," that is, to learn how to behave by understanding the wisdom by which God created the universe. The Wisdom of Solomon, a text that examines wisdom's manifestations throughout the history of the world, notes that wisdom "is found by those who seek her" (Wis 6:12).

Humans are no small part of the created order. Within its ancient Near Eastern context, the *imago dei* in which humans are created in Genesis 1:27 connotes humanity's role in representing God's real presence in the world. Humanity's ability to transgress its role, to try to become "like a god" (our translation of Gen 3:5), also attests to its unique role in maintaining God's created order. Natural elements, such as rocks, trees, and even animals, do not try to transgress the boundaries God has created for them. Humans, however, have a tragically unique capacity to transgress, a word that rightly captures one of Israel's most common definitions of sin. By transgressing divinely appointed boundaries, humans become vehicles for chaos, that is, for what stands opposed to God's creation. In ancient Near Eastern texts, including the Bible, human transgression affects not just human society, but all of nature: human evil leads to the flood (Gen 6:5-7); Ahab's support of Baal worship is accompanied by severe drought (1 Kings 16:29–18:46); Israel's famine in the days of Amos comes as punishment for sin (Amos 4:6-9). These are just a few examples.

The proverbial literature has a didactic purpose. It aims to teach rich young males to be "wise," a necessary attribute given their future potential for power. It is important to notice the ingrained hierarchy in the text. Wisdom books, such as Proverbs, are not addressed to everybody, nor do they contain the "wisdom" needed by all people. They are addressed to a particular social group that is defined by gender, ethnicity, and class. The men are instructed to observe the world and to act in ways befitting their station in life. They must handle money responsibly, pick good friends, arrange marriages with women who will be supportive of their leadership, feast as is their right, but within the limitations of decorum, etc. In other words, they must act in ways appropriate to their station within God's created order.

For Israelites, people who acted in ways that transgressed their social station became vehicles for chaos. Examples of this would include women who spoke and acted like men, poor people who had the pride of the rich, and rich males who acted like demure women. While certainly some acts were always wrong, the morality of other behaviors was affected by social context. Such a moral code works only if it is undergirded by the conviction that this knowledge of God and God's creation is accessible to all people. In other words, it works only if God's revelation is somehow accessible to all people. It might be argued that a book like Proverbs still depends on an inspired author to reveal God's teaching and, therefore, that the Old Testament always maintains the need for special revelation. Yet, the fact that the book is addressed to only one particular audience while maintaining that all are called to a moral life attests to the fact that the wisdom in the book is simply a model for how people everywhere must pursue wisdom. It is not only the inspired author who is called to be wise; all humans must pursue wisdom.

Wisdom is transformative. In other words, knowing God's revelation through creation results in a righteous life. Wisdom is not a set of principles or postulates, not a code of law; it is a transforming recognition of the reality of God as creator. The clear and unequivocal result of God's revelation through wisdom is a life lived in rectitude.

> For the LORD gives wisdom;
> from his mouth come knowledge and understanding;
> he stores up sound wisdom for the upright;
> he is a shield to those who walk blamelessly,
> guarding the paths of justice
> and preserving the way of his faithful ones. (Prov 2:6-8)

As the Wisdom of Solomon makes clear, the result of this righteous life is immortality, which "brings one near to God" (Wis 6:19).

### Summary

The Old Testament witnesses to a variety of ways by which God is made known to humanity. Prophetic revelation entails the direct communication between God and an individual of a message intended for the community. The Torah resulted from a particular direct revelation of God to the people of Israel at Sinai. All Israel knew what God required of them because of the eternal nature of this revelation. God is also revealed in creation. All of humanity knew something about God by becoming "wise" about God and God's plan embedded in this creation. While each of these three modes of revelation utilizes distinct vehicles of revelation (individual prophet, text-encoded law, and created order), all three see this revelation as life-changing, transformative.

## II. Revelation in the New Testament

In many respects, the New Testament bears important similarities to the Old Testament in what it tells us about revelation. However, the

New Testament's understanding of revelation is also definitively different from the Old Testament because of the incarnation of Jesus, God's Son. For example, in the New Testament, Christian prophecy is acknowledged to be the activity of God's Spirit and the writings of the Old Testament prophets are respected as the word of God. At the same time, the New Testament portrays Jesus as the prophet *par excellence* and describes the prophecies of the Old Testament as ultimately fulfilled in Jesus. Likewise, the New Testament confirms the revelatory character of the law, as understood in the Old Testament. At the same time, it identifies Jesus as the new Moses who calls for the perfection and fulfillment of the law. Finally, the New Testament carries forward from its Old Testament sources certain understandings about the revelatory character of the wisdom tradition. Moreover, it uses the imagery of the wisdom tradition to proclaim Jesus as the Wisdom of God and the revelation of God.

### Prophetic revelation and Jesus, the prophet

The gospels of the New Testament, particularly the gospel of Matthew, make frequent reference to the writings of the prophets. When they do, the presupposition is that these prophecies carry weight because they are the word of God, not only when they were first delivered, but now too as they are recalled in the situation of the New Testament. Thus, the author of Mark's gospel gives authority to the ministry of John the Baptist by saying, "As it is written in the prophet Isaiah..." (Mk 1:2). Likewise, in Luke's story of the rich man and Lazarus, Abraham responds to the rich man's request to send someone to warn his brothers of their fate by saying, "If they do not listen to Moses and the prophets, neither will they be convinced even if someone rises from the dead" (Lk 16:31). In this way, Luke's gospel affirms the words of the prophets as authoritative and as a heaven-sent call to repentance—whether or not their words are heeded!

When the gospels mention the prophets and refer to Jesus, they often do so to indicate that certain events in the life of Jesus conform to God's plan of salvation. Concerning the birth of Jesus, Matthew says, "All this took place to fulfill what had been spoken by the Lord through the prophet [i.e., Isaiah]" (Mt 1:22). Later, in the story of the holy family's flight to Egypt, Matthew says, "This was to fulfill what had been spoken by the Lord through the prophet [i.e., Hosea]" (Mt 2:15). By incorporating these fulfillment citations, Matthew takes for granted the role of the prophet as mediator of God's word, but he also asserts that

God's word, once spoken to Israel through the prophets, is now being fulfilled, that is, being made more clear, in the person of Jesus. Likewise, in John's gospel, when Philip invites Nathaniel to join him in following Jesus, he says, "We have found him about whom Moses in the law and also the prophets wrote, Jesus son of Joseph from Nazareth" (Jn 1:45).

In some cases, the gospel writers go a step further, not only citing the prophets of the Hebrew scriptures to describe who Jesus is and who he was destined to be, but also describing Jesus as the prophet *par excellence*. Just as many Old Testament prophets expected a life of trial, so too, in the scenes in which Jesus' prophetic character is revealed, his impending death hangs like a cloud. For example, the synoptic gospels contain a scene in which Jesus visits his hometown and is met with a great deal of suspicion. "Where did this man get this wisdom and these deeds of power?" (Mt 13:54; cf. Mk 6:2), they say. Apparently the gospel writers view Jesus' teaching and miracle working as akin to the work of the prophets, because they have Jesus respond, "Prophets are not without honor except in their own country and in their own house" (Mt 13:57; cf. Mk 6:4). Immediately following is the story of the death of John the Baptist, which prefigures in a way the death of Jesus (Mt 14:1-12; Mk 6:14-29). In another scene, when Jesus is confronted by a group of Pharisees and Sadducees who want him to produce a sign, presumably as evidence that he is God's prophet, he answers, "no sign will be given to it except the sign of Jonah" (Mt 16:4; cf. Mk 8:12; Lk 11:29). Of course, the sign of Jonah (three days in the belly of the whale) is a reference to Jesus' death and resurrection.

Luke's gospel places particular emphasis on Jesus as God's prophet. Again, these references are often connected with his healing activity or with his impending death. In the story of Jesus raising the widow's son at Nain, the crowd reacts with amazement, saying, "A great prophet has risen among us!" (Lk 7:16). Later Jesus is portrayed as delivering oracles of woe against the Pharisees (Lk 11:42-44) and the lawyers (Lk 11:46-52). In the second of these oracles, he says: "Therefore also the Wisdom of God said, 'I will send them prophets and apostles, some of whom they will kill and persecute,' so that this generation may be charged with the blood of all the prophets shed since the foundation of the world" (Lk 11:49-50).

Clearly "this generation" refers to the time of Jesus' death, so that Jesus stands as the culmination or sum of all the prophets. In another scene, when the Pharisees try to warn Jesus that Herod intends to kill him, he tells them to deliver a message to Herod. The message concludes, "I must be on my way, because it is impossible for a prophet to be killed outside of Jerusalem" (Lk 13:33). Of course, the prophet to whom the saying refers is Jesus. Finally, in the story of the disciples on the way to Emmaus, the risen Jesus is conversing with the disciples as they travel along the road. Without recognizing him, they talk about Jesus as "a prophet mighty in deed and word before God and all the people" (Lk 24:19). Later Jesus chides them for their slowness in believing "all that the prophets have declared," concerning the necessity of the messiah's suffering and death (Lk 24:25-27). In sum, Jesus as prophet and revealer of God's word must be understood in the context of his crucifixion. The crucified Christ is both the messenger (the prophet) and the message, the revealer and the revealed.

### Torah as revelation and Jesus, the new lawgiver

The writers of the New Testament and the earliest Christians took for granted the revelatory character of the Jewish scriptures. For example, in Acts of the Apostles, when Paul is brought to trial before Felix, the governor of Judea, he defends himself by saying, "I worship the God of our ancestors, believing everything laid down according to the law or written in the prophets" (Acts 24:14). Elsewhere in the New Testament, the law is understood to carry authority to direct one's activities in righteousness, precisely because it is revelatory literature. In Matthew's gospel, in the Sermon on the Mount, Jesus says, "In everything do to others as you would have them do to you; for this is the law and the prophets" (Mt 7:12). Later, in a critique of the scribes and Pharisees, Jesus scolds them for being overly concerned about tithes, while they have "neglected the weightier matters of the law: justice and mercy and faith" (Mt 23:23).

While holding firm to the revelatory character of the law, Matthew's gospel seems to go a step further and suggest that Jesus is the new Moses. The gospel itself is arranged in five blocks of narrative, each followed by a discourse section consisting of a collection of sayings of Jesus, often thought to parallel the five books of Torah. In the infancy narrative, Joseph is told to take Mary and the child to Egypt to escape the clutches of Herod. The narrator adds, "This was to fulfill what had been spoken by the Lord through the prophet, 'Out of Egypt I have called my son'" (Mt 2:15), referring to the Exodus. After his forty days in the wilderness, reminiscent of the Israelites' forty years in the wilderness, Jesus calls his first disciples. When the crowds gather, he ascends an unnamed mountain, reminiscent of Sinai, and begins to teach. This long discourse includes several statements from the law of Moses, to which Jesus adds a further command designed to clarify the true meaning of the law (Mt 5:21-47). Often the clarifications take the audience beyond the letter of the law to its true intent. This section ends with the saying, "Be perfect, therefore, as your heavenly Father is perfect" (Mt 5:48). In other words, living the true meaning of the law, "fulfilling" it, means a fundamental change in understanding who we are with respect to God.

At the same time, some New Testament writers speak of a reality greater than the law. The author of the letter to the Hebrews, in referring to the purificatory qualities of sacrifices prescribed by the law, says that the law is "only a shadow of the good things to come" (Heb 10:1). In contrast to those sacrifices, which must be repeated again and again and still cannot perfect its participants, the author proclaims, "It is by God's will that we have been sanctified through the offering of the body of Jesus Christ once for all" (Heb 10:10). In other words, this sacrifice of Jesus supersedes and perfects anything that is prescribed in the law.

In his teaching on justification by faith, Paul also writes of a reality greater than the law, or, perhaps more accurately stated, people's misunderstanding of the place of the law. As Paul uses the term, justification means right relationship with God or acquittal by God. Therefore, Paul's teaching on justification cannot be understood apart from his teaching on sin. It also cannot be understood apart from covenant, since Paul understands law to mean the commandments given to Moses. For Paul, sin is humanity's refusal to acknowledge God as God—and itself as God's creatures (Rom 1:21). Thus humans took it upon themselves to break relationship with God. They cannot repair that relationship by obeying the obligations of the covenant, because the covenant is not a covenant of equals. Only God can repair the relationship, only God can acquit humanity. Therefore, Paul says that justification by means of the law is impossible. Instead, justification comes through faith in Jesus Christ "whom God put forward as a sacrifice of atonement" (Rom 3:25). Through Jesus, God repairs, and therefore perfects, or fulfills, the covenant of law. Jesus makes the transformative power of the law accessible to all in faith.

### Jesus, the Wisdom of God

As already noted, Old Testament wisdom literature works from the assumption that God's revelation is accessible to everyone who is open to receive it. The New Testament works from the same assumption, except that Jesus is the Wisdom of God. For example, the author of the letter to the Colossians describes Christ as "God's mystery" and the one "in whom are hidden all the treasures of wisdom and knowledge" (Col 2:2-3). The author also incorporates a hymn about Christ, the Wisdom of God:

> He is the image of the invisible God, the firstborn of all creation;
> for in him all things in heaven and on earth were created,
> things visible and invisible, whether thrones or dominions or
>     rulers or powers—
> all things have been created through him and for him.
> He himself is before all things, and in him all things hold
>     together. (Col 1:15-17)

Like Lady Wisdom of the Old Testament, Jesus is described as the first of creation, the one through whom all things came to be, and the one who holds all things together. However, unlike Lady Wisdom, Jesus is proclaimed as the one in whom "all the fullness of God was pleased to dwell" (Col 1:19) and the one through whom God reconciled all things to himself "by making peace through the blood of his cross" (Col 1:20). In other words, the revelation of God is most fully manifest in Jesus and its purpose is realized in his crucifixion and exaltation.

Likewise, in the gospel of John, Jesus is portrayed as Wisdom and the revelation of God. The prologue proclaims Jesus, the Word of God, who like Lady Wisdom was with God from the beginning and through whom all things came to be (Jn 1:2-3; cf. Prov 8:22-31; Wis 7:24; 8:1). He is the glory of God and the light that shines in the darkness (Jn 1:5, 14; cf. Wis 7:25-26). He came to dwell with God's people, and not all received him (Jn 1:11, 14; cf. Prov 1:20-33), but to those who did, he became the revealer of God, the one who makes God known (Jn 1:18; cf. Prov 2:1-11). However, in contrast with Lady Wisdom who is described as God's throne partner (Wis 9:4, 10) and co-craftsperson in creation (Prov 8:30; Wis 9:9), Jesus is not simply a personified power of God. Rather, he is God's only Son, and the "wise" person knows Jesus, as Son, to be the sum and culmination of God's creative plan. Jesus *is* the revelation of God. In the words of *Dei Verbum*, "The most intimate truth thus revealed about God and human salvation shines forth for us in Christ, who is himself both the mediator and the sum total of revelation" (*DV* 2).

In general, the New Testament understands the Word of God to be wholly transformative for those who are open to being possessed by it. The letter to the Hebrews describes it as living and effective (Heb 4:12). It is living in the sense that it is the source of eternal life; it is effective because nothing can stop it from achieving its purpose. The Word of God is sharper than any two-edged sword, penetrating the innermost recesses of the heart and judging all our thoughts and intentions. In other words, because of the Word, every aspect of our lives is laid bare, making us painfully exposed to God to whom we must render an account of our lives (Heb 4:12-13).

In light of the Word's transformative power, it could be said that Jesus, as the Word of God and Wisdom of God, has the capacity to utterly consume us. At the same time, Jesus, precisely in his role as God's Wisdom, can be the source of all consolation. In Matthew's gospel, after identifying himself as the one who reveals the hidden things of God, Jesus issues an invitation that sounds much like Lady Wisdom's invitation to the simple ones to come and banquet with her. Moreover, he speaks to an unnamed audience as if to the whole world:

> Come to me, all you that are weary and are carrying heavy burdens, and I will give you rest. Take my yoke upon you, and learn from me; for I am gentle and humble in heart, and you will find rest for your souls. For my yoke is easy, and my burden is light. (Mt 11:28; cf. Prov 9:1-6)

Likewise, Paul in his first letter to the Corinthians talks about God's wisdom (Christ crucified) which was decreed before the ages, but which had remained hidden until this time. The "wise" of the world do not understand, he says, "'what God has prepared for those who love him'—these things God has revealed to us through the Spirit; for the Spirit searches everything, even the depths of God" (1 Cor 2:9-10). What blessed consolation for those who are open to receive it!

## Conclusion: Toward a scriptural approach to revelation in our day

People sometimes are tempted to think of the Bible, and therefore revelation, as a static thing—what is revealed to us in the pages of the Bible is readily available to us and, because it is the word of God, its meaning is eternal and unchangeable. Others sometimes think of the

Bible as a repository of divinely revealed "proof statements" used to establish the church's doctrines. However, neither of these positions accurately describes what it means to say the Bible is revelation. Likewise, neither of these positions reflects a *biblical* approach to revelation. After looking at what the Bible has to say about revelation, we can come to better conclusions about what characterizes a biblical approach to revelation today. First, let us summarize briefly what the Bible has to say about revelation.

We have seen that the biblical canon attests to several vehicles for God's revelation, all perfected in Christ. These include the prophet, the law, and wisdom. Although prophets are called to a more direct experience of God, revelation is not given for its own sake, or even for the sake of the prophetic recipient. Rather, direct revelation is given to the prophets, who, driven by a solemn responsibility to the community, speak God's word so that God's people can be transformed. Jesus, as both the prophet *par excellence* and the fulfillment, that is, fullness, of the message of the Old Testament prophets, is given to humanity so that we may know God's prophetic revelation more clearly.

Likewise, although the Torah was revealed to a person, Moses, it was revealed for a community, Israel. The Torah embodies the divinely revealed codes of Israel's life in covenant with God and it expresses the degree to which human response to God affects all aspects of human life. As Deuteronomy 22:6 states, it even governs what we do when we see a bird's nest on the ground. The purpose of the law was to transform the lives of God's people so that they might realize the full implications of the covenant. Yet for Christians, the law came to represent people's futile attempts to rectify a covenant shattered by human failure. Since God initiated the covenant, only God could repair it and only God could acquit humanity of its sin. Thus Jesus is the repairer of the breach. Jesus is the means by which God set the covenant in right order and brought the people again to a life transformed.

Finally, God was revealed not only to the elite in ancient Israel, those who could read and study Torah, but to all people. God is knowable by all people through God's purposeful act of creation. For Israel, and for us, "creation" is not just a moment in the historical past. Rather, the creative act involves the continual sustenance of a viable world. Humans, as the image of God, assist God in maintaining an inhabitable world by becoming "wise," that is, by knowing God's revealed design and preserving the fragile order necessary to sustain life on earth. As Christians, we see this design fully revealed in Christ, who is divine Wisdom. A positive response to Wisdom's invitation results in a changed life, paralleling what Bishop Lucker saw as a fundamental principle: that revelation is a life-changing experience. "I came to realize that all is centered on the revelation of God and our response in faith . . . Once you are touched—really *touched* by a few basic truths of faith, your life will be different" (Lucker, 511). To adapt the words of Bishop Lucker, Israel conceived of itself as a people "possessed by truth," a truth revealed by God to all people in multiple ways. By extension, Christians see themselves as a people possessed by the Word of God—namely, Jesus, the revelation of God and the full realization of God's plan of salvation.

What then can we say about a biblical approach to revelation today? Whether we are talking about the prophets of old, the Torah, the wisdom of the sages, the words and deeds of Jesus, or our encounter with the divine in creation, revelation is, first and foremost, *dynamic.* If the Bible is our guide to understanding revelation, then we know that revelation is never a passive encounter, but an experience that requires seeing, hearing, speaking, and acting. In the process of revelation, God inserts God's self in human history and humans, as recipients of revelation, make an active response. Implied in this statement is the recognition that revelation can be known only in and through particular historical and cultural contexts.

The dynamic character of biblical revelation can be seen in the church's recognition that God speaks through the human authors of the Bible and "in human fashion," making it necessary for us to "carefully search out the meaning the sacred writers really had in mind" if we are to ascertain what God wished to communicate (*DV* 12). At the same time, we who hear the word today must recognize that we are hearing (understanding and responding) in a different historical and cultural context. Therefore, we engage in a process of rereading the biblical text in light of new circumstances and drawing out its meaning for the contemporary situation. We also recognize that its meaning is shaped by the culture in which it takes root. As the inspired word of God, it is a *living* word that is effective today in our midst.

Second, a biblical approach to revelation today involves the recognition that revelation, whether public or private, is received in the context of *community* and is given for the sake of the community. This is a particular challenge to contemporary American culture, which upholds the rights of individuals sometimes to the detriment of the common good. However, the Bible itself provides a model. The documents that

eventually came to be known as the Bible were written for the edification of communities of faith. Likewise, the process of canon formation
was a community endeavor. In fact, one of the primary safeguards for
reliable interpretation of scripture is that it takes place within communities of faith (the tradition of the church). Even the action which is
called for by a biblical approach to revelation has a communal dimension; it is action on behalf of, or for the sake of, the community. Therefore, when we respond to God's revelatory activity today, we need to
be aware that we do it not as individuals but as members of a faith community and as members of a human community, called to fullness of life
in covenant relationship with God.

Finally, a biblical approach to revelation is *transformative*. In his
book, *Jesus: A Gospel Portrait*, the New Testament scholar Donald Senior
talks about how the Holy Spirit is detectable in the church's enduring
love of sacred scripture. He goes on to note that, in the long course of
its history, "when circumstances forced reform on the church—or, less
frequently, when she freely chose it—the church has turned to the
word of God to renew its life. There, in the portrait of Jesus, it finds re-
freshment and challenge. There it finds direction for its own ministry of
teaching, of healing, of reconciling..." (p. 157). Implicit in Senior's
statement is the communal dimension of the transformative encounter
with revelation. What Senior is saying is that, whatever else it does, sacred scripture transforms the community that receives it; it transforms
the church. The Pontifical Biblical Commission's "Interpretation of the
Bible in the Church" is even more explicit about the communal dimension of this transformation, localizing it in the church's theology. Thus
the commission asserted:

> One of the principal functions of the Bible is to mount serious
> challenges to theological systems and to draw attention con-
> stantly to the existence of important aspects of divine revela-
> tion and human reality which have at times been forgotten or
> neglected in efforts at systematic reflection. (Pontifical Biblical
> Commission, 520)

The interrelationship of these three characteristics of a biblical approach to revelation—dynamic, communal, transformative—is perhaps
already apparent from what has been said above. However, we would be
remiss if we did not call to mind the wisdom of the bishops of the Second Vatican Council, when they wrote: "Tradition and scripture make

up a single sacred deposit of the Word of God, which is entrusted to the church" (*DV* 10). What a powerful statement! Tradition by itself is not the revelation of God (in its fullest sense), but neither is sacred scripture. In fact, we cannot fully receive or understand the revelation of sacred scripture apart from the tradition. Thus, sacred scripture and tradition *together* are the revealed word of God. Moreover, they are the revelation of God *entrusted to the church*—for its edification, for its chastisement, for its consolation, for its salvation. Such is the dynamic, transformative nature of revelation that enlivens God's community, the church.

Thus we return to the place where we started. The bishops at the Second Vatican Council offered their teaching on revelation for "the whole world to hear the summons to salvation, so that through hearing it may believe, through belief it may hope, through hope it may come to love" (*DV* 1). This is the goal of revelation: the salvation or wholeness of humanity. When we come finally to abide in love, we are utterly transformed, because God is love.

## References and suggestions for further reading

Collins, Raymond F. "Inspiration." In *The New Jerome Biblical Commentary*. Ed. Raymond E. Brown, Joseph A. Fitzmyer, Roland E. Murphy. Englewood Cliffs, N.J.: Prentice Hall, 1990. Pp. 1023–1033.

Fitzmyer, Joseph A. *Scripture, the Soul of Theology*. New York: Paulist Press, 1994.

McKenzie, John L. "Aspects of Old Testament Thought." In *The New Jerome Biblical Commentary*. Ed. Raymond E. Brown, Joseph A. Fitzmyer, Roland E. Murphy. Englewood Cliffs, N.J.: Prentice Hall, 1990. Pp. 1284–1315.

Ord, David Robert, and Robert B. Coote. *Is the Bible True? Understanding the Bible Today*. Maryknoll, N.Y.: Orbis Books, 1994.

Pontifical Biblical Commission. "The Interpretation of the Bible in the Church." *Origins* 23 (1994): 499–524.

Senior, Donald. *Jesus: A Gospel Portrait*. New York: Paulist Press, 1992.

# 3
# A growing understanding of the Bible in the life of the church

CHRIS A. FRANKE AND VINCENT T. M. SKEMP

I n his copy of the documents of Vatican II, Bishop Lucker underlined, circled, and starred the following words from paragraph eleven of the Dogmatic Constitution on Divine Revelation: ". . . the books of Scripture teach firmly, faithfully and without error that truth which God, for the sake of our salvation, wished to see confided to the sacred scriptures." With this sentence, Vatican II confirmed and energized a growing appreciation of the Bible among Catholics. In particular, the Council confirmed and energized a non-fundamentalist approach to the Bible: the Bible is "for the sake of our salvation," a word given for the life of the church. In a pastoral letter to the people of his diocese at the beginning of Lent, 1980, Bishop Lucker announced that the diocese would begin sending out a month-by-month collection of the scripture readings from the church's renewed lectionary: "I can think of no better way to enter into the spirit of the season than by receiving the sacraments and meditating on the daily scripture readings" (Lucker, 119).

Our essay puts Bishop Lucker's efforts in the context of the radical growth of Catholic understanding of the Bible in the twentieth century. In Lucker's own lifetime, and with the support and advocacy of church people like him, the Catholic Church grew and changed in its teaching on understanding the Bible and its teaching on biblical translations. We focus on three areas here and have divided our essay into three parts corresponding to those areas. In part one, we will show the effects of Vatican II, in particular of *Dei Verbum*, on understanding the Bible. In part two, we focus on official church teaching since Vatican II, in particular the 1993 Pontifical Biblical Commission's instruction on "The Interpretation of the Bible in the Church," and most recently the 2002 document,"The Jewish People and Their Sacred Scriptures in the Christian Bible." In our third section, we will note some important recent Catholic contributions to biblical studies and future directions for Catholic biblical studies. In a brief conclusion to our essay, we will note the perennial need of the pilgrim Church to return to its scriptures. We write from our experience as biblical scholars of the Old and New Testament and from our experience of educating students in an appreciation of the Bible as professors at the College of St. Catherine.

## I. The Council thinks through what it means to call the Bible inspired

Vatican II's *Dei Verbum* was the culmination of an extended debate on the role of scripture and its interpretation in the life of the church. The conciliar constitution built upon Pius XII's revolutionary 1943 encyclical *Divino Afflante Spiritu*. The impact of these two documents cannot be adequately understood without a brief description of the state of Catholic biblical scholarship before Pius's encyclical.

In the years before *Divino Afflante Spiritu*, the Pontifical Biblical Commission, formed in 1902 largely to counter modernist influence, issued statements on how the Bible was to be interpreted by Catholic scholars. According to the commission, Mosaic authorship of the Pentateuch was affirmed and multiple authorship condemned. The Book of Isaiah could not be considered the work of multiple authors writing in different historical periods. Genesis 1–3 was to be interpreted as literal history. In the New Testament, the priority of Matthew among the synoptic gospels was asserted. Pauline authorship of the pastoral epistles and Hebrews was not to be questioned.

The first four decades of the twentieth century were a time of trial in Catholic biblical scholarship. In addition to the statements of the Pontifical Biblical Commission, two papal encyclicals were issued. In 1907 Pius X published *Pascendi Dominici Gregis,* which condemned modernism and those who applied historical criticism to the study of scripture. In 1920 Benedict XV released *Spiritus Paraclitus,* in which he rejected the use of literary forms. A former member of the Pontifical Biblical Commission, J. A. Fitzmyer, referred to some of these teachings as "retrograde and miserable." Bishop Lucker noted Avery Dulles's comment on the initial work of the Pontifical Biblical Commission that their decrees "proved with the passage of time [to be] unduly restrictive."

The results for Catholic biblical scholars and laity were devastating. A few examples will illustrate the harm done to those who used the findings of modern scholarship to advance biblical understanding. In 1910, Fr. Henry A. Poels, a Dutch Old Testament scholar at the Catholic University of America, was dismissed from the university when he questioned Mosaic authorship of the Pentateuch. The great Catholic Bible scholar Marie-Joseph Lagrange, O.P. (1855–1938), founder of the Ecole Biblique in Jerusalem and a pioneer in the use of historical criticism, suffered persecution for his ideas. In his 1903 book, *La méthode historique surtout à propos de l'Ancien Testament* (that is, *The Historical Method Especially as It Concerns the Old Testament*), he explained how historical criticism can enhance and enrich understanding of the ancient sacred texts. Vatican authorities ordered Lagrange to cease teaching and publishing in the field of Old Testament. Fearing dismissal from their positions and being silenced from even publishing scholarly opinions, other Catholic exegetes were hesitant to apply tools of modern scholarship to the Bible. Such was the climate in the early twentieth century.

Where did this leave the person in the pew? The only acceptable translation of the Bible for Catholics was the Douay Rheims, which was published in 1580, revised in 1750, and based on the Latin Vulgate. The faithful were warned against reading other translations, such as the King James version, and furthermore were not even encouraged to read the Catholic translation on their own for fear of the dangers of personal interpretation. This attitude continued until well after *Divino Afflante Spiritu*, especially on the pastoral level.

Still, with Pius XII's encyclical in 1943, the oppressive and threatening atmosphere of the previous forty years began to lift. Just as the Second Vatican Council opened the windows and let fresh air into the church, so this encyclical did likewise for Catholic scholars and readers of the Bible. Scholars were no longer forbidden to ask the difficult questions. They were permitted, encouraged, even required to do so. *Divino Afflante Spiritu* embraced methods of historical and literary criticism that had been condemned, thus overturning the previous prohibitions of the Pontifical Biblical Commission, and of *Pascendi* and *Spiritus*. Historical and literary criticism were adopted as legitimate methods of interpretation. Historical criticism interprets the Bible within the context of the events out of which the writings grew. Literary critics, on the other hand, focus on how a text was composed. Source critics examine how the Bible was put together over a period time using materials from different times, places, and authors. Form critics are interested in stereotyped patterns that biblical authors use. Source criticism, which refers to the Yahwist, Elohist, Deuteronomist, and Priestly authors as four different sources for the first five books of the Bible, is now so common that Pope John Paul II himself refers to the Yahwist. Bishop Lucker noted, "If [John Paul II] had said that in 1910 he would have been removed" (see Appendix: Moses—Author of the Pentateuch). Lagrange, once silenced, is now a candidate for beatification.

In 1964, the Pontifical Biblical Commission's instruction on "The Historical Truth of the Gospels" caused a seismic shift in strategies of New Testament interpretation and in how the gospels were to be understood. The instruction officially accepted historical criticism, endorsed form criticism for the gospels, and distinguished three stages of gospel tradition. It thus reaffirmed *Divino Afflante Spiritu* on the use of literary criticism to discover the purpose of the ancient authors, and it liberated Catholics from an outmoded and literalistic understanding of the gospels. The gospels were not to be viewed as presenting the details of Jesus' life in accurate chronological order or as providing throughout the *ipsissima verba Iesu*, the very words of Jesus. Instead, they were to be seen as reflections of the christological perspectives, proclamations, and experiences of early Christian communities approximately thirty-five to seventy years after Jesus' death and resurrection.

Vatican II's *Dei Verbum* reaffirmed many of the ideas presented by Pius XII in *Divino Afflante Spiritu*. It encouraged new translations of the Bible so that the scriptures could be available to the Christian faithful as well as to non-Christians for whom translations should be adapted. Like Pius XII's encyclical, it highlighted the importance of using the Septuagint, the Greek translation of the Hebrew Bible, and the earliest manuscripts of the sacred books in Hebrew and Aramaic in the work of translating. It encouraged open access to the Bible for all. It called for Bible scholars to renew their strength daily and to pursue their work so that the faithful could be nourished by the scriptures.

*Dei Verbum* has had a great impact on how people read the Bible and understand the nature of biblical inspiration. Bishop Lucker had cause to underline *Dei Verbum*'s understanding of inspiration as truth "for the sake of our salvation" (*DV* 11). This was the final statement approved by the Council as to the nature of biblical inspiration. However, the Council came to this decision only after serious discussion, much of it centered on the relationship between inerrancy and inspiration.

The inerrancy of scripture is a major issue in how people interpret the Bible and is closely related to different understandings of inspiration. Christian denominations define inspiration in many ways, and it is a major feature distinguishing fundamentalists and evangelicals from other Protestants and from Catholics. Fundamentalists and evangelicals tie it to inerrancy and assert that texts such as 2 Timothy 3:16-17 ("all scripture is inspired by God") mean that since the Bible is the word of God it is without any error whatsoever.

Other Christians view the matter of inspiration and divine authorship in a variety of ways, and try to account for the existence of errors within the Bible. The unusual Greek word in 2 Timothy 3:16, *theopneustos* ("inspired" or "inspiration" or literally "God breathed"), is not defined. 2 Timothy 3:16 explains how the scriptures can be used, but not how they came to be written down, nor how they came to be in the mind of the human writers. It does not explain the effect of inspiration on the texts or on the ancient writers. At the very least, whatever one might say of God as author of scripture, God is not author in the way we use the word today regarding human authors who take up a writing instrument and create a literary work. It is instructive that the Bible is called the word of God, not the words of God.

The relationship between inerrancy and inspiration was an item of protacted debate at Vatican II. Bruce Vawter, in his book *Biblical Inspiration*, described the process that led to the official formulation that captured the attention of Bishop Lucker. The first draft offered to the committee for discussion by the council fathers stated that "since divine inspiration extends to all things [in the Bible], it follows directly and necessarily that the entire Sacred Scripture is absolutely immune from error." This included "every error in every field, religious or profane," and was based on the notion that, since God is the supreme truth, it follows that God "can be the author of no error whatever." Nowhere in the Bible, however, is inspiration described in this primitive fashion. The equation of God as "supreme truth" with God as "author of no error" is an inadequate, literalistic notion of authorship, and it does not do justice to the meaning of God as supreme truth. The first draft was rejected as unsuitable even for purposes of discussion (see Vawter, 143–155).

Extensive debate took place before the acceptance of the final formulation of the nature of inspiration in scripture as truth which is necessary for the sake of salvation (*DV* 11). This reflects the idea of biblical truth (Hebrew *emet*) which has the sense of trustworthiness, constancy, faithfulness. A good example is found in Zechariah 8:16. "These are the things that you shall do: Speak the truth to one another, render in your gates judgments that are true and make for peace, do not devise evil in your hearts against one another, and love no false oath." The opposite of truth here is the devising of evil and false oath. The biblical notion of truth is not concerned so much with erroneous assertions as with intentional deceitfulness and treacherous behavior. Such an understanding of truth can free readers of the Bible from concerns about possible errors such as those having to do with scientific data, history, or prophecy and lead them to consider the more basic and profound truths of the Bible which have to do with divine and human faithfulness and trust. Regarding this crucial phrase in *Dei Verbum*, Bishop Lucker noted that it "leaves room for the more liberal-minded to admit error in the Bible where this does not affect its essential message."

An example of such an error is the historical inaccuracy in Luke 2:1-2. In these verses, Luke connects the birth of Jesus with a decree of Caesar Augustus ordering the registration of the whole Roman Empire, with the first enrollment when Quirinius was governor of Syria. This information is fraught with historical problems. Although there were a number of local censuses, there never was a census of the whole Roman Empire under Augustus. And the census of Judea, not of Galilee, took place in 6–7 C.E. under Quirinius, about ten years after the birth of Jesus. Such historical inaccuracies are understandable, given that Luke probably did not have access to Roman records and was writing his narrative about fifty years after Jesus' crucifixion. The important point is not the historical error but Luke's theological intention. By relating Jesus' birth to a worldwide census, Luke alludes to the universal significance of the Savior's birth.

For Catholics, the truth of a biblical passage is not necessarily tied to its historicity. What we have shown in this part of our essay is what a long and challenging journey it was for the Catholic Church to come to this position in its official teaching.

## II. Since the Council: Catholicism attempts to push its thinking further on how the Bible fits in the life of the church

A new Catholic translation of the Bible, The New American Bible, appeared in its entirety in 1970. The process was begun in 1944, soon after the appearance of *Divino Afflante Spiritu*. The American bishops requested that the members of the Catholic Biblical Association make a translation of the Bible from the best available texts. The first volumes of the Old Testament were published in the 1950s and parts of the New Testament in 1964, the latter made for use in the lectionary.

The translation published in 1970 was well received by Catholics and non-Catholics alike. However, the translation was not set in stone. For the Old Testament, the discovery and reconstruction of texts from the Dead Sea provided new information that was incorporated into revisions. The book of Genesis was translated anew to reflect updated scholarly findings. Liturgical use of the New Testament and of the Old Testament psalms showed the need for a new translation, and by 1986 a new revision and translation was produced. The members of the Catholic Biblical Association, mostly but not all Catholic, have worked for many years to make a careful translation from the original languages, one that fit the needs of the American reader of the Bible. Here we recall the words of John Paul II in his 1993 address to the Pontifical Biblical Commission: "Biblical thought must always be translated anew into contemporary language so that it may be expressed in ways suited to its listeners" (John Paul II, 1993, 6).

In the last half of the twentieth century scholars began to ask different questions about the Bible and to employ numerous new approaches to the text. Scholars discovered that data from many fields such as anthropology, sociology, and economics shed light on the Bible. Because of these new directions in biblical studies, the Pontifical Biblical Commission issued the document, "The Interpretation of the Bible in the Church" in 1993. While it endorses historical criticism as indispensable to biblical interpretation, it acknowledges that the method is insufficient and should be supplemented by other approaches. The document surveys various methods of and approaches to biblical interpretation and assesses the advantages and limitations of each. Among other things, it reflects on characteristics of Catholic biblical interpretation and its relation to other theological disciplines, and the role of biblical interpretation in the life of the church.

"The Interpretation of the Bible in the Church" is a document that every Catholic could benefit from reading. It describes the important contributions that biblical scholars have made in the area of ecumenism. Ecumenical dialogue has made progress in recent years because scholars and exegetes have adopted the same methods and hermeneutical points of view. For instance, scholars have collaborated on several new translations of the Bible such as the New American Bible and the New Revised Standard Version.

"The Interpretation of the Bible in the Church" condemns funda-
mentalist interpretation of the Bible while acknowledging that "this
kind of interpretation is winning more and more adherents, in religious
groups and sects, as also among Catholics" (Pontifical Biblical Commission, 509). Despite church teaching on the usefulness of the historical-
critical method and newer methods of criticism, opposition to historical criticism continues among ultra-conservative Catholics who cling to
a pre-critical approach to scripture akin to the literalism practiced
among Protestant fundamentalists. For example, the journal *The Wanderer* routinely lambasted the work of Catholic New Testament scholar
Raymond E. Brown. Much of this criticism was based on misstatements
attributed to Brown. Even after his death, a *Wanderer* obituary cast as-
persions on this great scholar and person of faith (see Fitzmyer, 1998).
Aside from the lack of charity, such criticism runs contrary to the long
Catholic tradition of intellectual excellence, which respects critical
thinking and the interaction between faith and reason. Catholic scholars
who explore scripture using modern approaches and methods do so
with the blessings of the church but not without some opposition from
both within and outside official Catholicism.

A landmark in ecumenical relations between Lutherans and
Catholics was the "Joint Declaration on the Doctrine of Justification" of
1999. Paul's teaching on justification by faith in his letter to the Ro-
mans was interpreted differently by Catholics and Lutherans and was a
factor in the sixteenth-century Reformation. The document states that
a consensus now exists between the Lutheran World Federation and
the Roman Catholic Church concerning basic truths of the doctrine of
justification. This doctrine is no longer considered an obstacle to
bringing about full communion: the condemnations drawn up in the
sixteenth century on the teaching of justification no longer apply. The
Catholic Church's growing understanding of the Bible created a climate that broke down barriers which had existed for centuries. This
ecumenical breakthrough became possible only when the Catholic
Church embraced historical criticism in the second half of the twentieth century.

A recent puzzling development related to the Bible, especially concerning textual criticism and Bible translations, has arisen with the re-
lease of *Liturgiam Authenticam* in 2001 by the Congregation for Divine
Worship. This document requires that all liturgical translations of the
Bible be made from the New Vulgate, a new Latin translation com-
pleted in 1979. *Liturgiam Authenticam* says the New Vulgate is the au-

thoritative text for translations of the Bible meant for liturgical use. If such a requirement were implemented it would mean a giant step backward for Bible translators and for all readers of the Bible.

*Liturgiam Authenticam* lays out rules for translation which are problematic. (1) Textual criticism, finding and using the best manuscript traditions of ancient texts, is proscribed. (2) Use of inclusive language is forbidden, though the document is inconsistent in this requirement. (3) Only one Bible translation should be used, whether in liturgy, study, or private reading. The implications of these requirements could have a deleterious effect on Bible translators, on lay people who wish to study and be enriched by the Bible, and on ecumenism.

A basic step in translating any biblical text is to establish the best readings from ancient manuscripts. To do this, the scholar must consult numerous manuscript traditions, must then make a judgment on which is the best reading, and finally must make a translation taking all these factors into account.

It is significant that the New Vulgate translation ignores the manuscript evidence from the Dead Sea Scrolls, texts discovered in 1947 that radically changed scholars' assessments of several manuscripts; for example, 1 and 2 Samuel, Sirach, and Tobit. Evidence from the Dead Sea Scrolls takes us back to a manuscript tradition almost one thousand years earlier than the next earliest Hebrew witness to the Old Testament. Since this important textual information is completely lacking in the New Vulgate, no biblical scholar would recommend its use for purposes of making an accurate and scholarly translation.

The Wisdom of Ben Sira, also called Sirach or Ecclesiasticus, and The Book of Tobit serve as examples of the serious problems inherent in the required use of the New Vulgate in the lectionary. In producing the Vulgate, Jerome reworked the Old Latin of Tobit and left the Old Latin of Sirach intact, with the result that the Vulgate of those books contains omissions, additions, and Christian reworkings that are absent in other forms of the ancient texts in the Semitic and Greek languages. In order to arrive at a critical version, modern scholars consult numerous ancient manuscripts and versions of these texts, in particular those found after 1947 at Qumran and at Masada, both near the Dead Sea. The Vulgate forms of those books are thus notoriously deficient in terms of modern textual criticism. The use of the New Vulgate in the liturgy, therefore, ignores more than half a century of official Catholic endorsement of textual criticism. Moreover, the New Vulgate could have deleterious spiritual effects on the laity by depriving them of the riches of a critical edition, since it inserts theological notions from a later time often far removed from the intentions of the original authors.

Just when Catholics are becoming more biblically literate and can read and respect the Bible on the same level as Protestants, the New Vulgate seems to require that these readers use a version of the Bible that has no legitimate standing among scholars and thus among the Bible reading public, whether Catholic, Protestant, or Jewish. This would be an unhappy development indeed. It stands in tension with *Dei Verbum,* which requires that access to the Bible must be wide open to the faithful by providing opportune and correct translations from the original texts.

It is unlikely, however, that this unhappy development will occur, given the way Catholics actually read the Bible today. Catholics avail themselves of many different translations. They participate in Bible study groups, some composed of Catholics, some of mixed groups of believers, using many different translations. This experience of sharing the Bible with a variety of believers has been enriching for Catholics in many ways. It is yet another example of how the church's growing understanding of the Bible has spilled into other areas of church life. Shared Bible exploration has led to a creative spirit of ecumenism, where not only scholars can understand one another, but also Christians and Jews are able to communicate in an irenic spirit.

Desire for a uniform Catholic Bible seems to have been a strong motivation behind the required use of the New Vulgate. Desire for a uniform translation in the vernacular was also strong in the fourth century during the time of Jerome and Augustine. Pope Damasus asked Jerome to revise the Old Latin Psalter to produce a uniform text out of the numerous manuscripts. The problem was that Psalter translations were not uniform. Christians were praying the psalms in slightly different forms depending on the region; e.g., North Africa, Southern Italy. After working on the Old Latin Psalter, which had been translated from the Septuagint, Jerome gradually came to realize the significance of the original Hebrew, which he referred to as the *fons veritatis*, "the source of truth." Jerome understood the problems inherent in translation and the need to consult the original as well as other ancient witnesses.

Augustine, however, was concerned that Jerome's new translation from the Hebrew differed from the traditional Old Latin translations used in liturgy and daily prayer. Augustine's main concern was the effect on the faithful, although he acknowledged the problem of the lack of a uniform text. The difficulty then and now is that a uniform text requires careful critical work based on numerous ancient manuscripts in several languages. To shortcut that process for any reason, even the desire for liturgical uniformity, is to misunderstand the value of biblical studies.

*Liturgiam Authenticam* makes little sense to biblical scholars in light of the hard-earned advances in Catholic biblical scholarship over the past sixty years. The New American Bible accomplished the desire of Vatican II that translations be made with non-Catholics so that all Christians would be able to avail themselves of an up-to-date translation. A translation from New Vulgate runs contrary to all of these important contributions. *Liturgiam Authenticum* shows little awareness of what modern biblical scholarship is about, of the location of Catholic biblical scholarship at the beginning of the new millennium, and of how Catholic lay people read and use the Bible in their daily lives.

A new document, "The Jewish People and Their Sacred Scriptures in the Christian Bible," was published in 2002 as we were completing our article. At this point the only available translations of the document are provisional. Our comments here can only touch on some features of this new document that relate to the question of growth in understanding the Bible.

The three main topics of the document are the relationship between the sacred scriptures of the Jewish people to the Christian Bible, themes in the Hebrew Scriptures and in Christian faith, and the Jews in the New Testament. The document makes many points that will be fruitful for a discussion of Bible translations and a growing understanding of the Bible. Following are examples of some of these points. "Without the Old Testament, the New Testament would be an unintelligible book, a plant deprived of its roots, and destined to dry up and wither." Not only is the Old Testament an essential part of the Christian Bible; Jewish methods of exegesis such as were used at Qumran and by certain rabbis must be studied to understand adequately the New Testament message because these same methods of exegesis are used by some New Testament authors. Christian exegetes can also learn much from the types of Jewish exegesis practiced over the past two thousand years.

The document is encouraging with respect to possibilities of Jewish-Christian dialogue on the scriptures. In the section on the contribution of Jewish reading of the Bible, Jewish and Christian readings of the Bible are compared to one another. Both Jewish and Christian interpretations of the Bible are "bound up with the vision of their respective faiths" and "both are irreducible." How can one account for these differences without denying either interpretation? "It cannot be said . . . that Jews do not see what has been proclaimed in the text." The difference between Jewish and Christian readings is that the Christian discovers an "additional meaning" in the text. This is consistent with the idea of inner biblical interpretation, that is, how within the Bible itself one section of the Bible will comment on, take issue with, or state differently what another section has to say. Numerous examples exist. The portrayal of David in 1 Chronicles is quite different from the portrayal of David in 2 Samuel. The writer of Deuteronomy radically reworks some of the Mosaic traditions found in Exodus and Leviticus.

The final portion of the document addresses in methodical fashion how Jews are presented in the New Testament. It discusses each of the gospels, the Pauline letters, and other writings, and addresses the matter of possible anti-Judaism in the New Testament. We look forward to learning more about this document in the days to come, and to discussing it with our Christian and Jewish colleagues. It is gratifying to see the progress that has been made in this important area.

In the last thirty years we have seen tremendous progress in ecumenical dialogue, biblical translations, and church documents investigating various aspects of biblical interpretation. This growth has led to a profound appreciation of scripture on scholarly and pastoral levels. Even today the Pontifical Biblical Commission is undertaking a three-year study of morality in the New Testament.

### III. The contributions of recent biblical scholarship and future directions for Catholic biblical studies

A quick glance at the various journals published under the auspices of the Catholic Biblical Association gives evidence of the growth in understanding the Bible. The list of the editors and contributors of the *Catholic Biblical Quarterly*, now in its sixty-fourth year and one of the most respected and widely read journals of the Bible in North America, is impressive. It shows a depth and breadth of scholarly achievement which has developed since the publication of *Divino Afflante Spiritu* and *Dei Verbum*. *Old Testament Abstracts* and *New Testament Abstracts*, which have been published for twenty-five years, are unique contributions for Bible scholars of all denominations. These publications are staffed by some of the foremost Catholic Bible scholars.

Catholic voices are also prominent in important non-Catholic commentaries and Bible dictionaries. The *Anchor Bible Commentary* series, a preeminent publication in the field of biblical studies, has a number of volumes written by Roman Catholic scholars. Several of the best sellers in this series were written by Roman Catholic scholars. Raymond Brown's two volumes on John served as a model for future volumes in the series. Numerous Catholic scholars were contributors to the *Anchor Bible Dictionary*, a permanent fixture in many libraries.

The Old Testament and New Testament commentaries published by Michael Glazier/Liturgical Press, Collegeville, Minn., are breaking new ground in the writing of commentaries, going beyond the historical-critical method to reveal new directions in biblical scholarship. The intent of the *Berit Olam* ("Eternal Covenant") series is to enable people to "hear afresh the life-giving words of God's everlasting covenant" and to present to the whole spectrum of Bible readers from lay people to professionals "the latest developments in the literary analysis of these ancient texts." Similarly, the goal of the New Testament series, *Sacra Pagina* ("Sacred Page"), is "to provide sound, critical analysis without any loss of sensitivity to religious meaning." The dynamic character of scholarly exploration of the revealed word of scripture enhances the life of faith.

The Catholic Study Bible (1990) is the newest edition of the New American Bible. It contains extensive notes and articles and is a helpful tool for anyone who wants to study the scriptural origins of faith. This translation fulfilled a real need for a Bible translation done in the idiom of a particular audience in a particular place and time. This translation was done for a late twentieth-century American audience using American English.

Such contributions to the larger world of scholarship and to the life of the church would not have been possible without the groundbreaking documents of the twentieth century and without the hard work of Bible scholars, "working in the vineyards of the Lord for these many years" (*DAS* 47). Before *Divino Afflante Spiritu*, Catholic scholars were discouraged from interacting with non-Catholic Bible scholars, and were not permitted to investigate and examine controversial issues. In the latter half of the twentieth century, Catholic Bible scholars could openly engage in critical textual and hermeneutical work, and this work continues to the present day. Catholic scholars stand on equal footing with their peers in biblical studies. They have legitimacy among other scholars. They are involved in a variety of criticisms including textual criticism, historical-critical readings of texts, literary studies, and feminist criticism. Catholic scholars have won respect and recognition for their work from their peers. In so doing, they have contributed to the growth of the church by giving access to the Bible to Catholic lay people, and helping them to have a greater appreciation of the richness of Catholic tradition.

Yet more remains to be done. Work on ecumenical relations continues, and a good foundation has been laid by mutual readings of the Bible. There is an awareness that no translation is perfect. New translations will always have to be made to address the changing situations of the faithful, much like the creation of the gospels themselves, which were composed with changing situations of the early communities in mind.

## Conclusion: The pilgrim church will always return to its scriptures, and will always be understanding them anew

As we have grown in our understanding of the Bible, we have come to see that biblical interpretation is an ongoing enterprise and that the pilgrim church will always seek more clarity and understanding of the word of God. *Dei Verbum's* assertion that "sacred Tradition, sacred scripture and the magisterium of the church are so connected and associated that one of them cannot stand without the others" (*DV* 10) is a call for increasing Bible understanding on all levels.

We have come a long way from the days of the early twentieth century when Bible study was a tool for a reaction against the modernist crisis. Most church documents including those from Vatican II, papal writings, and the Pontifical Biblical Commission have been responsible for the support and encouragement of sound biblical scholarship. These teachings and insights have not been fully implemented in some areas. Also problematic is a tendency visible in some church documents toward a pre-critical use of the Bible. The problem continues to influence how people from parishes to seminaries use the Bible. The Catholic Church needs to continue to press for more emphasis on sound Bible scholarship in its seminaries, its worship, its local churches, and its schools in order to fulfill the hope of *Dei Verbum* that the study of scripture be the soul of theology (*DV* 24).

In the introduction to this book, Bishop Lucker says that because Christ's prophetic character has been given to the whole church, we will all together continue to return to God's word and find in it, as Matthew's gospel says, "what is new and what is old" (Mt 13:52). Here

Lucker follows Vatican II's *Lumen Gentium,* chapter 2, on the church as "People of God":

> The holy people of God shares also in Christ's prophetic office: it spreads abroad a living witness to him, especially by a life of faith and love and by offering to God a sacrifice of praise, the fruit of lips confessing his name (see Heb 13:15)...The people unfailingly adheres to this faith, penetrates it more deeply through right judgment, and applies it more fully in daily life. (*LG* 12)

Like the Council, Bishop Lucker understood the church as the place of truth—the place where we return again to God's word, both written in the scripture and alive in our midst—in which together we are changed on our pilgrim way to God. In our essay we have shown both how much progress the church has made in understanding the importance of the Bible for its pilgrim way and how much further we have yet to go. We end with words from the same paragraph of *Lumen Gentium.* May we who teach and may those whose office it is to lead the church never "extinguish the Spirit, but...test all things and hold fast to what is good (see 1 Thess 5:12, 19-21)" (*LG* 12).

## *References and suggestions for further reading*

Bechard, Dean. "Remnants of Modernism in a Postmodern Age: The Pontifical Biblical Commission's Centennial." *America* 186 (February 4, 2002): 16–21.

Brown, Raymond. *Biblical Exegesis and Church Doctrine.* Mahwah, N.J.: Paulist Press, 1985.

Congregation for Divine Worship and the Discipline of the Sacraments. *Liturgicam Authenticam. Origins* 31/2 (2001): 17, 19–32.

Fitzmyer, Joseph. *A Christological Catechism: New Testament Answers.* New revised and expanded ed. Mahwah, N.J.: Paulist Press, 1991. (The appendix includes texts and commentary on the Biblical Commission's 1964 Instruction on the Historical Truth of the Gospels and Vatican Council II Dogmatic Constitution, *Dei Verbum.*)

Fitzmyer, Joseph. "The Interpretation of the Bible in the Church Today." *Irish Theological Quarterly* 62 (1996-1997): 84–100.

Fitzmyer, Joseph. "Raymond E. Brown, S.S. In Memoriam." *Union Seminary Quarterly Review* 52 (1998): 12–14.

Fogarty, Gerald P. "Dissent at Catholic University: The Case of Henry Poels." *America* 180 (October 11, 1986): 180–184.

Jensen, Joseph. "*Liturgiam authenticam* and the New Vulgate." *America* 185 (August 13-20, 2001): 11–13.

John Paul II, Pope. "Address on the Interpretation of the Bible in the Church." *L'Osservatore Romano*, English language weekly edition (April 28, 1993): 3–4, 6.

Lutheran World Federation and the Roman Catholic Church. *Joint Declaration on the Doctrine of Justification.* Grand Rapids, Mich.: Eerdmans, 2001.

Pontifical Biblical Commission. "The Interpretation of the Bible in the Church." *Origins* 23 (1994): 499–524.

Vawter, Bruce. *Biblical Inspiration.* Philadelphia: Westminster, 1972.

# II

# On Being the Church

## Re-reading *Lumen Gentium*
## for what it is asking of the church in our day

*Vatican II: "Already prefigured at the beginning of the world, the church was prepared in marvelous fashion in the history of the people of Israel and in the ancient alliance. Established in this last age of the world, and made manifest in the outpouring of the Spirit, it will be brought to glorious completion at the end of time ... The church—that is, the kingdom of Christ already present in mystery—grows visibly in the world through the power of God." (LG 2, 3)*

*Bishop Lucker: "We are just trying to figure out how to be a church. I am not trying to start my own church; we are just trying to figure out together how to be a church. How to be a good church. How to be a renewed church, and how to touch the hearts of people." (Introduction to this book)*

This section of the book opens with J. Michael Byron's essay on the theology of communion, the understanding of the universal church as a "communion of communions." Byron places Bishop Lucker's own interest in the relationship between the local and universal church in the context of Vatican II's overcoming of a Catholic tendency to overemphasize the institutional and hierarchical character of the church at least since the Reformation.

Susan Wood's essay, "The Bishop as Teacher: Proclaiming the Living Word of God in the Church," sums up Vatican II's understanding of the teaching role of bishops. She shows how the Council emphasized the dialogical and communal nature of the bishop's task. She reads twenty-five years of Bishop Lucker's pastoral letters as fulfilling well this mandate of the Council, and she underlines the importance of such dialogical communion for the future life of the church.

In the concluding essay of this section of the book, "Papal Apologies Embody and Advance Vatican II on the 'Tradition Poured out in the Church,'" William McDonough and Catherine Michaud show a hopeful coming together that could unite the disparate views on the relative importance of local and universal church. The recent papal apologies, and the literature that has been generated around them, acknowledge clearly that whatever the full "mystery of the church" (*LG*, chapter one) entails, no institution or denomination can claim to embody its fullness. Only by conversion, only by asking for forgiveness and starting out again on the road of faith, do any of us begin to find truth.

# 4
## *Communio* as the context for memory:
## On the universal-local church relationship

J. MICHAEL BYRON


Contemporary Roman Catholic ecclesiology is aware that the universal church and the local churches imply and indeed require one another. But the more immediate and existential task of upholding the integral identity of both in practice is a more complex challenge. It is a task that simply cannot be avoided, however, because the way this relationship is conceived affects virtually every other aspect of ecclesial life: how institutional structures are ordered; how ministers are selected; how authority is exercised; how the church legislates; how sacraments are celebrated; and so on.

It was Bishop Lucker's belief that ecclesiology is on a relatively more firm foundation when the essence of the One, Holy, Catholic, and Apostolic church is approached inductively rather than deductively. In other words, he was persuaded that our identity as the church universal is more reliably established in and through reflection upon the concrete life of the local churches. This preferred starting point for theology is to be contrasted with a method that sets out from an abstract universal definition and a proposed metaphysical essence. To begin with a consideration of what is visible and historical is in no way to remove from the church its radically transcendent quality as mystery. Rather, it is to make an option which accords relative priority to religious experience over religious ideas in the Catholic conversation about self-identity. Theologically, this instinct is rooted in the conciliar ecclesiology of *communio*.

The church of Jesus Christ is one and many, both universal and particular at the same time. There can be no church, properly so called, which has no concrete historical referents or subjects; such a thing would be no more than an idea about the church. On the other hand,

Catholic faith holds that any particular or local church (the term "local" ordinarily designating a diocese under the headship of a bishop) must be referred immediately to the church universal, and must be understood to express and constitute that universal church in a specific time and place. Apart from a universal referent, one engages something less than the church in its fullness.

Thus the ecclesiological paradox: the Christian church is neither divisible into component parts nor capable of being apprehended apart from its particular instantiations. In every concrete Christian community, overseen by a bishop who is in communion with the episcopal college and its head, there is found the church, the whole church, and nothing less than the church. At the same time, there is always a "more" to every particular ecclesial community, an orientation toward singularity and universality which can never be expressed adequately in a specific, concrete assembly.

The inevitable challenge in considering any universal reality is that it includes everything and everybody in general but nothing and nobody in particular. On the other hand, apart from recognizing the principle of universality it is difficult to understand how the multiple concrete expressions of ecclesial life are not simply distinct and particular.

This essay examines the tension between the universal and particular in the life of our church today. I proceed in four sections and end with a brief conclusion. In the first section, I summarize the over-emphasis on the universal aspect of the church's life in pre-Vatican II Catholic teaching and practice. In the second, I summarize the change in the church's thinking about its own nature that occurred at the Second Vatican Council. In the third, I both argue that *communio* is the best way to summarize the church's self-understanding and suggest what I think is at the center of this *communio* ecclesiology. In the fourth, I briefly indicate where this *communio* ecclesiology might lead us on three practical challenges in church life today, namely infallibility, ecumenism, and the authority of local and universal churches. In a brief conclusion I come back to Bishop Lucker's concern for the life of the local church.

## I. A church out of balance: Historical background to Vatican II

It is sometimes said that Vatican II was a historically unique council inasmuch as it was summoned without any apparent looming crisis in doctrine or pastoral practice. *Aggiornamento*, it is noted, was about a disposition rather than a definition. Yet the council fathers were certainly aware of the problematic imbalance of the local-universal relationship which was the legacy of a truncated ecclesiological reflection at Vatican I. It was widely recognized that the doctrinal lopsidedness of the church universal over the local churches articulated in 1870 in *Pastor Aeternus,* especially as that was reflected in the practical exercise of papal-episcopal ecclesial oversight, could not be sustained indefinitely. By the time of the calling of Vatican II it was apparent to the substantial majority of diocesan bishops that there was pressing ecclesiological work to be done. At issue was the very definition of "church," although the more explicit battle was to be waged over the question of episcopal collegiality.

The "universalist" ecclesiology so much in evidence in *Pastor Aeternus* was not novel in the nineteenth century. At least since the great schism of 1054 the idea of one flock/one shepherd, which language John's gospel (chapter 10) has Jesus using in order to speak about *himself,* had been applied to the pope more or less explicitly. It was precisely this universalist perspective against which the classic Protestant reformers reacted in the sixteenth century. Throughout the second Christian millennium one can find ample evidence that even the churches of the East recognized a certain primacy attached to the church at Rome, although surely not in the sense of a primacy of juridical authority envisioned at Vatican I and still broadly understood among many of the faithful today. With the exception, perhaps, of the conciliarist period during the Great Western Schism, this universalist ecclesiology describes roughly eight hundred years of Western history (see Henn, 102–116). A related outcome of this emphasis was that, by the time of Pius IX, discussion about the church had become overwhelmingly discussion about structural authority and the sources and limits of juridical power. Within this construal, unity was read as uniformity, and the role of the primacy was emphasized at the expense of the role of the episcopal college. Universalist ecclesiology necessarily brings an attendant downplaying of the importance of the local churches.

Yet even *Pastor Aeternus* was not unaware of the need to account for the divine institution of the episcopate. To appease those bishops at Vatican I who voiced concern about the language of "ordinary and immediate" papal authority, the third chapter of *Pastor Aeternus* was made to state that "the bishops who, under appointment of the Holy Spirit (see Acts 20:28), succeeded in the place of the apostles, feed and rule individually, as true shepherds, the particular flock assigned to them" (Denzinger-Schönmetzer, 3061). This section went on to quote Gregory the Great, expressing his desire to preserve the prerogatives of his brothers in the episcopate. Recall that it was Gregory who refused to be called "universal bishop" out of concern not to undermine the episcopal authority of all others. In brief, as Henn notes, "by acknowledging [the] divine institution of the ministry of bishops, Vatican I may be said to have sown the seeds of episcopal collegiality," and thereby preserved the integrity of the local churches (Henn, 140). This was not explicitly articulated, however, for nearly a century. Moreover, Vatican I declined to adopt the view, prevalent for decades previous, that the exercise of local episcopal jurisdiction was rooted in the primacy. Considering the practical limits which the fresh memory of nationalist controversies in Europe imposed upon what the Council could say positively about collegiality, *Pastor Aeternus* upheld the universal-local ecclesiological dialectic to the extent that this was possible. The subsequent clarification (1875) elicited from the German bishops in the light of Chancellor von Bismarck's claims of Roman papal monarchy further paved the way for the collegial discussions of Vatican II (Henn, 141).

Another strand of ecclesiological reflection which informed the context of Vatican II was the concept of the Mystical Body of Christ. Historically this image can be traced at least to the time of the German theological renewal of the early nineteenth century, but it did not receive sustained attention until the encyclical bearing that name was issued in 1943 by Pius XII. The Mystical Body metaphor, essentially, holds that the church is formed by the life which flows from its head to its members who, through the animation of the Holy Spirit, form the Body of Christ. This instinct is thoroughly Pauline in its biblical origin and its invocation was intended to introduce a fundamental spiritual dimension into ecclesiological reflection. The heavy emphasis in traditional theological discourse on visible structures and juridical authority were believed to have crowded out the understanding of the church as mystery.

Bishop Lucker found in Pius XII's encyclical a great personal inspiration for ecclesial life. In one of his last pastoral letters to the people of the Diocese of New Ulm, written in February 2000, Bishop Lucker reflected back upon the impact of the image of the Mystical Body in his own ministry:

> That encyclical became the basis for our course in the seminary on the church. It gave us a whole new view of the church; that is, that we are the Body of Christ, we share in the very divine life of God. God is our father. We are brothers and sisters of Jesus Christ, brothers and sisters of one another and united in one body through the grace and power of the Holy Spirit. I re-

call Fr. Godfrey Diekmann, OSB speaking about this at the National Liturgical Conferences. I responded, "Yes, this is it!"

Nevertheless, Pius did not go far enough. The nature and the mission of the church became a major theme of the Second Vatican Council. He identified the church of Jesus with the Roman Catholic Church. The council built on Pius XII's work, added to it and taught that the church of Jesus Christ is found in the Roman Catholic Church, but that it is broader than that and is found, although not fully, in other churches as well. (Lucker, 550)

The development of Mystical Body ecclesiology was but one of the many fruits of the intense theological reflection during the period between Vatican I and II. Among other things, new investigative methods brought to awareness something of the genesis and organic development of church structures. The recovery of many biblical and patristic images made for a much richer discussion. The image of church as primordial sacrament, for example, was one of the outcomes of the liturgical movement. It focused attention upon the church as a consecrated, holy people rather than seeing it primarily in terms of its visible structures. There were also great advances in ecumenical studies, which led to a re-appreciation of the ecclesiologies of the Eastern/Greek traditions, as well as to a less polemical evaluation of Protestant ideas on ecclesiology. It became more apparent that a strictly institutional model for church was a hindrance to dialogue and thereby, more importantly, a hindrance to the goal of Christian unity. It was also becoming clearer that such unity was a goal in the process of being realized, rather than an abstract reality which was already statically contained within the Catholic Church. This corresponded to a more general awareness that the church had a mission in and for the world. A prevalent Western existentialism served to reinforce the idea of a church situated in history, noting that it had a dimension which was human and developing (or at least capable of developing).

## II. Vatican II's understanding of church: The emergence of the idea of *communio*

As for Vatican II itself, it must be emphasized that every one of its ecclesiological articulations was put forward with keen awareness that the non-Catholic Christian world was watching. This utterly unique conciliar context must be held firmly in view in contemporary discourse, because it has been often either ignored or exaggerated in postconciliar reflections on the nature of *communio*. On one hand, the affirmations of *Lumen Gentium* about the relationship between the universal and the local churches did not intend to speak in solely apologetic tones to the wider ecumenical audience. On the other hand, the conciliar decrees on ecclesiology cannot be understood to concern themselves strictly with intramural Roman Catholic questions of self-identity.

Particular concern was expressed among Orthodox theologians both during and after the Council that the traditional Roman emphasis upon the absolute priority of the universal dimension and its juridical privileges was a violation of the eucharistic foundation of the church. Since every local church is possessed of a bishop and a valid sacramental life, most notably the Eucharist, each is integrally the church. Thus, as Orthodox theology understands it, it is contrary to the essence of ecclesial identity to subordinate any one church, or many, to the authority of another.

Always lurking just beneath the surface of many anxieties over the right relationship between the universal and the local churches is the question of juridical power: Can the universal and the local exercise of ecclesiastical authority be conceived in a way such that the *munera* (ministries or offices) of teaching, sanctifying, and governing are not unidirectional? Is there a way to understand the role of the church universal in reciprocal terms, wherein its singular dimension is retained but where there is also a theological imperative to attend to the concrete life witness of the local churches in discerning ecclesial identity itself? If so, this imperative must be reflected in those visible structures through which power is exercised.

This was the conviction of the majority of bishops at Vatican II. Many of them had become concerned with the perceived diminishment of the status of local ordinaries to the point that they were regarded in practice as agents of the Roman curia. For this reason there was a concerted effort at the Council to stress the role of the local bishops in the governance of the universal church. There was also a protracted struggle undertaken to reform and to internationalize the curia itself. Particularly in *Lumen Gentium*'s treatment of hierarchical office (chapter 3: "The Church Is Hierarchical"), as well as in the reflections on the episcopate in the Council's Decree on the Pastoral Office of Bishops (*Christus Dominus*), there was a desire to restore greater reciprocity in the authority and prestige of the college of bishops vis-à-vis the primacy.

For example, where *Pastor Aeternus* had considered the nature of the episcopate within the context of the papacy, *Lumen Gentium* reversed that schema and *began* with the episcopacy. The practical effects of this decision were substantial. *Lumen Gentium* 21 teaches that each and every bishop enjoys the fullness of the sacrament of orders directly from Christ. This affirmation was expressly opposed to a notion of reserving that dignity to the primate who then could share it with others as a kind of secondary source. This meant that, as *Lumen Gentium* 22 states, "Together with its head, the Supreme Pontiff, and never apart from him, [the order of bishops] is the subject of supreme and full authority over the universal church . . ." Some bishops saw this as a flat-out contradiction of the teaching of *Pastor Aeternus,* in which supreme authority was stated to have been vested in the Roman pontiff. Yet most of the bishops of Vatican II saw precisely the opposite: episcopal collegiality is a complement to and completion of the exercise of the primacy.

The Council was quite specific in teaching that episcopal consecration is a sacrament, and in fact it is *the fullness* of the sacrament of orders. This represented the retrieval of patristic theological reflection and was also a rather dramatic reversal of the sacramental imagination which had held the field for hundreds of years previously. Prior to Vatican II it was almost universally *denied* that consecration was a sacrament. It was the *priest* who was the recipient of the sacrament of orders in its fullness, while consecration was ordered toward jurisdictional empowerment. By contrast, the Council deliberately stepped away from the long-dominant dichotomy between the so-called powers of order and of jurisdiction in the episcopate. This distinction emerged in the medieval West and resulted at length in a notion of sacrament which was seen solely in terms of the power to sanctify. The power to govern was thought to be rooted in a deputation from an ecclesiastical authority. *Lumen Gentium* regarded this as an artificial distinction, and proposed instead the ministry of the bishop as being of a single piece. This recovery of ancient theological instincts meant that all three of the offices proper to the mission of Christ are bestowed in their fullness upon every bishop: the office of teaching, the office of sanctifying, and the office of governing or "jurisdiction." In *Lumen Gentium* the college of bishops is presented as the successor to the college of apostles, and it is the subject of supreme and full authority over the universal church, provided that this college is never to be imagined without its head. Moreover, according to *Lumen Gentium*, the episcopal college is not fundamentally constituted for the exercise of juridical power. Although that is an inescapable dimension of collegial authority, its ecclesiological purpose articulated at Vatican II is to be the visible expression of *communio.* It follows that episcopal rank is an ecclesial *munus* rather than a personal possession or an individual privilege. Its ultimate meaning is realized in partaking in the mission of Christ for the building up of the church. It is to be viewed as having an innate universal quality not only because the *mission* is universal, but also because a bishop is a bishop only when identified with the college.

It has been suggested by many that the concept of church as communion, or *communio,* is an image that captures the essential features of the two most prominent metaphors expressed in *Lumen Gentium*: Body of Christ and People of God. Avery Dulles, Walter Kasper, Jean-Marie Tillard, and Susan Wood have been among the significant contributors to the post-conciliar discussion on *communio.* To speak of the church in this manner is to speak of a community of communities, or a church of churches. It envisions a number of concrete local communities which live alongside one another in a bond of faith and charity. Explicit *communio* vocabulary in present discourse is more directly derived from Protestant sources roughly contemporaneous with Vatican II, but it has sunk deeper roots in Roman Catholicism during the post-conciliar period. *Communio* is a far more rich category than has often been recognized. While frequently telescoped into the quite specific question of visible institutional structures, this is neither the only nor the most important aspect of such ecclesiology.

Ultimately the source of Christian *communio* is God, and more specifically the grace of God's Holy Spirit as encountered in the sacrament of baptism and culminating in the celebration of the Eucharist. This is all prior to the other visible expressions of unity among the churches. To acknowledge this is not to evaluate those other expressions as unimportant; it is simply to say that they flow out of something primordial and transcendent which is common to all Christians. Again, to be identified with the Roman Catholic Church is necessarily to partake in two realities at the same time: a communion that is singular and universal as well as a communion that is local and particular. A church that is solely universal is an invisible abstraction, while a church that is only local is not Catholic. Our theology of incarnation holds that God does not dwell among us as an abstraction or an idea or a philosophy. Rather, the Christian's relationship with God is realized as mediated through particular historical realities and, as Michael Himes has observed, not "above, below or around" those realities (Himes, 150). The supreme instance of this principle is the singular man, Jesus the Christ. At the same time, it is acknowledged that no particular mediation can fully contain or exhaust the transcendent Mystery of God.

During the first centuries of the church, basic structures were developed to make this dual reality visible and concrete: for example, a residential bishop, an order of episcopate, a presbyteral college, deacons, and various other kinds of ministers. Each of these exercised, and continue to exercise, a role that is *both* lived out in the daily activity of the community *and* represented at the celebration of the Eucharist. *Communio* is realized and sacramentalized in one's own time and place, in a here-and-now, or it is not realized at all. To profess the solidarity and *communio* into which we are summoned with all humanity is nothing other than to announce in an abstract, universal way that we are summoned to love the neighbor who is concrete and immediately present. As 1 John 4:20 puts it, our love for the God (and by extension for the church universal) which we cannot see is actualized in the love for the brother/sister in the local, visible church.

But, acknowledging this, the local community is then summoned in effect to "lose itself" within the *communio* of the whole church. To be centered solely on the local church would be to forsake what is transcendent in it. "Each local community is called to love the other local communities," and the gifts given to each are intended for the good of all. Each local communion, in turn, shares in the riches of the whole (Himes, 150). This is ritually enacted at the Eucharist, which is never the Eucharist of any single parish or diocese, but always and only that of the church universal. Indeed, the Eucharist as the ongoing culmination of baptism is the *source* as well as the summit of the Christian life, as Vatican II said in *Sacrosanctum Concilium* 10. No community that fails to celebrate Eucharist can possibly live as a part of the greater church.

This sacramental bond leads into a necessary distinction in the theology of ministry. The distinction is between Christian ministry in a generic sense and that particular ministry which is exercised by the bishop. Certainly this was part of what the bishops of Vatican II had in mind when they distinguished in *Lumen Gentium* the ministries of clergy and laity and specified that it was a distinction of kind and not only of degree. While all Christians participate in the summons to ministry (including liturgical ministry) by virtue of their baptism, the fact that there is a component of *eucharistic leadership* involved in the ministry of the bishop bestows it with some particular qualities. Among other things, in the bishop is to be located a principle of communion with all other churches. This is by virtue of his membership in the universal college, which is the concrete and visible expression of *communio*. Thus, episcopal ministry presumes presidency at the Eucharist, but it must be emphasized again that the visible ministry of the local bishop is not the *source* of *communio*. The Holy Spirit of God is that source. St. Paul emphasizes that the many gifts which are given for the purpose of *communio* are exactly that: gifts from God. And the greatest of these gifts is love, which compels each local church to place its charisms in service to the good of the others and of the whole. As the gospel and letters of John so frequently repeat, it is the presence of love which is the mark by which Christian disciples recognize one another and are recognized by others. And the primary visible *sign* of the presence of such love is communion (Himes, 150).

This means that while there can be no meaningful visible expression of the *communio* of churches apart from the bishops in college, the college per se is not enough: the college *presumes* a meaningful lived experience of *communio* at the local level, both within and among the churches of which each bishop is in some sense the representative. The representative function of the local bishop is a dual one, for his ability to reflect the mind of the universal church both conditions and is conditioned by his ability to reflect the faith of his local church. Each local bishop necessarily speaks for both, and in conciliar theology there is no perceived contradiction in that. In practice it is a more ambiguous undertaking, as my concluding remarks will demonstrate. This dialectical-collegial structure of the individual bishop and the episcopal college as a whole is so ordered because of the very nature of what the church *is* as a communion of communions.

## III. From Vatican II forward:
## *Communio* as the source of tradition

Himes has pointed out that this sense of *communio* is also at work behind what Catholic theology describes as the "Tradition" (Himes, 151–152). It had become commonplace, particularly after the Council of Trent and through the nineteenth century, to construe the theological "Tradition" in terms of a body of truth-propositions handed on as a deposit of information from one generation to the next. While it may indeed include that, in its full sense "Tradition" points to the shared life of the church "which finds expression in the act of passing on the community's grasp of revelation in one generation to subsequent generations" (Himes, 152). Truth *arises from* the life shared among Christians in the communion of the churches, rather than being *proposed to* the church extrinsically as a kind of second source of unwritten revelation alongside the Bible. So while it is necessary to have doctrine properly articulated, this too is insufficient to be an expression of true *communio*. It is because *communio* is effected and sustained by the Spirit that the whole church has the capacity to discern accurately what Christ has revealed. And it is the daily concrete life of the local churches that is the context for this discernment. Communion gives birth to the clarification of doctrine. Tradition, then, is "a source of revelation not in the sense of a body of truths not contained in scripture," but rather as the communal and organic unfolding of meaning around the singular salvific event of Jesus Christ. Therefore, one cannot claim to have a grasp of the truth of "revelation" apart from living the life of Christian *communio* (Himes, 152). This is merely to say that one cannot understand the gospel without living it concretely in a local communion of love. That is the local church: not only an assembly of people with a correct and informed grasp of official church teaching (though that is important enough), but the concrete, organic community in which doctrine finds a source as well as an expression.

Himes notes that this principle of *communio* as source and locus may further be applied to the matter of discerning right faith and morals, as in the matter of the *sensus fidelium* explicated in *Lumen Gentium*. The theological roots of this principle can be traced back at least as far as Newman, who proposed that the faithful ought to be consulted in the articulation of doctrine. "He did not intend to claim that all the faithful have theological expertise, let alone some sort of infused knowledge. Rather he meant that those who consistently attempt to live in communion with one another in the local community and with the communion of communities . . . have by that fact a connaturality with the truth of revelation," that is, a reliable intuition for right doctrine (Himes, 152). Once more, this *communio* finds its source ultimately in the Spirit and is not the end product of Christian believers working diligently at getting along.

Thus, to speak theologically of "Tradition" is to refer not merely to the handing on of doctrinal propositions from age to age, although it includes that as a second-level reality. It refers rather to the whole *communio* of ecclesial life as it comes to visible expression in prayer, action, teaching, relating, speaking, and working. *Communio*, therefore, suggests a weight to the notion of "Tradition" that is greater than the mere accumulation of information. Catechisms and historical theological investigations certainly reflect that "Tradition," but they do not entirely account for it. This point is worthy of emphasis because the *communio* into which Christians are summoned is a duty in which more is at stake than may be apparent. Being a functioning *communio* is the precondition for the ability to discern God's own truth properly. Thus, the notion of the *sensus fidelium* affirms that academic theology and doctrinal scholarship, while hardly insignificant or unimportant, are modes of knowing and discerning which are qualitatively different from the mode of lived *communio*.

A further implication of *communio*, Himes points out, concerns the theological notion of "reception" of faith and doctrine. Here too the ultimate source of this gift is the Holy Spirit, who directs the particular churches in communion to hear and recognize universal truth. In that sense, the local churches serve a reciprocal ratifying function. Such a mutual recognition, which is the fundamental ground beneath the idea of reception, is not the same thing as obedience (Himes, 155). Because there is no particular church which enjoys a pre-emptive higher status in terms of its ability to discern and articulate religious truth, reception cannot be reduced to the docile and unreflected acceptance by one local church of teaching proposed in another local church. The fact that the bishop of Rome, for example, enjoys a certain primacy or status magisterially does not derive from the idea that there is something about that *place* which has unique access to truth to the denigration of all other places. It derives from the fact that the bishop of Rome is the visible principle of unity in the college of bishops. The church of Rome, and hence its bishop, enjoys a primacy by virtue of its relatedness with all other churches and their bishops.

Reception suggests not some kind of parliamentary procedure for determining juridical force, but rather the recognition in and by the local churches that a particular teaching or doctrine is "grounded upon the original apostolic witness," which is ongoing in every local church (Himes, 155). In other words, the criterion for reception is truth, and not the role that any particular church may have had in the articulation of doctrine. In the same manner, the teaching of a council is not deemed to be binding because it is taught by a council; rather, a council teaches things because they have been found to be true (Himes, 155).

In earlier periods of Catholic theology it was customary to make the distinction between what was called the *ecclesia docens* and the *ecclesia discens*, between that part of the church which teaches and that part which is taught. But the Vatican II call to universal responsibility for the church in all its aspects among all the baptized takes away the utility of this distinction. All are both teachers and learners, albeit each one in a way commensurate with his or her status or vocation in the visible structure of the church. So it is not the case that one person or one group or one local church teaches while all others submit passively to that teaching. This need not in any way diminish the proper role of the hierarchical magisterium in definitively articulating faith and morals. What the principle of reception does require, though, is the displacement of the idea that the majority of the church simply receives teaching while a minority proposes it.

The exercise of *communio* in this fashion reminds us that the mystery of the church does not cohere neatly with any other known political structure. The church as *communio* is neither a democracy nor a monarchy. The kind of *obsequium* which authoritative magisterial teaching calls for is neither of a kind in which local churches are free to ratify or reject it nor of a kind in which extrinsically enforced obedience is possible (see *LG* 25). It is not accidental that *obsequium* itself is a Latin word which resists translation into other languages, because the quality of adherence which it is meant to elicit is an utterly unique one. Every merely political analogy or model positively distorts the mystery of what *communio* is (Himes, 156).

## IV. Contemporary challenges for a *communio* ecclesiology: Infallibility, ecumenism, authority

One cannot avoid in this discussion the matter of the magisterial charism of infallibility. Vatican I and subsequent teachings have explicitly noted that the subject of this charism is the church as a whole. It is not a proprietary gift which attaches to discrete persons who inhabit or even lead the church. Thus, what is expressed as the "faith of the church," whether infallible or otherwise, has to arise from the *life* of the church as it is expressed in particular churches. Spiritual gifts shared in common are received in many different ways at different times, and the experience of such gifts may be variable in different contexts. This means that every local church is directly responsible not only for the discernment of truth but for creating the conditions by which it can be recognized. In a very real sense, infallibility as an exercise of the church is *dependent* upon the way that the concrete lives of the particular churches are carried out. *Communio* is what guarantees that a matter is the faith of the *church,* and not only of some portion of it.

The bishop can be understood in this regard as a kind of corporate personality, the local church symbolically projected onto a singular person. This is a very ancient instinct in theology. It is why, for example, Ignatius of Antioch could write to the members of a church which he had never visited that he "knew" them because he had met their bishop (Himes, 153). The bishop is the bridge figure who speaks in two directions: both "as the voice of the episcopal college to the local community, and as the voice of the local community to the Church at large" (Himes, 153). And because every bishop holds the responsibility of the whole, each bishop teaches with the authority of the entire college. Further, every local church is a particular instantiation of the church universal; it is not something less than the full church, not a portion or a franchise of a more complete local church someplace else. Thus, when a bishop articulates the faith of his local church, he speaks in some sense of the faith of the whole. For this reason there has always been the concern in the episcopal college that teaching must be done with a certain "moral unanimity" or clear consensus. Such express doctrinal *communio* is what gives evidence that the teaching is authentic.

In the same way, the pope as bishop of Rome functions as a type of corporate personality by embodying in his person the episcopal college (Himes, 154). This, and only this, is the reason why the pope as a single person enjoys the charism of infallibility proper to the church of Christ, as Vatican I put it. He is, so to speak, the "head of the head" in addition to being servant of the servants. The episcopal college cannot be said to exist apart from its visible head, and likewise there can be no head without the college. Vatican II ecclesiology was concerned that neither side be ignored in that delicate equation. Both college and head are intrinsic to the nature of the church as a visible expression of *communio.*

The post-conciliar period has thrust upon ecclesiology with even greater urgency the question of *communio* and ecumenism. How is the Catholic Church to be understood as being in a communion with other Christian bodies? The final report issued by the extraordinary meeting of the Synod of Bishops in 1985, which was summoned by the pope in order to reflect upon the state of the church twenty years after the council, included a strong affirmation of the principle of ecumenical dialogue: "Basing itself on the ecclesiology of communion, the Catholic Church at the time of the Second Vatican Council fully assumed her ecumenical responsibility. After these 20 years we can affirm that ecumenism has inscribed itself deeply and indelibly in the consciousness of the church. We bishops ardently desire that the incomplete communion already existing with the non-Catholic churches [*sic*] and communities might, with the grace of God, come to the point of full communion" (Synod of Bishops, 449).

To a great extent this question turns on the issue of how the exercise of the Petrine ministry is carried out. Theologically speaking, it seems to be a uniquely Catholic instinct that communion with the bishop of Rome is one of the foundational elements of the church, without which it would not be what it is. Other Christian churches and ecclesial bodies may have various degrees of appreciation for the Petrine office, but none regard the absence of it as jeopardizing the very essence of what the church is. This is an aspect of *communio* that requires dialogue with others in order to be worked through, because it raises the critical question of how the one faith of the Christian church is adjudicated and by whom. Are Catholics able unilaterally to define the content of Christian faith which is binding upon all the baptized? Who speaks for the Great Church, and with what warrant? Even in light of the Roman Catholic claim to be the body in which the fullness of faith subsists, the matter is not settled, because it is still an imperative role of the episcopal college to be responsible for Christian unity.

There is today a fair consensus in ecumenical theology that the issue of the primacy and its relationship to the episcopate is a question which simply has to be confronted in the quest for Christian unity. As far back as 1967, Pope Paul VI stated that "the pope—as we all know—is undoubtedly the gravest obstacle in the path of ecumenism" (cited by Hebblethwaite, 9). Again in the encyclical letter *Ut Unum Sint* (1995), Pope John Paul II stated that the office of the bishop of Rome "constitutes a difficulty for most other Christians, whose memory is marked by certain painful recollections" (*UUS* 88). Much of Orthodox theology emphasizes the traditional role played by the pentarchy—those five ancient patriarchates of the sixth to the eighth centuries. Even though it is admitted that the see of Rome enjoyed a certain pre-eminence among the five, Orthodoxy does not understand this status as one of universal legislative power. Thus, whenever the exercise of the primacy is presented as a power *over* other bishops and their churches, this is contrary to Orthodox theology. Instead, they contend, the primacy must be viewed as being rooted in the episcopacy itself; it is the synod of bishops which is the ordinary subject of the exercise of the primacy.

Western Protestants also, particularly Lutherans and Anglicans, are quite well-disposed to the principle of the ministry of a universal primacy, but there are strong hesitations expressed over the likelihood that the rights and duties of the local bishops will be usurped in practice. Richard Gaillardetz notes in this regard, "It is difficult to imagine a formalized unity among the Churches that does not include some shared understanding of doctrinal teaching authority. Even so, Roman Catholics cannot afford the hubris of thinking that their structures and understandings of authority *in toto* and as presently constituted provide the only viable possibility. If there lies in the future of Christianity a formalized unity among some of the various Christian traditions, no one can know at this point what precise form the structures and manner of exercise of ecclesial authority will take" (Gaillardetz, 275–276). He goes on to suggest that any effort in the quest for unity will require some recognition of the gap that is widely perceived between what Catholics say is their *vision* of authority in the church and the way in which present structures actually function. Vatican II stated in its Decree on Ecumenism (*Unitatis Redintegratio*): "In ecumenical work, Catholics must assuredly be concerned for the members of separated christian communities . . . but their primary duty is to make a careful and honest appraisal of whatever needs to be renewed and done in the catholic household itself, in order that its life may bear witness more clearly and more faithfully to the teachings and institutions which have been handed down from Christ through the apostles" (*UR* 4).

The concrete way in which the bishop of Rome has functioned as a source for unity has changed many times throughout the course of history, and there is no need to believe that it cannot change again. Change here does not mean undermining or doing away with; it simply recognizes that this ministry is in service to an end greater than itself. The pope today is many different things simultaneously: the bishop of the diocese of Rome, the patriarch of the Latin church, the head of the episcopal college, and the supreme pontiff and successor of Peter. Distinguishing these roles more carefully will be a necessary part of the effort toward Christian unity.

There is a certain ambiguity over the degree to which current hierarchical leadership is willing to re-imagine such institutional structures of authority. Noteworthy in this discussion is an oft-cited letter published by the Sacred Congregation for the Doctrine of the Faith (CDF) in 1992, titled "Some Aspects of the Church Understood as Communion." Its contents came in for some serious theological criticism because it was viewed as being far too universalist in tone. The letter intended to be a kind of instruction in proper interpretation of the concept of *communio*, reiterating that this is a most useful image for considering the reality of the church. It quoted Pope John Paul II as saying that the concept of communion "lies at the heart of the church's self-understanding" (CDF, par. 3). It emphasized that the church's *communio* is always both invisible and visible at the same time, and that these two realities correspond. Further, it noted that this *communio* involves not only those presently alive on earth, but also the eschatological community which it called "the heavenly church" (par. 6). This *communio* includes the saints and especially the Blessed Virgin Mary.

It was the second section of the letter which was the cause for greatest dispute. On one hand, it affirmed that there are now and have always been "manifold particular expressions of the saving presence of the one church of Christ." Further, these local communities "are in themselves churches because, although they are particular, the universal church becomes present in them with all her essential elements" (par. 7). On the other hand, however, the letter identified perceived dangers to *communio* which it called expressions of "ecclesiological unilateralism." The critical text came in the course of this discussion, and said that the universal church "is not the result of the communion of the churches, but in its essential mystery it is a reality ontologically and temporally prior to every individual particular church." This sounded to many ecclesiologists like the equal and opposite error of radical centralism. It went on to say: "Indeed, according to the fathers, ontologically the church-mystery, the church that is one and unique, precedes creation and gives birth to the particular churches as her daughters. She expresses herself in them; she is the mother and not the offspring of the particular churches" (par. 9). The criticism for this text came from the perception that it was attempting to describe the church as it exists in the mind of God, a church without any people in it, utterly severed from its historical dimension. The letter is illustrative of how subtle is the necessary vocabulary for speaking of the church as *communio,* and how easily one can slip into making statements that threaten to dissolve the tension between the one and the many.

## Conclusion: Bishop Lucker and change in a church lived as *communio*

From the folio of articles which Bishop Lucker kept on matters concerning the local-universal church dialectic, it appears that he remained frustrated with the degree to which the instincts of Vatican II have yet to be made real in ecclesial practice. Two areas of particular interest to him were the manner in which bishops are appointed and the reluctance in official theology to acknowledge historical change in law, doctrine, and pastoral praxis. A perusal of articles gathered and generously glossed, authored by thinkers such as Hebblethwaite, McBrien, Bernardin, Dulles, Komonchak, and Granfield, reveals a passion for linking ecclesiological theory with life on the ground in actual Christian dioceses and parishes. To do this is to introduce ambiguity, contingency, subjectivity, and history into ecclesiological deliberation. It is telling that the singular repeated word scratched into the margins of so many of these collected articles is "change." As Bishop Lucker seems to have felt, change is neither an ideological war cry nor a postmodern plot to undermine authority; it is simply descriptive of the historical record. To acknowledge change is an exercise in honesty.

But this impinges on doctrine only if the concrete life of the local churches bears a critical weight in theological thinking. For Bishop Lucker, it does. This is clear from the 1991 mission statement of the Diocese of New Ulm:

> The local church is the diocese. We form one people, all of us in this fifteen county area—bishop, priests, religious and laity. We are bound together as a communion (community) of one faith, one divine life, one call to love, celebrating the same sacraments with Jesus as our center and the Holy Spirit as our source of life and power. We are united with other local churches throughout the world in proclaiming our Holy Father, Pope John Paul II as the visible head of the universal church. We begin with people. That is what we are, the people of God—bishop, priests, parish ministers, religious, men and women—all of us. (Lucker, 356)

There too in the folio is a reflection published by Clifford Longley in *The Tablet* just a few weeks before Bishop Lucker's death (see Longley, 970). He devoured it while lying in his hospice bed. The article analyzes the recent public debate carried on between Cardinals Ratzinger and Kasper over the dialectics of the church universal and the local churches (see Kasper, 8–14). There are dozens of underlined sentences and several cross references scrawled in the margins. But there are exactly three circled words: "challenge" and "collegiality" and "nullified."

Clearly, there is further work to be done in bringing *communio* from the Council to the countryside and from the countryside back to the curia.

## References

Congregation for the Doctrine of the Faith (CDF). "Some Aspects of the Church Understood as Communion." *Origins* 22/7 (June 25, 1992): 108–112.

Denzinger-Schönmetzer. *Enchiridion Symbolorum*, 36th ed. Freiburg: Herder, 1976.

Gaillardetz, Richard. *Teaching with Authority: A Theology of the Magisterium in the Church.* Collegeville, Minn.: The Liturgical Press, Michael Glazier Books, 1997.

Hebblethwaite, Peter. *Paul VI: The First Modern Pope*. New York: Paulist Press, 1993.

Henn, William. *The Honor of My Brothers: A Brief History of the Relationship between the Pope and the Bishops.* New York: Crossroad Publishing Co., 2000.

Himes, Michael J. "The Ecclesiological Significance of the Reception of Doctrine." *The Heythrop Journal* 33:2 (April 1992): 146–160.

Kasper, Walter. "On The Church." *America* 184/14 (April 23-30, 2001): 8–14.

Longley, Clifford. "Opening up the Big Questions." *The Tablet* 25 (July 7, 2001): 970.

Synod of Bishops. "The Final Report." *Origins* 15/27 (December 19, 1985): 441, 443–450.

# 5
# The bishop as teacher:
# Proclaiming the living word of God in the church

SUSAN K. WOOD, S.C.L.

S ince the church is a people united in the profession of the apostolic
faith, it needs to have a common understanding of its faith, for apostolic faith is normative for those who call themselves Christian.
Since apostolic times, new questions have arisen and conflicts in understanding have occurred. Hence the church needs teachers with pastoral
authority to act as judges in matters of faith. Catholics believe that the
bishops have inherited a teaching mandate which Christ gave to his apostles. As successors of the apostles, bishops receive from Christ "the mission of teaching all peoples, and of preaching the Gospel to every
creature . . ." (*LG* 24). Bishops have the task of determining authoritatively
the correct interpretation of the scripture and tradition committed to the
church and judge for the church the accuracy of the presentation of this
revelation by others (National Conference of Catholic Bishops, par. 2).

Bishops exercise their teaching authority both personally and collegially. Vatican II taught that their authority is "proper, ordinary and immediate" (*LG* 27) although it is ultimately controlled by the supreme
authority of the church and can be limited by that authority. This means
that their authority is theirs by virtue of their ordination to the episcopate and is not simply a mediation of papal authority. They exercise
their own authority by their own right by virtue of their office as bishop
and are not merely branch offices of the Vatican.

Their authority is also communal and collegial, for they are made
members of the episcopal college by virtue of their ordination and
communion with the Bishop of Rome. Even when they are teaching individually in their own dioceses, they are teaching in communion with
the other bishops and with the Bishop of Rome. The whole episcopal

college in union with the pope exercises the supreme teaching authority of the church, either when gathered together in an ecumenical council or when dispersed throughout the world (*LG* 25). The pope, as head of the episcopal college, also exercises this supreme teaching authority. The Second Vatican Council (1962–1965) is the most recent example of an ecumenical council. However, bishops also convene to teach pastorally in national conferences of bishops (John Paul II, 1998, *Apostolos Suos*) and they offer a consultative voice to the pope in their participation in synods.

The American bishops in preparation for their pastorals, "The Challenge of Peace" (1983) and "Economic Justice for All" (1986), consulted widely with the laity, thereby demonstrating that the teaching of bishops involves a discerning listening to the life of the church. The *sensus fidelium* can never be reduced to an opinion poll, but it does focus on the witness of the whole church in matters of faith and its ability to penetrate more deeply into that same faith through right judgment and to apply it more fully to life (*LG* 12). Listening to the *sensus fidelium* belongs to the communal dimension of episcopal teaching.

Bishop Lucker underlined this communal-dialogical nature of episcopal teaching in his ministry. The present essay examines three characteristics of communal-dialogical episcopal teaching, both in universal church teaching and in the pastoral ministry of Bishop Lucker. First, the essay examines the "hierarchy of truths" as the idea pertains to episcopal teaching. Second, it shows how the primary instance of episcopal teaching, both for Bishop Lucker and the larger church, is in the preaching of the bishop. Third, the essay juxtaposes the Second Vatican Council's understanding of the office of the bishop as a prophetic office with writings on this same theme by Bishop Lucker. The essay's conclusion comes back briefly to the communal-dialogical nature of bishop's role in the church.

## I. The "hierarchy of truths": An ongoing debate about truth in the church

The pastoral authority of bishops is limited to what pertains to Christian faith or to the Christian way of life. The object of their teaching is explicitly or implicitly contained in revelation or is necessary to defend or explain some revealed truth. However, not all church teaching is equal in its relation to the foundation of the Christian faith. Thus, the Decree on Ecumenism reminds us that "when comparing doctrines with one another, they [Catholic theologians] should remember that in catholic doctrine there exists an order or 'hierarchy' of truths" (*UR* 11). In his teaching Bishop Lucker identified six different levels of teaching, all requiring a different kind of response: (1) Divinely revealed truth, that is, doctrine definitively and infallibly taught by the church as revealed. The response is faith. (2) Definitive non-revealed truths proposed as infallible; these are matters of faith and morals that, even though not revealed themselves, are required to safeguard the integrity of the deposit of faith, to explain it rightly, and to define it effectively. The response is firm assent. (3) Authoritative but non-irreformable teaching that aids in promoting a better understanding of revelation and makes explicit its contents. The response is religious submission in respect and obedience of will and intellect. (4) Disciplinary rules that may be either universal laws of the church or particular laws of a diocese, such as liturgical norms or church practices. The response is obedience. (5) Theological opinions. These invite agreement. (6) Pious practices and devotions. These invite imitation.

It is worth examining the evolving theological understanding of the first three levels of church teaching outlined by Bishop Lucker. First, infallible teaching is a judgment that a teaching is irreformable and irrevocable even though the *expression* of the doctrine may need to change in order to remain comprehensible over time. Only the supreme teaching authority of the church, the episcopal college or the pope, can teach infallibly. An individual bishop does not have this authority by himself, although collectively the bishops, even when dispersed throughout the world, can teach definitively (*LG* 25). The most common means of teaching infallibly is through an ecumenical council, although the pope can also exercise this teaching authority when he teaches *ex cathedra*. This has occurred only twice: the proclamation of the doctrines of the Immaculate Conception (1854) and the Assumption (1950). The bishops at Vatican II chose not to teach infallibly, although bishops had done so at previous ecumenical councils such as Vatican I (1870) and the Council of Trent (1545–1563). Examples of infallible doctrines include the Blessed Trinity, the full humanity and divinity of Jesus Christ, the real presence of Christ in the Eucharist, the bodily resurrection of Christ, and our redemption by Christ. Non-acceptance of these truths results in heresy.

The last ten years have witnessed an expansion of the second category, definitive non-revealed truths proposed as infallible. These are what were traditionally called "secondary objects of infallibility," those truths it was necessary to uphold in order to preserve divinely revealed truth. Previously, all definitive truths, those in the first and second category of teaching, were considered to be infallible. Furthermore, the criteria for infallible teaching were fairly clear. The pope needed to define doctrine explicitly *ex cathedra* while exercising his official office. Ecumenical councils distinguished between pastoral teaching, disciplinary teaching, and doctrinal teaching, although Francis Sullivan in his book, *Creative Fidelity,* has shown the intricacies of interpreting the authoritative nature of these documents. Since some of the early councils were convened initially as regional councils, their ecumenical status became clear only later, during a process of reception of their teaching. However, once they had been accepted as ecumenical, the first seven ecumenical councils' teaching became normative for the church.

In the last ten years, the term "definitive" has been applied by the pope in his apostolic letter *Ordinatio Sacerdotalis* (1994) to teaching prohibiting the ordination of women. He declared "that the Church has no authority whatsoever to confer priestly ordination on women and that this judgment is to be definitively held by all the Church's faithful" (*Ordinatio Sacerdotalis* 4). Yet an apostolic letter does not constitute infallible teaching and is not an instance of the pope teaching *ex cathedra.*

In addition, documents issuing from curial congregations are labeling teaching as "definitive." For example, in its response to a *dubium* (doubt) concerning whether the church can ordain women, the Congregation for the Doctrine of the Faith said, "This teaching requires definitive assent, since, founded on the written word of God and from the beginning constantly preserved and applied in the tradition of the church, it has been set forth infallibly by the ordinary and universal magisterium" (CDF, 401).

The congregation appealed to the infallibility of the ordinary magisterium, that is, the definitive teaching of the bishops when dispersed throughout the world (*LG* 25). However, with the exception of some doctrines which, although they have never been explicitly defined, are certainly dogmas of faith, it is not easy to verify the conditions for the infallibility of this universal ordinary magisterium.

The Pontifical Council for the Family in "*Vademecum* for Confessors Concerning Some Aspects of Conjugal Life" (1997) said that the teaching on the intrinsic evil of contraception is to be held as "definitive and non-reformable" (par. 4). Curial congregations do not have the authority to teach infallibly. Therefore, these teachings are declared to be "definitive," but they cannot be said to be "infallible." However, only infallible teaching is truly irreformable and irrevocable. All other teaching is fallible, reformable, and revocable. This change in the use of the term "definitive" to mean irreformable, but not infallible, represents a new use of the language of authority, one not represented in Bishop Lucker's six levels of teaching. Theologians are still trying to sort out what this means for the interpretation of church documents.

A third level of teaching, non-definitive or non-infallible teaching, is authoritative and requires an attitude of willingness to accept the teaching. This type of teaching exists for the pastoral good of the church at specific times in history and is subject to change. Bishop Lucker traces changes in authoritative, non-irreformable teaching that have already occurred in the history of the church and includes among them teachings on academic freedom, animal rights, biblical criticism, the relationship between church and state, communism, creation in six days, democracy, ecumenism, Galileo, usury, religious freedom, and slavery. His papers indicate that he would also include the following issues as authoritative but non-irreformable teachings or church practices: those having to do with the validity of Anglican orders, birth control, capital punishment, the celibacy of the clergy, communion of the divorced and remarried, the authority of the curia, the use of nuclear weapons for deterrence, limitations on general absolution in the sacrament of penance, homosexuality, the ordination of women (at least to the diaconate), and the absence of light matter in sexual sin. These are very contested issues within the life of the church, issues that show the difficulty both in determining how we know what is a definitive teaching and in developing church practices of discerning types of teaching. Bishop Lucker advocated free, open, and lengthy discussion of issues to discover definitive teaching. Then, when we have come to the conclusion that something is definitive, he said: "In the end, we bow in the face of definitive teaching" (Introduction; note that Bishop Lucker's lists on non-irreformable teaching appear as an appendix to this volume).

## II. The ministry of the word of God in the church: The bishop as preacher

The threefold office of sanctifying, teaching, and governing in imitation of Jesus Christ who was priest, prophet, and king functions as a structuring motif in *Lumen Gentium*. The document describes the people of God in chapter 2, bishops and priests in chapter 3, and the laity in chapter 4, thus indicating that sanctifying, teaching, and governing are qualities of the church as a whole before they are qualities designating any particular person or office within the church. Such an approach fits Bishop Lucker's conviction that the bishop's special ministry of teaching lies within the context of the broad ministry of the word of God in the church (Lucker, 367). This means that the teaching ministry of the bishop carries out a function of the entire church. It is not just a personal ministry; it is an ecclesial one. It also means that bishops are not above the word, but are able to teach it because they have first listened to it as embodied in the scriptures and in the living tradition of the worship and life of the church (*DV* 8).

Bishop Lucker's reflections on the teaching ministry of the diocesan bishop were occasioned by the document approved November 14, 1991 by the U. S. Bishops, "The Teaching Ministry of the Diocesan Bishop: A Pastoral Reflection." Since the present volume represents an attempt to complete the book that Bishop Lucker undertook, it seems appropriate to quote extensively from his pastoral letter, dated February 1992, listing what he considered to be important ideas dropped from the first draft of that text along with his reflections on them. Bishop Lucker lists five such ideas:

> [First,] the teaching ministry of the diocesan bishop is seen in the context of the total teaching ministry of the church. Jesus taught the good news to ordinary folk, sinners, publicans, the sick and the lame, outcasts, and women. This group formed the community of disciples. Jesus, the Word, is teacher in what he is, in what he does, and in what he says. He gathered all who believed in him. All members are called to hand on their faith with others. All are called to teach. This includes parents, catechists, priests, teachers, and theologians. The apostles were chosen from among these followers of Christ and were entrusted with a special task. The teaching ministry of the apostles was part of the teaching mission of the church. The bishops, as successors of the apostles, have a special role.

> [Second,] the ministry of the word is concerned with the revelation of a hidden God and faith, our response to that good news of God. By what God said and did, God revealed the mysteries of the Trinity, of creation, of Jesus, of the Holy Spirit, the church,

the sacraments, of everlasting life, and a Christian way of life. We are invited to a deep and total human response to that revelation. The Word of God is filled with life, dynamism, and with God, a faithful, loving, gracious Lord. We respond with awe and reverence. The ministry of the word includes, therefore, evangelization, catechesis, liturgical preaching, and theology as well as the official teaching office of pope and bishops.

[Third,] there are different levels of teaching in the church. Not all church documents and statements are taught with the same authority. Some teaching revealed by God can never change. Some teachings are so closely connected with revealed truths that they are also definitively taught. This is the central core of teaching revealed by God, which is unchangeable. There is a widespread acceptance within the church of this core context of faith. All teachings are expressed in human language and in a particular historical context. Some teachings are reformable; that is, while not taught definitively, they apply the gospel to issues of today in conformity with the truths of faith. Some call for a response of faith; others call for assent; still others call for obedience of mind and heart. For many hundreds of years, theologians showed the levels of teaching by what was called "theological notes."

[Fourth,] the earlier draft noted that in the past the church made errors and mistakes, not on essential teachings but in reformable statements of the teaching church. It is refreshing to recognize and admit this and to acknowledge that we can grow in our understanding of the message of revelation and in the expression and application of the teaching of the church, given to us by Jesus, to different times and different cultural expressions. The Holy Spirit continues to guide us.

[Fifth,] bishops of the United States have exercised a special teaching role as they teach together in the Conference of Bishops. In a number of our recent pastoral letters, we developed a manner of instruction that involved widespread consultation and progressive revisions, which prepared our people for the reception of the pastoral letters. (Lucker, 367–369)

Bishop Lucker believed that the document was drastically weakened by changing its tone and by dropping the part dealing with the teaching role of the whole church and placing the teaching ministry of the bishop in this context. He criticized the document on the floor of the bishops' meeting, asking: "Where is the life, the dynamism, the beauty of the Word of God? Where is humility? Where is mystery? Where is reverence?" In his opinion, the final draft was concerned almost exclusively with heresy, error, and dissent expressed in a cold, juridical tone (Lucker, 369). Bishop Lucker affirms that the bishop is called to defend the church's teaching against error and to supervise the ministry of the word in the diocese, but much more positively he is called to preach, teach, write, and communicate the word of God and to encourage others in their teaching ministry.

Too often when we think of the teaching office of the church or the bishop as teacher, we think first of dogmas and truths, church creeds and councils, and documents that issue from them. Various levels of teaching and their interpretation can appear to be very technical and even tedious. These definitely belong to the teaching office of the bishop and are necessary to preserve the apostolic faith of the church. Yet it would be a pity if we allowed them to obscure the essential teaching task of the bishop—to proclaim the word of God as living for us today. A bishop teaches most frequently in his exercise of what we call the ordinary magisterium of the church through the pastoral work he does day in and day out in his local church. The bishop is primarily a teacher through his preaching of the gospel, his principal responsibility (*LG* 25, *CD* 12). Other ways the bishop teaches are through his pastoral letters or columns in the diocesan newspaper and talks he gives to various groups in the diocese, such as catechists and school teachers. The pastoral advice he gives to individuals or groups is yet another form of teaching.

The purpose of preaching is not merely to communicate information or give catechetical instruction, but to elicit faith. Faith is both a relationship with God and intellectual belief in the content of our faith. Although Bishop Lucker noted that both are necessary, the focus of his pastoral teaching was to emphasize the importance of developing a relationship with God. He defined faith as "the response of the human person to the living Word of God, which is expressed both in our relationship with God who has first loved us and in our assent to the truths which God has revealed" (Lucker, 425). He said that unless we had that relationship, the next step would be impossible. Before we can say "I believe in what you have revealed. I want to learn more about you. I want to learn about what you have taught us," we must have that relationship. The main point in Bishop Lucker's teaching was that God loves us, and God is present in our lives. He did not just talk *about* God and church teaching, but handed on his personal faith, his relationship with a living and loving God (Lucker, 418). The bishop is a teacher who leads us in the way of faith and teaches by embodying what he proclaims. He is able to proclaim the faith because he first lives it and is able to bear personal witness to it. There is a transparency between the man and the message that is not obscured by the formalities of office. At least that was the power and influence of Bishop Raymond Lucker.

Bishop Lucker regretted that he did not devote enough of his time to teaching the word of God; he asked the priests of his diocese to schedule the sacrament of confirmation on weekdays if possible, so that he could spend weekends at parishes to worship with the people and preach the word of God (Lucker, 20). He also enjoyed speaking to groups of religion teachers, as he believed that the Lord had blessed him with special gifts in the teaching of theology.

In effective preaching, the preacher first resonates with the word of God and gets in touch with his own faith. Then he speaks the word so that it resonates with the faith of the hearer in such a way that something new comes to awareness. The word may prophesy, announce, transmit, recall, nurture life, teach, exhort, edify, console, persuade, judge, or give testimony. God's creative word is accomplished in what is proclaimed, so that we can say "What you hear is what you get."

In the proclamation of the scriptures, the text proclaimed becomes present in the life of faith of the Christian community. The past events of salvation history become the autobiography of the present community, for the past experience of the people of God becomes the living word of God for us today. The community interprets its own present experience in the light of the scripture texts proclaimed in faith and thereby finds its identity in them. The sense of the faith, what we call the *sensus fidelium*, is this resonance between the faith of the people of God and the proclamation of the gospel.

The bishop has a special role in this process. As an ordained person entrusted with an apostolic office and as a member of the college of bishops, the successor to the college of the apostles, he both witnesses to the authoritative nature of the scriptures, presenting the living word of God to the community, and represents the community, witnessing that the word proclaimed represents its faith. Thus his role with respect to his prophetic office parallels his role in his priestly office. His role in the Liturgy of the Word parallels his role in the Liturgy of the Eucharist, reflecting the unity between pulpit and table. In both he acts *in persona Christi*, representing Christ to the community, and *in persona ecclesiae*, representing the community to Christ. As an extension of this role, he oversees the preaching and teaching of the gospel within his diocese, making sure that the faith proclaimed in his diocese is the same faith proclaimed by the apostles. Thus, his church is kept in continuity with its apostolic foundations and secure in its Christian identity.

A constant theme in Bishop Lucker's pastoral letters is that the bishop does not do this alone, but shares the responsibility for passing on the faith and proclaiming the word with the entire Christian community. For example, he exhorts his people: "We have an identity as Catholics . . . We wish to hand on this identity. We wish to hand on our faith, our worship, and our way of life to our children, to one another, and to the society in which we live. The most important thing I could say to you is that it is not so much what you know, but it is rather who you know. Our identity is Jesus Christ. Everything flows from this relationship" (Lucker, 425). This "proclamation of Christ by word and the witness of their lives" is what we call evangelization (*LG* 35).

Bishop Lucker describes an evangelist as "one who proclaims the good news—that God loves us, that Jesus is our Lord and savior who lived and rose again in order to share his divine life with us. And through the power of the Holy Spirit we form one body, one people in Christ" (Lucker, 68). From this description it is clear that the bishop is the first evangelizer in his church and that his task is to call his people to evangelize, for "handing on the faith is a responsibility of every member of the church" (Lucker, 68).

### III. Vatican II and Raymond Lucker on the bishop's prophetic office: Twelve teaching duties of a bishop

A survey of the duties related to the prophetic office of the bishop in the various documents of Vatican II shows that this office is thoroughly pastoral and practical. Significantly, each duty pertains to the bishop's participation in the ordinary magisterium of the church, since no single bishop aside from the Bishop of Rome can exercise the extraordinary magisterium. Many of these duties are reflected in the pastoral letters of Bishop Lucker. This section of my essay lists the duties of the bishop as articulated by Vatican II and cross-references them to some of the writings of Bishop Lucker on each duty. According to the Vatican II documents, in their teaching function bishops must perform at least the following twelve duties.

First, bishops must call all people to faith or strengthen them in living faith (*CD* 12). Bishop Lucker frequently wrote words like these: "I especially want to talk to you about evangelization . . . Handing on the faith is a responsibility of every member of the church" (Lucker, 68; see also 234–236, 417–419, 425–428).

Second, the Council holds that a bishop should expound the mystery of Christ in its entirety, including those truths ignorance of which is ignorance of Christ (*CD* 12). Bishop Lucker wrote: "Where do we find the central teachings of our faith? We find them in the Creed. We find them in the prayers of the church. We find them in the celebration of the church year" (Lucker, 451; see also 66–67, 333–334, 335–336).

Third, a bishop is to point out the way divinely revealed for giving glory to God and thereby attaining eternal happiness (*CD* 12). Bishop Lucker wrote: "Nothing touches our everyday lives more than the way in which the church worships . . . [Liturgical changes] have enriched our lives and our faith to the extent that we have prepared for them, understood their meaning and opened our hearts to the action of the Holy Spirit" (Lucker, 293–294; see also 158–160, 435–436, 437–439).

Fourth, the Council says a bishop must show that the material things of life and human institutions can also be directed to the salvation of humanity and contribute substantially to building up the body of Christ (*CD* 12). In 1997, Bishop Lucker wrote a pastoral letter explaining what he had learned in a diocesan capital campaign:

> I learned that the campaign's success came from the contributions of the many ordinary people who live in the diocese. I learned that if you give people a chance, present them a clear need and goal, they will respond. I learned that people really appreciate the ministry of the priests of the diocese. I learned that we would not have been able to be successful without an outside consultant. I learned that people want information. (Lucker, 494; see also 56–58, 340–341, 490–492)

Fifth, a bishop must expound in accord with the teaching of the church the inestimable value of the human person; her or his freedom and bodily vitality; the family and its unity and stability; the begetting and educating of children; social structures with their laws and professions; labor and leisure, arts and technology; poverty and affluence (*CD* 12). Bishop Lucker wrote, among other things: "I see so many connections between pollution of soil, water and land, and sexual exploitation . . . Every [one of us] is called to transform the world. And that is particularly needed in economics and sexuality; in the world of work and in the family" (Lucker, 276; see also 24–26, 74–75, 138–140, 183–185, 212–214, 224–226, 532–534).

Sixth, bishops must propose methods for finding an answer to questions of the utmost gravity: the ownership, increase, and just distribution of material wealth; peace and war; the effective fellowship of all peoples (*CD* 12). Bishop Lucker's writings on war and peace, and especially on the connections between peace and economic development, are treated by Amata Miller, I.H.M., in another essay in this book. But even a short listing shows something of the extent of his concern here. (See Lucker, 24–26, 166–168, 172–174, 185–188, 203–205, 208–210, 288–289, 360–361, 433–434.)

Seventh, the bishop is to present the doctrine of Christ in a manner suited to the needs of the times. Such teaching should deal with the most pressing difficulties and problems which weigh people down. The bishop is to preserve this doctrine and teach the faithful themselves to defend it and spread it (*CD* 13). In 1989, Bishop Lucker dedicated four pastoral letters to what he called "the essential elements of Catholic teaching—what can change and what remains the same?" (Lucker, 326). In the last of those four letters, he stressed that "our faith is the response of the *total* person to the living Word of God . . . We also need to place emphasis on the change of heart and conversion that are essential to our profession of faith" (Lucker, 334; see also 68–70, 326–334).

Eighth, the Council says bishops are to make evident the maternal solicitude of the church for everyone, whether they are believers or not (*CD* 13). Bishop Lucker wrote a pastoral letter in response to the flood that western Minnesota experienced in 1997. He wrote: "The church is not just the gathering of people for worship and for religious education. The church is on the dikes and feeding the sandbaggers . . . The flood, tragic as it is, is also a reminder of what we are called to be as followers of Jesus and members of the Body of Christ" (Lucker, 489).

Ninth, bishops must take particular care to further the interests of the poor and the underprivileged to whom the Lord has sent them to preach the gospel (*CD* 13). In a pastoral letter entitled "Greed," Bishop

Lucker wrote of its opposite: "I am edified by the generosity of the people in this diocese, especially toward the poor of the world. Your gifts to the missions and especially to our mission in Guatemala are exemplary..." (Lucker, 197; see also 126–128, 237–239).

Tenth, the bishop is to make an approach to people, seeking and promoting dialogue with them. If truth is constantly to be accompanied by charity and understanding by love, in such salutary discussions they should present their positions in clear language, unaggressively and diplomatically. Likewise, they should show due prudence combined with confidence, for this is what brings about union of minds by encouraging friendship (CD 13). Bishop Lucker wrote of his concern that any emphasis on the teaching authority of the ordained in the church not adopt "a tone and manner [toward the laity that is] negative and not especially helpful" (Lucker, 505).

Eleventh, the Council asks bishops to employ the various means of communication which are at hand at the present time to make known Christian doctrine. This applies especially to preaching and catechetical instruction, which clearly come first in order of importance (CD 13). Bishop Lucker's twenty-five years of pastoral letters in the local diocesan paper are surely an example of this. In his final pastoral letter, he wrote: "I have taken seriously my responsibility to proclaim the Word of God. I have written over two hundred pastoral letters... expressing my views on parish renewal, spiritual life, my own personal spiritual journey, and on issues of concern in the diocese and in our church" (Lucker, 569).

Last, bishops are to be especially concerned about catechetical instruction given to children, adolescents, young people, and even adults. They should also ensure that, in giving this instruction, teachers observe a suitable order and method, accommodated not only to the subject matter but also to the disposition, aptitude, age, and environment of the hearers. Bishops should make sure that this instruction is based on sacred scripture, tradition, liturgy, the teaching authority and life of the church. They should see that catechists are properly trained for their work. They should take steps to restore or improve the adult catechumenate (CD 14). Bishop Lucker, who was director of the Department of Christian Formation of the United States Catholic Conference from 1969 to 1971, wrote frequently on catechesis. Here is one of his most characteristic convictions:

> I expect each Catholic, especially each Catholic adult, to be
> able to know and explain the Apostles' Creed. I am asking

each young person to study it and be prepared to explain it as part of his or her preparation for confirmation . . . The words of the first article of the Creed are so filled with meaning . . . We fall down in awe and reverence. And we cry out, "I believe, Lord. But help my lack of faith (Mark 9:24)." (Lucker, 332; see also 6–8, 48–50, 81–83, 141–143, 227–230, 360–361, 433–434, 443–444)

It is worth noting here that the words from Mark's gospel that Bishop Lucker cites in the letter above were his episcopal motto. In the gospel, the words were spoken by a father who had brought his epileptic son to Jesus for healing. They are also the final words Bishop Lucker wrote in the last of his 202 pastoral letters:

I look back on twenty-five good years. Through all of this I have felt the support of the community I live with in New Ulm, of my numerous family, and above all, the love and care of the Lord Jesus.

The motto I chose when I was appointed a bishop was, 'I believe. But help my lack of trust.' That has guided all of my ministry in these years. (Lucker, 569)

## Conclusion: The bishop as communal-dialogical teacher

The very nature of episcopal pastoral teaching requires that it be communal and dialogical, for the bishop must address men and women within their total environment. The Second Vatican Council said that "we must be aware of and understand the aspirations, the yearnings, and the often dramatic features of the world in which we live" (GS 4). A bishop cannot teach unless he knows his audience, and he does not know his audience without listening to the hopes and fears, problems and joys, failures and achievements, questions, doubts, and convictions of his people. There is a complementary relationship between the bishop and the rest of the community. Through their sense of the faith (*sensus fidei*) the faithful recognize God at work in the bishop's teaching and exercise of authority. The bishop, on the other hand, listens to the sense of the faith within the people because the Holy Spirit also rests on them and the whole community of believers is blessed with the inerrancy of the faith (*LG* 12).

Church structures must be in place to facilitate this dialogue. Many bishops have listening sessions throughout their diocese and pastoral councils which include lay people. There is provision for diocesan synods within canon law (canon 460). The voice of the laity is less evident, however, in synodical structures beyond the diocese. "The Gift of Authority," the 1999 ecumenical document of the Anglican-Roman Catholic International Commission, suggests an agenda for the Roman Catholic Church to strengthen the communal and dialogical nature of episcopal teaching: "The Second Vatican Council has reminded Roman Catholics of how the gifts of God are present in all the people of God. It has also taught the collegiality of the episcopate in its communion with the bishop of Rome, head of the college. However, is there at all levels effective participation of clergy as well as lay people in emerging synodal bodies? Has the teaching of the Second Vatican Council regarding the collegiality of bishops been implemented sufficiently?" (ARCIC, 57).

The participation of bishops within the Synod of Bishops is also limited. As Archbishop Quinn has pointed out, the synod is called by the pope who determines its agenda. Preliminary documents are not made public. Its deliberations and recommendations to the pope are secret. The procedures consist of a series of eight-minute speeches without necessarily any connection, response, or discussion. The pope then writes and issues the final document after the conclusion of the synod. A structure allowing a freer and more open exchange of ideas would enhance the quality of dialogue within the synod.

The liturgy gives us a model for a communal and dialogical style of governance. The church is most fully manifested "in the full, active participation of all God's holy people in the same liturgical celebrations, especially in the same Eucharist, in one prayer, at one altar, at which the bishop presides, surrounded by his college of priests and by his ministers" (SC 41). Within a diversity of roles, ministries, and responsibilities, all those present fully participate. Communal and dialogic governance elicits the full, active participation of all the baptized in the mission of the church.

Bishop Lucker was a great supporter of two proponents of dialogic consultation—Archbishop John Quinn, former archbishop of San Francisco and former president of the National Conference of Catholic Bishops, and Cardinal Joseph Bernardin, archbishop of Chicago and founder of the Catholic Common Ground Project. Archbishop Quinn called for open discussion of church issues, new ways of selecting bishops, a reform of the procedures for the Synod of Bishops, and for an-

other ecumenical council. Cardinal Bernardin called for dialogue on serious pastoral concerns, such as the changing roles of women, the experience that Catholics have of the eucharistic liturgy, the meaning of
human sexuality, and the gap between church teaching and the convictions of many faithful, the image and morale of priests, and lay leadership in the church. The Catholic Common Ground Project remains
committed to bringing all parties to the dialogue table in an effort to
end "the polarization that inhibits discussion, cripples leadership, and
threatens the church in the United States" (Lucker, 469).

Bishop Lucker took his prophetic office seriously. He approached
these responsibilities from a communal perspective with a focus on
consultation and dialogue. In his reflections on twenty-five years as
bishop of the diocese of New Ulm, he highlighted this style of pastoral
leadership, saying, "I committed myself to pastoral planning which involves listening to the people of the diocese in formulating diocesan
goals and programs that would be in tune with our mission . . . I committed myself to a process of consultation taking seriously the recommendations of the Diocesan Pastoral Council and the Priests' Council in
the formation of diocesan policies" (Lucker, 567).

Bishop Lucker loved to teach—in the pulpit, in the classroom, in
the diocesan paper. He supported Catholic schools and frequently addressed catechists. His basic message was as simple as it was profound:
Jesus Christ loves us and is present to us today.

## References and suggestions for further reading

Anglican-Roman Catholic International Commission (ARCIC). "The Gift of Authority." *Origins* 29/2 (1999): 17, 19–29.

Congregation for the Doctrine of the Faith (CDF). "Reply to the *Dubium* Concerning
the Teaching Contained in the Apostolic Letter *Ordinatio Sacerdotalis.*" *Origins* 25/24
(1995): 401, 403.

Gaillardetz, Richard R. *Teaching with Authority*. Collegeville, Minn.: The Liturgical
Press, 1997.

John Paul II, Pope. Apostolic letter *Ordinatio Sacerdotalis. Origins* 24/4 (June 9, 1994):
49, 51–64.

National Conference of Catholic Bishops (NCCB). "The Teaching Ministry of the
Diocesan Bishop: A Pastoral Reflection." *Origins* 21/30 (1992): 473, 475–492.

Pontifical Council for the Family. "*Vademecum* for Confessors Concerning Some Aspects of Conjugal Life." *Origins* 26/38 (1997): 617, 619–632.

Quinn, John R. *The Reform of the Papacy: The Costly Call to Christian Unity*. New York: Crossroad Publishing Co., 1999.

Sullivan, Francis A., S.J. *Magisterium: Teaching Authority in the Catholic Church*. Mahwah, N.J.: Paulist Press, 1983.

Sullivan, Francis A., S.J. *Creative Fidelity: Weighing and Interpreting Documents of the Magisterium*. New York: Paulist Press, 1996.

# 6
# Papal apologies embody and advance Vatican II on the "tradition poured out in the church"

WILLIAM MCDONOUGH AND CATHERINE MICHAUD, C.S.J.

O n the First Sunday of Lent, 2000, during Mass at St. Peter's Basilica in Rome, Pope John Paul II and seven cardinals asked God's forgiveness for "the sins of all believers." In his homily the pope explained this public confession and repentance as a "purification of memory":

> One of the characteristic elements of the great jubilee is what I described as the *purification of memory* (*Incarnationis Mysterium*, 11). As the Successor of Peter, I asked that "in this year of mercy the Church, strong in the holiness which she receives from her Lord, should kneel before God and implore forgiveness for the past and present sins of her sons and daughters" (*Ibid.*). Today... seemed to me the right occasion for the Church, gathered spiritually round the Successor of Peter, to implore divine forgiveness for the sins of all believers. Let us forgive and ask forgiveness! (John Paul II, 2000a, 649)

The seven sections of the reconciliation service, each introduced by a cardinal or archbishop, included repentance for sins against the service of truth, against Christian unity, the Jewish people, human rights, women's dignity, the poor and oppressed people of the world, and the fundamental rights of people.

Stories that appeared in the *New York Times* reflect some of the reactions that the papal apologies evoked. Vatican spokesperson Joaquin Navarro-Valls told the press: "This is an entirely new thing... it will take years for the Church to absorb it" (*New York Times*, March 13,

2000). Another story claimed that the pope "overcame cardinals' objections to carry out what he considered a hallmark of his papacy. . . a sweeping apology for the errors of the Catholic Church going back 2,000 years" (*New York Times*, May 26, 2002).

How will the pope's "universal prayer, confession of sins, and request for forgiveness" be regarded? Will it be regarded, as the pope believes, as a "hallmark" of his papacy? Or will it be dismissed as an inadequate exercise, a missed opportunity because it failed to acknowledge straightforwardly that, in the words of theologian Francis Sullivan, "not merely 'certain of her sons and daughters' but some official policies of the Catholic Church had been in contradiction to the Gospel"? (Sullivan, 22).

A third story, this one written about church responses to the sexual abuse scandals, gives a way of considering the two possibilities here:

> Some scholars draw an important distinction between seeking forgiveness and offering an apology. Forgiveness requires an act of contrition. "You are opening a dialogue if you ask for forgiveness, but when you say you are sorry you are shrugging it off," said Garry Wills, a professor of history at Northwestern University. . . Mr. Wills said he believes Roman Catholic bishops and priests involved in the sexual abuse scandals couldn't be forgiven unless they admit wrongdoing and try to undo it. (*New York Times,* May 26, 2002)

Time will fully reveal whether the pope's gestures amounted to a mere apology or constituted an act of contrition.

Yet, to take a word from Bishop Lucker, surely something "remarkable" is at work in the pope's apologies. Through the 1990s Lucker had noticed the pope's increasing determination to make repentance a central focus for the Jubilee Holy Year of 2000. John Paul II had written as much in his 1994 apostolic letter, "On the Coming of the Third Millennium":

> It is appropriate that, as the Second Millennium of Christianity draws to a close, the Church should become more fully conscious of the sinfulness of her children, recalling all those times in history when they departed from the spirit of Christ and his Gospel and, instead of offering to the world the witness of a life inspired by the values of faith, indulged in ways of thinking and acting which were truly *forms of counter-witness and scandal.* (John Paul II, 1994, par. 33)

Bishop Lucker was moved by the words the pope had written to the world's cardinals in calling them to the consistory out of which the apostolic letter later came even more than by the words in the pope's apostolic letter. Italian journalist of Vatican affairs, Luigi Accattoli, quoted a portion of the pope's letter to the cardinals in his book, *When a Pope Asks Forgiveness: The Mea Culpa's of John Paul II* (1998). These words caught Bishop Lucker's attention:

> How can we be silent about so many kinds of violence perpe-trated in the name of faith? . . . In the light of what Vatican II has said, the Church must on its own initiative examine the dark places of its history and judge it in the light of Gospel principles . . . It could be a grace of the coming Great Jubilee. It would not in any way damage the moral prestige of the Church; on the con-trary, it would be strengthened by the manifestation of loyalty and courage in admitting the errors committed by its members, and in a certain sense in the name of the church. (Accattoli, 57–58)

After reading these words, Bishop Lucker wrote a pastoral letter of his own—"When a Pope Asks Forgiveness"—to the people of his dio-cese in February, 1999. He quoted the concluding words above and then added:

> These are remarkable words, especially when for a long time it was difficult for us as a church to admit that we ever make mis-takes, errors, or sins. Yes, the church is holy and "without spot or wrinkle" because it is the Body of Christ. Yet, as the Second Vatican Council reminds us, it is made up of a sinful people on pilgrimage. (Lucker, 525)

Our aim in this essay is to support and extend Bishop Lucker's con-viction that something "remarkable" is under way in the papal apologies. We will argue here that the pope's actions embodied and advanced the teaching of Vatican II. We are particularly interested in the apologies as an instance of what the Council's Dogmatic Constitution on Divine Rev-elation (*Dei Verbum*) called the "tradition . . . [whose] riches are poured out in the practice and life of the believing and praying church." For the Council, this tradition includes "everything that serves to make the peo-ple of God live their lives in holiness and increase their faith." Lives fash-ioned according to the Word of God become the message handed down from Jesus and the Apostles, continuing through words and actions to vitalize Christ's Body.

The Council understood that tradition is only secondarily a deposit of theological and doctrinal statements and creeds. It is divine revelation transmitted and made operative in the present. It is not simply transmitted from one generation to another as a kind of treasured heirloom; it continues to develop and grow in the church. In sum, the Council taught the dynamic nature of truth in the church; the recent papal apologies underline that teaching by embodying it.

This article comprises two main sections and a conclusion. In the first section we show that the apologies embody and advance the Council's teaching in *Dei Verbum* that tradition "makes progress in the church" (*DV* 8). The apologies show *how* tradition makes progress in the church, namely through repentance. In the second section, we show how the apologies embody and develop the Council's understanding of the role of popes and the bishops as teachers. In *Lumen Gentium* the Council states that the pope and bishops are "authentic teachers [who] . . . under the light of the Holy Spirit cause the faith to radiate, drawing from the storehouse of revelation new things and old" (*LG* 25). The apologies make clear that the pope (and the bishops with him) exercise the proper role of the magisterium in acts of public repentance in deed and word. The papal apologies, we suggest here, should lead Catholics away from an intellectualistic understanding of the teaching role of bishops in the church toward a more dynamic, participative one.

## I. The papal apologies embody and extend Vatican II on how tradition makes progress in the church: Repentance

We submit that the papal apologies, an explicit call to conversion for the whole church, have put into action the vision of Vatican II in the historical present. We concern ourselves here with a favorite text of Bishop Lucker from *Dei Verbum*: "The tradition that comes from the apostles makes progress in the church, with the help of the Holy Spirit" (*DV* 8).

The apologies were part of the eucharistic liturgy of the first Sunday of Lent: they followed the pope's homily that day, and preceded the Liturgy of the Eucharist. After the pope introduced the ritual, his delegate began with a general confession of sins:

Let us pray that our confession and repentance will be inspired
by the Holy Spirit, that our sorrow will be conscious and deep,

and that, humbly viewing the sins of the past in an authentic "purification of memory," we will be committed to the path of true conversion.

In a prayer concluding the ritual, Pope John Paul II himself prayed:

Most merciful Father, your Son, Jesus Christ . . . in the humility of his first coming redeemed humanity from sin, and in his glorious return he will demand an account of every sin. Grant that our forebears, our brothers and sisters, and we, your servants, who by the grace of the Holy Spirit turn back to you in wholehearted repentance, may experience your mercy and receive the forgiveness of our sins. (John Paul II, 2000b, 648)

Thus, a pledge to seek conversion and a plea for forgiveness frame the papal apologies. Within this frame, the pope and his fellow bishops acknowledge six particular areas of sin: those committed in service of truth, those harming the unity of the Body of Christ, those against the People of Israel, those against love, peace, and the rights of peoples and respect for cultures and religions, those against the dignity of women, and those against the fundamental rights of the person. The first five of these apologies reveal how the church's language has changed in the almost-forty years since the Council. The last apology, which addresses "sins in relation to the fundamental rights of the person," does not fit the pattern, both because it is more general than the other five, and because it is the only apology that does not directly mention Christians as guilty of the sins confessed. In each of the first five cases, we illustrate the development of tradition implicit in the apology (1) by citing the ritual of forgiveness in which a cardinal or archbishop named specific actions and attitudes as sinful, and for which the pope asked God's forgiveness; (2) by connecting the apology to its conciliar precedent; and (3) by noting the development in the years since the Council.

### Confession of sins committed in the service of truth

*Cardinal Ratzinger:* Let us pray that each one of us, looking to the Lord Jesus, . . . will recognize that even men of the Church, in the name of faith and morals, have sometimes used methods not in keeping with the Gospel in the solemn duty of defending the truth . . .

> *Pope John Paul II:* Lord . . . have mercy on your sinful children and accept our resolve to seek and promote truth in the gentleness of charity. (John Paul II, 2000b, 647)

The clearest conciliar precedent for this apology is in *Gaudium et Spes.* There the Council acknowledged the rift that had developed between faith and science:

> The humble and persevering investigators of the secrets of nature are being led, as it were, by the hand of God, even unawares, for it is God, the conserver of all things, who made them what they are. We cannot but deplore certain attitudes, not unknown among Christians, deriving from a short-sighted view of the rightful autonomy of science; they have occasioned conflict and controversy and have misled many into opposing faith and science. (*GS* 36)

This conciliar text acknowledges the conflict between science and religion that in the past amounted to a crisis and today remains to some degree unresolved. Walter Kasper describes more thoroughly the relationship between church and science at the time of the Council:

> Since the unhappy trial of Galileo in the seventeenth century an ominous schism developed between Church belief and a world stamped by modern science. In the eighteenth century the Church lost most of the intellectuals and in the nineteenth most of the workers. A synod in Würzburg called it an advancing scandal. (Kasper, 12; our translation from the German)

While the Council acknowledges that short-sightedness was "not unknown among Christians," it does not acknowledge that the church's leaders themselves held short-sighted attitudes toward science. The Council's only specific allusion to Catholic Church and magisterial involvement in short-sighted rejection of science appears in a general reference to Galileo in *Gaudium et Spes*, footnote 7 of chapter 3.

In 1992, John Paul II carried conciliar teaching further by directly acknowledging the "tragic mutual incomprehension . . . between science and faith" evidenced in the Galileo case (see John Paul II, 1992, 373). The papal apology of 2000 is more explicit than either the Council or John Paul's previous statement: "men of the Church . . . have sometimes used methods not in keeping with the Gospel." Although the apology does not specify that these "men of the Church" have included popes and bishops, it does bring the Council's acknowledged rift a step closer to the institutional life of the church. And the papal apology locates the problem more precisely than any previous church statement had. What John Paul had called a "tragic mutual incomprehension" in 1992, he calls "intolerance and [a failure to be] faithful to the great commandment of love" in the apology. The apology then makes explicit what the Council and previous papal statements had only implied, that is, that the rift between science and faith is a sin needing to be forgiven: "Have mercy on your sinful children and accept our resolve . . ." (John Paul II, 2000b, 647).

There is a twofold extension of the Council here that occurs in the other apologies as well: first, the apologies acknowledge the reality of the church's culpability and go further than the Council in explicitly naming the sinful action—in this case, of using "methods not in keeping with the Gospel in the solemn duty of defending the truth"; second, the apologies explicitly ask for forgiveness.

### Confession of sins that have harmed the unity of the Body of Christ

*Cardinal Etchegaray:* Let us pray that our recognition of the sins which have rent the unity of the body of Christ and wounded fraternal charity will facilitate the way to reconciliation and communion among all Christians.

*Pope John Paul II:* Merciful Father . . . we urgently implore your forgiveness, and we beseech the gift of a repentant heart, so that all Christians . . . will be able to experience anew the joy of full communion. (John Paul II, 2000b, 647)

Here is the one apology that perhaps does not go beyond the position that the Council had already taken. The only direct apology made at the Second Vatican Council was in the *Decree on Ecumenism:*

St. John has testified: "If we say we have not sinned, we make him a liar, and his word is not in us" (1 Jn 1:10). This holds good for sins against unity. Thus, in humble prayer we beg pardon of God and of our separated sisters and brothers, just as we forgive those who trespass against us. (*UR* 7)

The papal apology does little more than reiterate the Council's statement, which acknowledges that Catholics bear much of the responsibility for "sins against unity" and begs forgiveness for these sins. In his book, Accattoli calls paragraph seven of the Decree on Ecumenism the "central confession of the Second Vatican Council," and shows how Pope Paul VI led the way by himself asking "for forgiveness from the separated brethren at the opening of the second session of the . . . Council in September, 1963" (Accattoli, 29, 21).

Pope Paul's apology was preceded by the first ecumenical apology made by the Protestant World Council of Churches in 1948 (Accattoli, 21). The 1948 Protestant apology, followed fifteen years later by Paul VI's, led to the conciliar apology. This, the Second Vatican Council's only explicit apology, led the way to more post-conciliar doctrinal development in the area of ecumenism than in any other area. The document of the International Theological Commission (ITC) that accompanied the apologies, "Memory and Reconciliation: The Church and the Faults of the Past," holds up ecumenism as its signal exemplar of "doctrinal development animated by mutual love" (ITC, 639). It is another indication that progress in tradition happens by repentance.

### Confession of sins against the people of Israel

> *Cardinal Cassidy:* Let us pray that, in recalling the sufferings endured by the people of Israel throughout history, Christians will acknowledge the sins committed by not a few of their number against the people of the covenant and the blessings . . . and in this way will purify their hearts.

> *Pope John Paul II:* God of our fathers . . . asking your forgiveness, we wish to commit ourselves to genuine brotherhood with the people of the covenant. (John Paul II, 2000b, 647)

This apology finds its precedent in the Council's Decree on the Relation of the Church to Non-Christian Religions (*Nostra Aetate*). That decree states:

> Since Christians and Jews have such a common spiritual heritage, this sacred council wishes to encourage and further mutual understanding and appreciation. This can be achieved, especially, by way of biblical and theological enquiry and through friendly discussions . . . The church reproves every form of per-

secution against whomsoever it may be directed. Remember-
ing, then, its common heritage with the Jews and moved not by
any political consideration, but solely by the religious motivation of christian charity, it deplores all hatreds, persecutions,
displays of anti-semitism levelled at any time or from any
source against the Jews. (*NA* 4)

Although the Council's language intends indirectly to include
church anti-Semitism among the hatreds to be deplored, this text does
not directly acknowledge that Christians shared in the deplorable attitudes or actions. Moreover, the Council expresses no apology here.
Michael O'Connor explains the Council's failure in relation to the Jews:

> The inadequacies of *Nostrae Aetate* stem from (its) overly broad
> focus . . . The treatment of Judaism in particular is further
> flawed, first, because of the failure to talk about the Nazi exter-
> mination of European Jewry. This neglect is understandable,
> since the *Shoah* had scarcely been broached as a topic of inquiry
> even among Jews in the 1960s. (O'Connor, 506)

Neither the Council nor the apologies specifically mention the
Holocaust (see "The Pope's Apology," *New York Times,* March 14, 2000).
We Christians have much further to go in our relations with Jews, and
yet the point is still true: the apologies develop what was begun in the
Council. The pattern in this apology is the same as that in the one about
truth-seeking: the church more explicitly acknowledges that Christians
have been anti-Semites and then it directly asks forgiveness. Accattoli's
claim of 1998 that "Pope John Paul II has much to say to the Jews, both
in words and in deeds," but that "he has not yet made an explicit request
for forgiveness" is no longer the case (Accattoli, 115).

One other development in this apology for treatment of the Jews
that reaches beyond the Council's position is in the encouragement to
remember. The Council's Declaration on the Relation of the Church to
Non-Christian Religions voiced a plea to "all to forget the past, and
urges that a sincere effort be made to achieve mutual understanding"
(*NA* 3). In a provocative contrast, the apologies ask for the opposite of
forgetting: "In recalling the sufferings endured by the people of Israel
throughout history, Christians will acknowledge the sins . . . and in this
way will purify their hearts." The Council sought "mutual understanding" with both Muslims and Jews, but in neither case did it say such understanding would be achieved through memory of sin and the effects

of sin. In part two of our essay we will investigate the pope's more developed understanding of memory in his hope that the apologies would inspire a "purification of memory."

### Confession of sins committed in actions against love, peace, the rights of peoples, and respect for cultures and religions

> *Archbishop Hamao:* Let us pray that . . . Christians will be able to repent of the words and attitudes caused by pride, by hatred, by the desire to dominate others, by enmity toward members of other religions and toward the weakest groups in society. . .

> *Pope John Paul II:* Lord of the world . . . Be patient and merciful toward us, and grant us your forgiveness! (John Paul II, 2000b, 647)

The conciliar precedent for this apology was in the Council's change of attitude toward religious freedom and dissent. Two conciliar texts are pertinent here, the first on the church and freedom of religion; and the second on the church and atheism:

> The church, therefore, faithful to the truth of the Gospel, follows in the path of Christ and the apostles when it recognizes the principle that religious liberty is in keeping with human dignity and divine revelation and gives it its support. Through the ages it has preserved and handed on the doctrine which it has received from its Master and the apostles. Although, in the life of the people of God in its pilgrimage, through the vicissitudes of human history, there have at times appeared patterns of behavior which was not in keeping with the spirit of the Gospel and were even opposed to it, it has always remained the teaching of the church that no one is to be coerced into believing. (DH 12)

> Not infrequently atheism is born from a violent protest against the evil in the word, or from the fact that certain human ideals are wrongfully invested with such an absolute character as to be taken for God . . . Believers themselves often share some responsibility for this situation. For, in general, atheism is not present in people's minds from the beginning. It springs from various causes, among which must be included a critical reaction against religions and, in some places, against the christian

religion in particular. Believers can thus have more than a little to do with the rise of atheism. (*GS* 19)

The first text from the Council's Declaration on Religious Liberty is often pointed out as comprising one of the clearest instances of doctrinal development at Vatican II. What comes through in reading the text now is the Council's emphasis on the continuity of its position with the preceding tradition: "It has always remained the teaching of the church that no one is to be coerced into believing."

The second text, from the Pastoral Constitution on the Church in the Modern World, more explicitly acknowledges that the Council is doing something new. Although there is no direct apology here as there is in the Decree on Ecumenism, this text is one of only three direct conciliar admissions of failure within the Christian community itself: "Believers themselves often share some responsibility for this situation" (*GS* 19). The other two admissions concerned ecumenism and the science-faith rift.

The Council here, as elsewhere, is understated in its diagnosis of the situation. Kasper fills in the details underlying these two relatively dispassionate conciliar calls for change on religious freedom:

> Paul VI called the rupture between Christian faith and modern culture the drama of our age. Between the divided Churches there was a three-to-four-hundred-year-long ice age. Ecumenical dialogue and sincere dialogue with non-Christian religions was at least at the level of the institutional Church not even envisioned; in fact, the initial pioneers of this dialogue were treated with suspicion, hindered, and reprimanded. Hans Urs von Balthasar spoke at the time of a needed "demolition of the bastions." (Kasper, 12)

As in other areas, so in the area of religious freedom the apologies extend the Council in the familiar twofold pattern. First, the apologies explicitly name the problems that the Council described more circumspectly; second, they directly ask for forgiveness: "Be patient and merciful . . . and grant us your forgiveness!"

### Confession of sins against the dignity of women and the unity of the human race

*Cardinal Arinze:* Let us pray . . . for women, who are all too often humiliated and emarginated, and let us acknowledge the forms of acquiescence in these sins of which Christians too have been guilty.

*Pope John Paul II:* Lord God, our Father, you created the human being, man and woman in your image and likeness . . . At times, however, the equality of your sons and daughters has not been acknowledged . . . Forgive us and grant us the grace to heal the wounds still present in your community on account of sin. (John Paul II, 2000b, 648)

Although the conciliar precedent is less developed here than in any of the apologies, it is present nonetheless. *Gaudium et Spes* does not speak of past failures, but says:

At present women are involved in nearly all spheres of life: they ought to be permitted to play their part fully in ways suited to their nature. It is up to everyone to see to it that women's specific and necessary participation in cultural life be acknowledged and developed. (*GS* 60)

The modesty of the Council's insight here is noted well by theologian Enda McDonagh: "There is no sign of foreseeing the immense impact the women's movement was about to make on society, Church or theology" (McDonagh, 301–302). Still and once again, the apologies have taken a seed planted by Council and let it grow. Women have been "humiliated and emarginated" by "Christians too." And the church directly asks for forgiveness and change.

This survey of the first five apologies shows that there are at least two remarkable elements about the papal apologies in relation to the Council. First, in no case do the apologies suggest, as the Council sometimes did, that the church had always in some fashion been right in its words or actions. On the contrary, in each case the words and actions are acknowledged as those of Christians and "men of the Church." Second, they are confessed as sinful, with the pope explicitly asking for pardon and affirming that God's forgiveness is needed so that "we" may change our lives.

What was not clear in the Council is made clear by the apologies: progress in the tradition happens by conversion, by "kneeling before God and confessing the errors of the past." In an essay written shortly after the conclusion of the Council, theologian Gregory Baum foresaw what the apologies would later add to conciliar teaching:

Growing in the understanding of the Gospel always involves an element of conversion. It seems to me inadmissible to think of doctrinal development in the Church simply as a passage from truth to greater truth. What takes place is often also a passage from blindness to seeing. The ecclesiastical magisterium, though equipped with the gift of infallibility, is again and again led to acknowledge its blindness on certain issues, to confess that while God had spoken it had not really listened, and to avow with gratitude that the Spirit, speaking in the Church or even outside the Church, brought the understanding of what God had revealed from the beginning. It seems to me that this is verified in the doctrinal development of our day. (Baum, 79)

Baum's point is "verified" in the Council, but it was not directly articulated there. It is directly articulated in the papal apologies. In sum, we have in the apologies an acknowledgment of the defects of church tradition and an affirmation that such defects are remedied through repentance.

The apologies make it clear that tradition progresses in the pilgrim church when that church remembers "the faults of the past," when it names them and brings them to God for healing. The papal apologies bring light to *Dei Verbum*'s true but dimly lit statement that the tradition makes progress in the church by revealing how this happens. Progress happens by kneeling and confessing sin. In the conciliar texts, clear expression of the church's need for "kneeling before God and begging pardon" is hard to find, but in the apologies this need is made clear with each apology. The apologies demonstrate how progress happens in church teaching: namely, by repentance. By acknowledging and repenting of its own defects, the pilgrim church moves closer to the unchanging "deposit" of revelation.

## II. The apologies embody and extend Vatican II's understanding of bishops: They teach by leading the church in repentance

If the apologies clarify how church teaching grows, they also clarify what church teaching is and who bishops as teachers are. That is, if the apologies clarify the intent of *Dei Verbum*, they also clarify a claim made in *Lumen Gentium* that bishops are "authentic teachers . . . who preach to the people assigned to them the faith which is to be believed and applied in practice; under the light of the holy Spirit [they] cause that faith to radiate, drawing from the storehouse of revelation new things and old" (*LG* 25). Our claim here is that the apologies, specifically as "an authentic purification of memory," are an instance of the "authentic teach[ing]" that *Lumen Gentium* refers to in the text above.

Catholics are not used to thinking of the church's teaching as acknowledgments of sin framed by prayers for memory and pleas for pardon and healing. Are we not accustomed to thinking of "church teaching" in a much more schematic fashion? For, whether we have agreed with specific instances of church teaching or disagreed with them, have we not all become used to thinking of church teaching as theological instruction on what Catholics believe? American Catholic moral theologian Germain Grisez expresses such an understanding of church teaching and his view of the response owed it:

> By the authorization of her divine founder, the Catholic Church, speaking through her magisterium, teaches all her members what they must do to be saved. So, faithful and clearheaded Catholics consider the moral guidance offered by the Pope and the bishops in communion with him to indicate moral truths by which they must form their consciences. Therefore, for faithful and clearheaded Catholics, the duty to follow one's judgment of conscience *cannot* conflict with the duty to live according to the moral teachings which the magisterium proposes. For unless they fulfill the latter duty, they have only their own subjective opinion to follow, not an authentic judgment of conscience. (Grisez, 14)

But *Lumen Gentium* represents the Council's articulation of a more dialogical understanding of church teaching by placing magisterial responsibility within the bishop's role as preacher. Paragraph 25 opens with these words: "Among the more important duties of bishops, the preaching of the Gospel has pride of place" (*LG* 25). This conciliar understanding was enacted in the papal apologies. They were introduced by the pope's homiletic words that "the recognition of past wrongs serves to reawaken our consciences to the compromises of the present, opening the way to conversion for everyone" (John Paul II, 2000a, 649).

The apologies should help us see that church teaching is more preaching and witnessing than formal theological instruction. Liturgical theologian Dominic Serra explains the relationship between teaching and preaching in this way:

> The homily is not a theological lecture, but surely not less. The homily must be based on sound exegetical work, but it must go far beyond exegesis. The language of theology and exegesis, as we currently know them in Roman Catholicism, is primarily discursive and governed by the laws of analytical reasoning. Using these, the homily must go much further. Just as the liturgy is an epiphany of God in our midst, so the homily must seek to reveal the Mystery rather than to study or analyze it . . . Only then is the Mystery no longer held at arm's length by our analysis but embraced by faith to become our very being. (Serra, 32)

The apologies, positioned between the homily and the Eucharistic Prayer in the Sunday liturgy, became part of "the epiphany of God" in the midst of the assembly. They are a truth that must be "embraced by faith to become our very being." In this sense, the apologies embody the Council's understanding of magisterial teaching and they add to it the quality of prophetic preaching. In ways that the Council could not, the apologies employ the Christian liturgical practice of "memory," of *anamnesis*. When the pope asks that the apologies become "an authentic purification of memory," he is invoking *anamnesis,* the sacramental recollecting of the saving acts of God that makes them present again now.

Liturgical theology helps us understand *anamnesis,* as Serra again explains:

> Our relatively recent recovery of the Jewish image of liturgical remembrance, or *ziccharon,* and of the New Testament *anamnesis,* has produced the insight that such remembrance . . . allows us to participate in the events announced when they are placed in juxtaposition to our lives in such a way as to reveal the present act of worship as an event in salvation history . . . In fact, [by] this anamnetic participation in the deeds of salvation . . . we come to know ourselves as saved because we are members of the People created by God's word . . . Understanding the Word of God in its liturgical context helps us to see that its creative dynamism is linked to its anamnetic quality. As anamnesis, it makes present what it proclaims by making the hearers participants in the events of salvation. (Serra, 29–31)

Preaching—one facet of magisterial teaching—is integral to liturgical worship that seeks to make its hearers "participants in the events
of salvation." The apologies—a form of magisterial teaching—seek also
to make the faithful "participants in the events of salvation"; they are
meant to purify our memory so that "we will be committed to the path
of true conversion" (John Paul II, 2000b, 645). The pope's International
Theological Commission explained the purpose of the apologies as the
anamnetic participation in the "purification of memory." It requires

> eliminating from personal and collective conscience all forms
> of resentment or violence left by the inheritance of the past on
> the basis of a new and rigorous historical theological-judgment,
> which becomes the foundation for a renewed moral way of acting
> . . . The entire process of purification of memory. . . needs to
> be lived by the church's sons and daughters not only with the
> rigor of [the correct combination of historical evaluation and
> theological perception], but also accompanied by a continual
> calling on the help of the Holy Spirit . . . [For example], in the
> case of the Reformation . . . the way that has opened to over-
> come these differences is that of doctrinal development ani-
> mated by mutual love. (ITC, 638–639)

We mentioned this text above in part one of our essay when we
juxtaposed the conciliar and papal apologies on ecumenism. Remem-
bering the past "becomes the foundation for a renewed moral way of
acting" and for "doctrinal development animated by mutual love." Magisterial teaching in this perspective is dynamic, dialogical, conserving,
and renewing. In *Lumen Gentium* 25 the Council asserted that bishops
"under the light of the holy Spirit cause the faith to radiate, drawing
from the storehouse of revelation new things and old." The apologies
demonstrate the Council's understanding of magisterial teaching as
evoking anamnetic participation in the deeds and words of salvation. We
are saying that the apologies embody and extend *Lumen Gentium*'s understanding of magisterial teaching as prophetic preaching leading us all
into an active, participative response of faith.

The International Theological Commission's companion document
to the apologies introduces a distinction between "magisterial acts" and
acts of mere "authority" that has not been made explicitly in any official
or unofficial magisterial statement before it:

It is necessary to specify the *appropriate subject* called to speak about the faults of the past, whether it be local bishops, considered personally or collegially, or the universal pastor, the bishop of Rome. In this perspective, it is opportune to take into account—in recognizing past wrongs and the present-day subjects who could best assume responsibility for these—the distinction between magisterium and authority in the Church. Not every act of authority has magisterial value, and so behavior contrary to the Gospel by one or more persons vested with authority does not involve per se the magisterial charism. (ITC, 641)

Some institutional church acts lack "magisterial value." Which ones? Clearly, any that are "contrary to the Gospel." The apologies clarify that we now know six realities that—wherever they may appear in any past, present, or future institutional actions or doctrinal formulations—are mere acts of authority without magisterial value: namely, violence in service of truth, harming the unity of the Body of Christ, anti-Semitism, failure to respect the rights of peoples and their cultures and religions, failure to respect the dignity of women, and abuses of the fundamental rights of the person.

The apologies add two clarifications to the Council's understanding that teaching makes progress in the church. First, the pope and the bishops need participation from the laity and of theologians in order to teach. That participation is needed so we may all live into the "magisterial" core in what is taught in official church statements. Pope John Paul II had explicitly said as much in his 1993 encyclical, *Veritatis Splendor*:

The truth of the moral law—like that of the "deposit of faith" —unfolds down the centuries: the norms expressing that truth remain valid in their substance, but must be specified and determined . . . in light of historical circumstances by the Church's Magisterium, whose decision is preceded and accompanied by the work of interpretation and formulation characteristic of the reason of individual believers and of theological reflection. (*VS* 53)

As preaching is a moment within the dialogue of the liturgy, so church teaching is a moment—"preceded and accompanied"—within the dialogical life of the church.

Second, the apologies add another clarification to the Council's understanding that teaching makes progress in the church: not only does teaching make progress by repentance, but such repentance by church officials becomes a kind of "second magisterial moment" preceding and accompanying both magisterial decisions and the interpretations and formulations of believers. We should expect further apologies from the magisterium in the future. Renewed doctrinal affirmations flow from them.

One final affirmation in the International Theological Commission's document helps us sum up our understanding of popes and bishops as teachers. That document explains and develops the teaching in *Lumen Gentium* on the church as mother, that all of us embody at different times both mother church and children of that mother:

> The Church, Vatican II affirms, "by means of the word of God faithfully received, becomes a mother, since through preaching and baptism she brings forth children to a new and immortal life who have been conceived by the Holy Spirit and born of God" . . . The church is continually realized in the exchange and communication of the Spirit, from one believer to another . . . By virtue of this living communication, each baptized person can be considered to be at the same time a child of the church in that he is generated in her to divine life, and mother church, in that by his faith and love he cooperates in giving birth to new children for God. He is ever more mother church the greater in his holiness and the more ardent in his effort to communicate to others the gift he has received. (ITC, 635; the text cited from the Council is *LG* 64)

The strangeness of the International Theological Commission's language ("*He* is ever more mother church . . .") should not obscure the remarkable substance of its theological point. The church's bishops are more and less mother church depending on their holiness and ardor, that is, on their conversion and their willingness to lead others toward conversion. This is what a prophet does, and *Lumen Gentium* designates bishops as our prime prophets. In this second part of our essay, we have shown how the apologies help us understand and live out the understanding of bishops as authentic teachers described in *Lumen Gentium* 25.

## Conclusion: What will repentance as development of truth ask of us now?

We conclude this essay by going back to two concerns raised at its beginning. First, Francis Sullivan expressed concern that the apologies did not clearly acknowledge that some teachings of the church were wrong. Sullivan's charge is correct in that the apologies offer no lists of church doctrines now needing to be changed. Second, Garry Wills distinguished between apologizing and seeking forgiveness. He is also right. Insofar as the church understands penance as a free gift of forgiveness from God effective in the ongoing conversion of persons, it will not allow for mere apologizing. "The love and mercy of God untiringly re-insert the human being into the dynamic of a positive fundamental option, and re-open to one the possibility of realizing one's life, step by step, in the ethical effort of continuous conversion" (Hidber, 117).

Unless the institutional church roots out instances of what it now proclaims to be sin, it undermines its own nature. The teaching church has announced that any teaching or practice that does not reflect this growth in understanding is an act of authority without magisterial value. It will be the task of theologians and believers to help point out the practical implications of these apologies and to propose to the magisterium possible reformulations of doctrine. It will be the task of the magisterium to make new doctrinal formulations and continue to repent of what is not magisterial in existing ones. It will be the task of all Christians to live in this deepening circle of faith.

Because it is the Mystery of God in Christ that we are trying to live into, "progress" in church teaching will always remain both possible and necessary. In an act of magisterium, Mother Church has announced and asked pardon for what it now knows to be contrary to the gospel. We see the Mystery more clearly now and, to use the words of Dominic Serra, we must "embrace it by faith to become our very being." To do so is to participate in the tradition poured out in the church.

## References

Accattoli, Luigi. *When a Pope Asks Forgiveness: The Mea Culpa's of John Paul II*. Trans. Jordan Aumann. Boston: Pauline Books and Media, 1998.

Baum, Gregory. "The Magisterium in a Changing Church." *Man as Man and Believer. Concilium*, vol. 21. Ed. Edward Schillebeeckx and Boniface Williams. New York: Paulist Press, 1967. Pp. 67–83.

Grisez, Germain. "The Duty to Follow One's Conscience." *Linacre Quarterly* 56/1 (1989): 12–23.

Hidber, Bruno. "From Anguish to Re-found Freedom: Penance in the Tension between Sacraments and Ethics." *Worship* 68/2 (1994): 98–117.

International Theological Commission. "Memory and Reconciliation: The Church and Faults of the Past." *Origins* 29/39 (March 16, 2000): 625–644.

John Paul II, Pope. "Lessons of the Galileo Case." *Origins* 22/22 (November 1992): 369, 371–375.

John Paul II, Pope. Apostolic letter *On the Coming of the Third Millennium: Origins* 24/24 (November 24, 1994): 401, 403–416.

John Paul II, Pope (2000a). "Jubilee Characteristic: The Purification of Memory." *Origins* 29/40 (March 23, 2000): 648–650.

John Paul II, Pope (2000b). "Service Requesting Pardon." *Origins* 29/40 (March 23, 2000): 645–648.

Kasper, Walter. *Kirche—wohin gehst du? Die bleibende Bedeutung des II. Vatikanischen Konzils.* Bonifatius Verlag: Paderborn, Germany, 1994.

McDonagh, Enda. "The Church in the Modern World (*Gaudium et Spes*)." *Contemporary Catholic Theology: A Reader*. Ed. Michale Hayes and Liam Gearen. New York: Continuum, 1999. Pp. 295–315.

O'Connor, Michael Patrick. "The Universality of Salvation: Christianity, Judaism, and other Religions in Dante, *Nostra Aetate*, and the New Catechism." *Journal of Ecumenical Studies* 33 (1996): 487–511.

Serra, Dominic. "The Homily as Liturgy." In *In Service of the Church: Essays on Theology and Ministry Honoring Rev. Charles Froehle*. Ed. C. Athans and V. Klimoski. St. Paul, Minn.: University of St. Thomas, 1993. Pp. 27–37.

Sullivan, Francis. "The Papal Apology." *America* 182/12 (April 8, 2000): 17–22.

# III

# Celebrating the Mystery of All Life

## Re-reading *Sacrosanctum Concilium* for what it is asking of the church in our day

*Vatican II: "It is very much the wish of the church that all the faithful should be led to take that full, conscious, and active part in liturgical celebrations which is demanded by the very nature of the liturgy, and to which the Christian people, 'a chosen race, a royal priesthood, a holy nation, a redeemed people' (1 Pet 2:9, 4-5) have a right and to which they are bound by reason of their Baptism." (SC 14)*

*Bishop Lucker: "There is a story told about an Italian family who decided to immigrate to America. They saved and saved to get enough to be able to purchase the passage for husband, wife, and children. They had nothing else but the few belongings they carried. The people in their village had a going-away party and gave them bread and cheese that they brought with them on the ship. They were in steerage for the two-week trip. Every day they had bread and cheese, bread and cheese. Finally, one of the little kids, curious about the rest of the ship, started to explore, and found on the next deck a big dining room with a table filled with food. There was fresh bread and butter, fruit, meat, soup, and all kinds of things. Everyone was invited. He was told by the steward, eat and enjoy. This food was part of the passage. He went down to tell his parents, to invite them to the abundant food . . .*

*I believe that the Eucharist and the celebration of the sacraments is at the very heart of what we are as a church . . . I believe so much in the centrality of the Eucharist, and in light of this we need to consider the issue of obligatory celibacy of the clergy." (Lucker, 447, 516)*

This section of the book begins with a close reading of one paragraph of Vatican II's Constitution on the Sacred Liturgy. In *Sacrosanctum Concilium* 47, which opens that constitution's chapter on "The Sacred Mystery of the Eucharist," J. Michael Joncas sees a whole theology connecting the church's liturgy with the "liturgy of life." The *convivium* of the Eucharist both expresses our "living together" and feeds us so that we can, as Joncas writes, "employ imagination and thought to find ways in which all God's creatures can 'exist together' in interdependence and harmony." Joncas's essay addresses the concern Bishop Lucker expressed in this book's introduction that our commitment to the sacramental life go hand-in-hand with our commitment to the life of the world.

Paul Feela's essay, "The Eucharistic Heart of Reconciliation and the Sacrament of Penance in the 'Order of the Faithful,'" reflects on "order" in the life of the church. Church order attempts to serve our ordinary life, the way we live with each other and in the world. As Catholics rediscovered the Eucharist as the ordinary means of our forgiveness, our perception of the sacrament of penance changed drastically. Feela asks about the future of penance in the lives of believers.

Shawn Madigan's essay, "Christ Given 'For You and for All': Vatican II, A Theology of Sacramental Inculturation and Its Need for Further Development," broadens Joncas's and Feela's more specific focus on Eucharist and penance. She asks about changes in the forms of celebration in the entire sacramental life of the church. How could we expect that prayer texts formulated by limited human beings would ever constitute the final form of all praying? Madigan follows the uneven attempts to work out a theology of sacramental inculturation in the years since the Second Vatican Council.

She follows Bishop Lucker's own interest in those historical "heroes" who found ways to broaden the church's life of prayer, as well as Lucker's concern that his local church could find unity among all its members, the descendants of European immigrants and the newest immigrants, the farm workers of mostly Hispanic origin. Her essay makes clear that we will be learning from each other how to pray for the rest of history.

# 7
# Memorial, sacrament, sign, bond, and banquet: The Eucharist and social life

J. Michael Joncas

As we read in the introduction to this collection of essays, in the last weeks of his earthly life Bishop Raymond Lucker shared with William McDonough a text from the Roman Rite Liturgy of the Eucharist that had come to have special meaning for him: "Through the mystery of this water and wine, may we come to share in the divinity of Christ who humbled himself to share in our humanity." Even though this text accompanies a rather minor liturgical act of mixing water and wine during the preparation of the gifts, Bishop Lucker had discovered in it a deeper meaning: it "is about the holiness of daily life."

Earlier liturgical commentators had also been struck by this action and its accompanying text. In all likelihood, the mixing of water and wine began as a purely functional act conforming to the Mediterranean custom of drinking diluted wine. Almost immediately, however, Christians saw in this act a reference to the water and blood flowing from Christ's side in the Johannine passion narrative. Later commentators divined in this liturgical act a deeper mystagogical meaning. Some, especially in the Christian

Note: All English translations of liturgical texts and of the General Instruction of the Roman Missal are by Jan Michael Joncas from *Missale Romanum ex decreto sacrosancti oecumenici Concilii Vaticani II instauratum auctoritate Pauli Pp. VI promulgatum Ioannis Pauli Pp. II cura recognitum. Editio typical tertia.* Urbs Vaticanis: Typis Vaticanis, 2002. These translations are not intended for liturgical use or as veiled critiques of the translations already approved; rather they attempt to give as "literal" a translation of the Latin originals as possible for scholarly reflection. References are to page numbers (e.g., MR2002: 125–126) or to articles of particular documents contained in the *Missale* (e.g., GIRM2002 #15).

East, allegorized the wine and water to stand for the two natures (divine and human) indissolubly joined in the one person of Christ. Those understanding liturgical symbols as mere illustrations of dogma had difficulty with this interpretation, since it does not square with the affirmations of the Athanasian Creed: *Unus omnino, non confusione substantiae, sed unitate personae* ("Christ is one, certainly not by a mingling of his substances, but by the unity of his person"). Others, especially in the Christian West, identified the wine with the risen Lord and the water with humanity: by the power of the Spirit operative in the liturgy, humanity is indissolubly united to Christ. Again those reducing liturgical symbols to dogmatic snapshots had difficulty with this interpretation, since it suggested that human beings once joined to Christ were incapable of being separated from him, a suggestion that denies the real possibility of sinful separation from Christ even in those who have been baptized and share the life of the sacraments (Jungmann, vol. 2, 38–41).

Bishop Lucker, less interested in allegorizing the liturgical action and more concerned to develop the theological implications of the liturgical text, found that these words challenge us to "think more deeply about the relationship between the Eucharist and our social lives as human beings." In so doing he confirms an insight from Paul Ricoeur dear to the heart of liturgists: "The symbol gives rise to thought" (Ricoeur, 347–357). Although Bishop Lucker spoke these words and performed this action (or observed a deacon, as the proper minister of this ritual, do so) every time he celebrated Mass in the vernacular, it took years of engagement with this liturgical symbol for him to generate new insights into its meanings.

In the forty years since the Constitution on the Sacred Liturgy was promulgated by the fathers of the Second Vatican Council, Roman Catholics have gained a new appreciation for the centrality of the Eucharist. Not only was the entirety of *Sacrosanctum Concilium*'s chapter 2 devoted to "the sacred mystery of the Eucharist," but Roman Rite Catholics have had their eucharistic worship enriched with five Latin editions of the General Instruction of the Roman Missal (hereafter GIRM), three Latin editions of the Roman Missal, two Latin editions of the Lectionary for Mass, a revised Roman Gradual, dozens of curial implementation documents and *responsa*, and hundreds of papal, episcopal, and scholarly writings on the topic. But new insights into the mystery of the Eucharist have also arisen from new ways of celebrating the Mass over the past forty years: engagement with the symbolic language of the liturgy gives rise to theological thought.

In previous writings I have argued that the Council fathers decreed a revision of the liturgical books oriented toward a reform of liturgical practices intended to lead to a renewal of [Catholic] Christian life (Joncas, 1997). In this article I will concentrate on one aspect of this process: the recovery of the connections between eucharistic celebration and the church's vision of social life, connections dear to the heart of Bishop Lucker. To that end I will discuss five aspects of the mystery of the Eucharist as adumbrated in *Sacrosanctum Concilium*:

> Our Savior, on the night on which he was handed over, instituted the Eucharistic Sacrifice of his Body and Blood at the Last Supper, by means of which he perpetuated the Sacrifice of the Cross unto the ages when he would come again and thus entrusted to the Church, his well-beloved Bride, a memorial of his Death and Resurrection: a sacrament of responsibility, a sign of unity, a bond of charity, a paschal banquet in which Christ is consumed, the soul is filled with grace, and the pledge of future glory is given to us. (*SC* 47; my translation of the Latin original)

I will examine how understanding the Eucharist as a memorial of Christ's death and resurrection, a sacrament of responsibility, a sign of unity, a bond of charity, and a paschal banquet all contribute to deepening the Church's vision of human community, in a small attempt to honor a man whose episcopal ministry touched and enriched my life.

## I. Memorial of Christ's death and resurrection

*Sacrosanctum Concilium* 47 lists *memoriale . . . Mortis et Resurrectionis [Christi]* as a first dimension of the mystery of the Eucharist. The notion of liturgical memorial is difficult to communicate in a culture in which "memorial" usually means a purely mental recalling of a past event, evoked precisely as "past," i.e., not present. This is quite different from the idea of liturgical memorial enshrined in technical terms such as *anamnesis* (Greek) or *zikkaron* (Hebrew). Here the reality of a past event is evoked, not so much as "past and gone," but as setting up a trajectory of power: grounded in the past, influencing the present, and brought to fulfillment in the future. Thus Jews "memorialize" the Exodus from Egypt in their Passover seder, not as simply recalling a scattered group of slaves successfully fleeing their overlords ca. 1250 B.C.E., but as the pattern of God's dealing with human beings, drawing them to freedom in the present and manifesting ultimate freedom to be encountered in the future. Christians "memorialize" the death and resurrection of Jesus Christ, not merely recounting the torture and execution of a first century C.E. Jewish reformer followed by the triumph of his message, but by appropriating his passage through death to life individually and communally in the present, for the sake of a future revealed to be not only possible but trustworthy. In a real sense, Christian liturgical memorial "remembers the future," i.e., understands Christ's resurrection as a divine disclosure of the intended future of humanity transformed by self-giving love, whose power is unsurpassably localized in Jesus of Nazareth and continues to transform his followers and their world.

While all liturgical celebrations—sacraments, sacramentals, and the Liturgy of the Hours—memorialize the death and resurrection of the Lord, the dominical sacraments of Christian initiation and Eucharist offer the densest concentration of these thematics. And while all the texts proclaimed and sung, gestures made and postures assumed, personnel deployed and objects hallowed during the eucharistic liturgy memorialize the paschal mystery, I believe the Eucharistic Prayers offer the clearest expression of this memorial:

> Holy Father, you so loved the world that when the fullness of the times was completed, you sent your Only-Begotten as Savior for us. Incarnate from the Holy Spirit and born of the Virgin Mary, he was transformed into the form of our condition in all things but sin. He preached the gospel of salvation to the poor, redemption to captives, and happiness to those sad at heart. So that he might fulfill your dispensation he handed himself over into death and, rising from the dead, he destroyed death and renewed life. And, so that we might not live more for ourselves, but for him who died for us and arose, he sent the Holy Spirit from you, Father, as first fruits to believers, so that, perfecting his work in the world, he might accomplish all sanctification . . . (Eucharistic Prayer IV; MR2002: 592)

> Remembering, therefore, your Son, Jesus Christ, who is our Passover and our most certain peace, we celebrate his death and resurrection from the dead and, awaiting his blessed coming, we offer to you, who are the faithful and merciful God, the offering which reconciles human beings with you. With kind-

ness look, most merciful Father, on those conjoined to you by the sacrifice of your Son, and perform in such a way that, by the power of the Holy Spirit, those sharing from this one bread and cup may be gathered into one body in Christ, by whom all division is borne away. Deign to preserve us always in communion of mind and heart, one with our Pope, N., and our Bishop, N. Assist us, so that as we await the coming of your reign, so we may remain until the hour at which we will stand before you, holy among your holy ones at the heavenly throne, with the blessed Virgin Mother of God, Mary, the blessed Apostles and all the saints, and our dead brothers [and sisters], whom we suppliantly commend to your mercy. Then, freed from the wound of corruption and fully established as a new creature, rejoicing we will sing the thanks of your Christ, living unto eternity. (Eucharistic Prayer for Masses of Reconciliation I; MR2002: 678–679)

Therefore we bless you, almighty Father, through Jesus Christ your Son, who comes in your name. He is the Word of salvation for human beings, the hand that you extend to sinners, the way by which your peace is made available to us. When we had turned ourselves away from you, Lord, on account of our sins, you led us back to reconciliation, so that, having been turned back to you, we might love one another through your Son, whom you have handed over into death for us . . . Therefore, making memory of the death and resurrection of your Son, who left to us this pledge of his love, we offer to you what you have entrusted to us, the sacrifice of complete reconciliation. Holy Father, we, suppliant, pray that you would hold us acceptable along with your Son and that you would deign to discharge his Holy Spirit on us in this salvific banquet, which bears away all those things which make us alien to each other. May that very Spirit make your Church among human beings a sign of unity and an instrument of your peace and preserve us in communion with our Pope, N., and our bishop, N., and all the bishops and all your people. Now that you have gathered us at the table of your Son, so align us with the glorious Virgin Mother of God, Mary, with your blessed Apostles and all the saints, with our brothers [and sisters] and with human beings of whatever race and language, [and] with those deceased in your

friendship at the banquet of eternal unity, in the new heavens and
the new earth, where the fullness of your peace shines forth.
(Eucharistic Prayer for Masses of Reconciliation II; MR2002:
682, 684)

Note that these powerful texts expressing the liturgical memorial
of Christ's death and resurrection have appeared in the Roman Rite
only since the time of the Second Vatican Council. If one accepts the
axiom of Prosper of Aquitaine that "the law of praying establishes the
law of believing" (lex orandi legem statuat credendi), then these prayers
surely enshrine the church's contemporary vision of social life, where
humans live "no longer for themselves," "in communion of mind and
heart," working "together for the coming of the kingdom," "that new
world where . . . people of every race, language and way of life [will]
share in the one eternal banquet." Since the Council fathers also decided to allow liturgical texts to be proclaimed in the vernacular, these
texts are not only the possession of those who read Latin, but, proclaimed aloud in the Christian assembly's mother tongues, can insinuate
their message into the consciousness of those regularly participating in
the Eucharist. Since Vatican II, as well, memorial acclamations have
been inserted for congregational recitation or chanting immediately
after the consecration, the first of which in literal English translation
reads: "We proclaim your death, Lord, and we confess your resurrection, until you come" (Mortem tuam annuntiamus, Domine, et tuam resurrec-
tionem confitemur, donec venias). Clearly, celebrations of Roman Rite Eucharist according to the so-called Novus Ordo Missae have highlighted the
Mass as a memorial of the death and resurrection of Christ with implications for humanity's social life.

## II. Sacrament of responsibility

A second aspect of the mystery of the Eucharist that Sacrosanctum
Concilium 47 details is its disposition as sacramentum pietatis. Since the
phrase is taken from Augustine's Sermon 36 on the Gospel of John,
sacramentum here does not bear all of the theological nuances that later
Catholic theology will place upon it; however, it does carry the sense of
"a sign of a sacred thing" conjoined with the nuance that this sign, in
some way, embodies the reality to which it points, i.e., it functions as a
symbol. Pietas, while perhaps the quintessential Roman civic virtue, is

extraordinarily difficult to define. Its semantic field includes "parental honor," "sense of duty," "loyalty," "tenderness," and "goodness." Clearly it does not convey the debased notion of demonstrative and hypocritical religiousness associated with the term "pious" for many English speakers in the twenty-first century. I have thus translated this phrase as "sacrament of responsibility," suggesting that the Eucharist is an efficacious sign (i.e., symbol) of the mutual responsibility of God and humanity for the created order.

It would be safe to say that one of the strains in Catholic spirituality is world-denying, manifesting a profound sense of the transitoriness of this world of space and time with a deep longing for the world to come. One could point to statements of patristic figures such as Jerome or Simon Stylites, monastic writers such as John Cassian or the early Cistercians, medieval authors such as Joachim of Fiore or Thomas à Kempis to support this thesis. A telling example of such a world-denying strain in Catholic spirituality appears in the Marian antiphon "Salve Regina," where those at prayer identify themselves as "poor banished children of Eve" and the world they inhabit as "this valley of tears," "our exile."

But Vatican II's Dogmatic Constitution on the Church (*Lumen Gentium*) and, even more, the Pastoral Constitution on the Church in the Modern World (*Gaudium et Spes*) emphasize a spirituality that takes this world seriously and positions the church at the heart of the transformation of history:

> The council exhorts Christians, as citizens of two cities, to perform their duties faithfully in the spirit of the Gospel. It is a mistake to think that, because we have here no lasting city, but seek the city which is to come, we are entitled to evade our earthly responsibilities; this is to forget that because of our faith we are all the more bound to fulfill these responsibilities according to each one's vocation. But it is no less mistaken to think that we may immerse ourselves in earthly activities as if these latter were utterly foreign to religion, and religion were nothing more than the fulfillment of acts of worship and the observance of a few moral obligations. One of the gravest errors of our time is the dichotomy between the faith which many profess and their day-to-day conduct . . . Let there, then, be no such pernicious opposition between professional and social activity on the one hand and religious life on the other. Christians who shirk their temporal duties toward their neigh-

bor neglect God himself and endanger their eternal salvation. Let Christians follow the example of Christ, who worked as a craftsman; let them be proud of the opportunity to carry out their earthly activity in such a way as to integrate human, domestic, professional, scientific and technical enterprises with religious values, under whose supreme direction all things are ordered to the glory of God. (*GS* 43)

This aspect of the mystery of the Eucharist appears in a variety of ways in the post-Vatican II Order of Mass. Every Eucharistic Prayer manifests the responsibility of the Christian community for other humans when it intercedes on behalf of the living and the dead, including prayer for "all the dead whose faith is known to [God] alone" (Eucharistic Prayer IV; MR2002: 595). Some Eucharistic Prayers explicitly intercede on behalf of non-[Catholic] Christians:

May this sacrifice of our reconciliation, we pray, Lord, advance the peace and salvation of all the world . . . (Eucharistic Prayer III; MR2002: 588)

Open our eyes so that we may recognize the needs of [our] brothers [and sisters]; inspire our words and actions to comfort those laboring and heavily burdened; make us serve them sincerely, according to the example and commandment of Christ. May your Church exist as a living witness of truth and freedom, of peace and justice, so that all be roused into a new hope . . . (Eucharistic Prayer for Various Needs and Occasions I; MR2002: 690–691)

A rubric of the 2002 *General Instruction of the Roman Missal* notes that, in addition to presenting bread and wine to the celebrating priest or deacon at the time of the Preparation of the Gifts, "money or other gifts for the poor or for the Church, brought to or gathered in the church building, may also be received" (GIRM2002 #73; MR2002: 36).

Yet it is in the restored Prayer of the Faithful that the Eucharist as sacrament of responsibility is most clearly manifest:

In the Universal Prayer, or Prayer of the Faithful, the people in a certain way respond to the Word of God received in faith and, exercising the office of their baptismal priesthood, offer prayers to God for the salvation of all. It is expedient that in Masses with the people this prayer would, as a rule, be offered, so that intercessions might be made for the holy Church, for those who rule over us in power, for those oppressed by various needs, and for all people and the salvation of the entire world.

The customary order of intentions would be:
a) for the needs of the Church,
b) for those governing the nation and for the salvation of the entire world,
c) for those oppressed by whatever difficulty,
d) for the local community. . .
(GIRM2002 ##69–70; MR2002: 34–35)

Two things should be noted. First, by positioning the general intercessions as the final act of the Liturgy of the Word, the liturgy intimates that successful engagement with God's word at the eucharistic celebration will inevitably draw the assembled worshipers into a deeper sense of their responsibility for and to one another, the church and the churches, the nations of the world, those who have a right to their prayer—indeed, bringing the "joys and hopes, the grief and anguish . . . especially of those who are poor or in any way afflicted" (GS 1) to explicit consciousness in the assembly gathered by and before God in the power of the Spirit. Second, the very order of the intercessions constitutes a school of prayer: Christians pray for their individual and local needs only in last place, after they have opened their hearts to share the compassion of God for his creation, accepting their responsibility to be stewards of the family of humankind and co-creators with God of humanity's future.

## III.  Sign of unity

A third notion of the mystery of the Eucharist listed in *Sacrosanctum Concilium* 47 is its character as *signum unitatis*. The human unity proclaimed and embodied in the church is an eschatological reality, a manifestation of the unity-in-diversity that constitutes the "interior" life of the Triune God. It is not a merely humanly constructed unity in which diversity is unified by conceptual categorization (by gender, race, language, class, etc.) or by external coercion (the obliteration of differ-

ences in a sterile uniformity). Romano Guardini has perceptively written of deformations of the liturgical assembly: when, on the one hand,
the congregation is not so much gathered in Christ to make a common
act of worship, but juxtaposed individuals simply pursuing their private
devotions in the same place, or, on the other hand, individual tempera-
ments and spiritualities are crushed in mindless mob activity:

> Every individual Catholic is a cell of this living organism . . . a
> member of [Christ's] Body. The individual is made aware of the
> unity which comprehends her on many and various occasions,
> but chiefly in the liturgy. In it he sees himself face to face with
> God, not as an entity, but as a member of this unity. It is the
> unity which addresses God; the individual merely speaks in it,
> and it requires of him that he should know and acknowledge
> that he is a member of it.
>
> It is on the plane of liturgical relations that the individual
> experiences the meaning of religious fellowship. The individual
> —provided that he actually desires to take part in the celebra-
> tion of the liturgy—must realize that it is as a member of the
> Church that he, and the Church within him, acts and prays; he
> must know that in this higher unity he is at one with the rest of
> the faithful, and he must desire to be so. (Guardini, 143–144. I
> have not altered Guardini's use of feminine pronouns to refer
> to the church and masculine pronouns to refer to members of
> the church. Though this usage is unacceptable in our day, all at-
> tempts to re-phrase the text end in confusion.)

*Sacrosanctum Concilium* and the General Instruction of the Roman
Missal offer five concrete ways in which the eucharistic celebration can
become a sign of unity:

> In the liturgy, apart from the distinctions arising from liturgical
> function or sacred Orders and apart from the honors due to civil
> authorities in accordance with liturgical law, no special prefer-
> ence is to be accorded any private persons or classes of persons
> whether in the ceremonies or by external display. (*SC* 32)

> In the celebration of the Mass the faithful enact [the reality of
> their existence as] a holy people, a people acquired [by God]
> and a royal priesthood . . . Thus they should avoid all impres-

sions whether of individualism or of division, having before their eyes the fact that they have a single Father in the heavens and that therefore they are all to be brothers [and sisters] among themselves. They should form one body, whether by hearing the Word of God, or by taking part in the prayers and in singing, or especially by common offering of the sacrifice and by common participation at the table of the Lord. This unity is made beautifully apparent by the gestures and postures communally adopted by the faithful. (GIRM2002 ##95–96; MR2002: 41)

First, in contrast to societies where social status may depend on accumulation of capital, media attention, professional credentialing, etc., the only membership card needed to participate fully in the liturgical assembly is baptism. There is even carefully ritualized recognition of various categories of the non-baptized moving toward full communion with the Church—inquirers, catechumens, elect—at various liturgical celebrations. For extraordinary breaches of ecclesiastical discipline, the baptized may lose their right to participate fully (i.e., sacramentally) at Eucharist by decree of excommunication, but they are still welcome to take a place among the baptized gathered for prayer. The fact that "no special marks of honor" are to be given to particular persons or classes of persons in liturgical celebrations indicates that the customary divisions of secular life cede their power before the radical unity of all in Christ.

Second, to receive and to respond to the word of God in faith—the purpose of the Liturgy of the Word—confers a unity on participants other than the ties of blood, gender, or nationality. Anthropologists speak of the power of myth and ritual to establish and reinforce social identity. Thus, my Polish grandmother, even as she traced her ancestry to the Old Country, could still speak of her "Pilgrim forefathers" when she celebrated Thanksgiving in her adopted home, the United States. The unity she felt with her own blood-kin was enriched by the unity she experienced with others who had made America their home through the myth and ritual of European settlers banqueting with native Americans on the produce of the new land: turkey, corn, and pumpkin. Christians of differing nationalities, ethnicities, classes, and political ideologies find their identity underscored and their unity enhanced by claiming the same "master narrative" witnessed in the Hebrew and Christian Scriptures. During the Liturgy of the Word, these texts are not received as more or less intriguing evidence of behaviors and belief systems of past civilizations, but as a "living word" enshrining the core beliefs and proposed values founding Christian identity.

Third, verbal participation—spoken and sung—in eucharistic texts is a sign of unity. Unlike a drama at which the spectators are asked to keep silence for the performance, Christian worshipers at communal prayer are a "performing audience," in Bernard Huijbers' suggestive phrase (see Huijbers). It is not for nothing that the word the congregation is asked to recite most frequently is "Amen"; taken from a Hebrew root meaning "firmness" or "strength," this technical term indicates both the assent the unified assembly gives to liturgical proclamations and its pledge to live in solidarity with the sentiments expressed. It is not for nothing that even in cultures where group music-making has almost disappeared as mass media broadcast music for consumption, the congregation is still asked to sing together as part of their liturgical experience; as the General Instruction of the Roman Missal avers:

> From the Apostle [Paul] the Christian faithful who gather together into one while awaiting the coming of their Lord are encouraged to sing as one at the same time psalms, hymns, and spiritual songs (cf. Col 3:16). For singing is a sign of exultation of heart (cf. Acts 2:46). Thus St. Augustine rightly says: "To sing is [an act] of a lover," and from antiquity comes the proverb: "The one who sings well prays twice." (GIRM2002 #39; MR2002: 28)

Common recitation or chanting of liturgical texts is both a sign of unity achieved and an impetus toward unity yet to be established.

Fourth, sacramental participation in consuming the consecrated bread and drinking the consecrated wine is the deepest expression of the "holy communion" established between God and humanity, individual humans and other humans, and human beings and the created non-human world. I treat this aspect of the eucharistic sign of unity in more detail below under the heading "paschal banquet."

Finally, the General Instruction of the Roman Missal observes that bodily participation in the Eucharist by means of common postures, gestures, and movement is both a sign and an instrument of unity (GIRM2002 #96). For example, when the assembly stands to greet the proclamation of the gospel with sung "Alleluias," when the assembly-members sign their forehead, lips, and breast while reciting silently: "May the message of the Gospel be in my mind, and on my lips, and in my heart," when thurifer and candle-bearers accompany the deacon as he processes from the altar to the ambo with the Book of the Gospels, common postures, gestures, and movement unify the assembly's focus of attention and manifest its veneration of the word of God. As the General Instruction of the Roman Missal wisely notes:

> A common stance of the body, assumed by all participants, is a sign of the unity of the members of the Christian community assembled at the sacred Liturgy: for it both expresses the thought and feeling of the participants and it fosters them. (GIRM2002 #43; MR2002: 29)

## IV. Bond of charity

According to *Sacrosanctum Concilium* 47, a fourth understanding of the mystery of the Eucharist is its nature as *vinculum caritatis*. *Vinculum* is easy to translate: it means "chain," "bond," or "fetter." However, just as I noted above that it is difficult for twenty-first century English speakers to catch the semantic field of *pietas*, similar difficulties attend the term *caritas*. Contemporary English speakers identify "charity" as an act of benevolence conferred by private institutions or individuals on undeserving recipients. Where the state provides "welfare" for its needy citizens (explicitly conceptualized as different from "charity"), private citizens contribute to "charities" dedicated to ameliorating the lives of the unfortunate. According to this notion, a "fetter of charity" would be incomprehensible: by definition, charity goes beyond obligations of justice and results from the altruistic feelings of those endowed with excess resources.

However, in the Catholic theological tradition, *caritas* is the usual translation of the biblical term *agape*. Greek and Latin knew at least four terms for what is covered by the English word "love": *storge* (Latin *pietas*) is familial love, the loyalty one has for one's blood-kin and country; *philia* (Latin *amicitia*) is friendship, the delight one takes in another grounded in mutual interests; *eros* (Latin *amor*) is attraction to beauty, the desire to meld with the person one finds attractive or to possess the object one finds desirable; *agape* (Latin *caritas*) is an act of the will, the deliberate choice to act for the welfare of another, whether or not that person is kin, one receives any mutual enrichment from the other, or one finds the other attractive. The Johannine literature identifies *agape* with God (1 Jn 4:16) and makes it the distinctive commandment given by Jesus to his followers in the context of the Last Supper: "Love one another as I have loved you" (Jn 13:34). In this context, the "bond of charity" is precisely the stipulation imposed and accepted in the baptismal covenant: Christians are to love one another (and by extension all humanity and the non-human created order) with the same self-sacrificing generosity manifested in Jesus' words and actions.

The restoration of the kiss of peace in the *Novus Ordo Missae* is perhaps the clearest expression of the Eucharist as a bond of charity. As the General Instruction of the Roman Missal observes:

> The Rite of Peace follows, by which the Church implores peace and unity for itself and for the entire human family, and the faithful express for themselves ecclesial communion and mutual charity, before they commune in the Sacrament. (GIRM2002 #82; MR2002: 37)

In the light of this directive, it is interesting to observe how problematic the implementation of this ritual has been, at least in the United States. Some refuse to perform the rite at all, including clerics who misread the rubric indicating that a deacon or priest may invite the community to share the Rite of Peace to mean that the rite itself is optional (what is optional is the clerical invitation, not the rite itself). Others are disturbed that this rite occurs so close to the reception of holy communion, feeling that it "distracts" them from preparing to receive the consecrated bread and wine. Some gesture this rite with a handshake, or an embrace, or by waving two fingers in a "peace" sign; none of these gestures seem to bear the weight of the mystery being enacted. Others use the rite as an opportunity to greet family and friends, those well known to them, when the force of the rite is clearly to manifest the agapaic love that Christians must bear not only for those they find attractive and compatible, but for those they do not know, and even for their enemies. If Roman Rite Eucharist is to increase its potential to manifest the "bond of charity," participants must gain a deeper insight into the symbolic import of the Rite of Peace.

## V.  Paschal banquet

A fifth understanding of the mystery of the Eucharist in the view of *Sacrosanctum Concilium* 47 is that of *convivium paschale*. The term "paschal" makes reference to the Jewish Passover (*Pascha*), a ritual meal at which the Exodus from slavery in Egypt was memorialized in recited texts, songs, prescribed cups of wine, and particular foods. The term was applied by Christians at baptism and Eucharist to the death and resurrection of Christ, understood as both *passio* (suffering) and *transitus* (passage). The idea of a "paschal banquet" arises from ancient aristocratic Roman evening meal practice in which the feasting comprised two segments: the *cena* (Greek *deipnon*), the meal proper consisting at least of bread, condiments, and liquid, and the *convivium* (literally "living together") (Greek *symposion*), a drinking party marked by conversation and entertainment (see Joncas, 2000). Thus, to recognize one aspect of the mystery of the Eucharist as a "paschal banquet" is to emphasize its character as a communal festive meal, providing nourishment from suffering and celebrating the transition from slavery to freedom, from death to life.

Since the notion of the Mass as a sacrificial meal is quite familiar to post-Vatican II worshipers, it may surprise them to note that many Roman Rite Catholics attended Eucharist in the second Christian millennium without receiving sacramental communion. The causes for this are multiple: the restriction of communion in the form of consecrated wine to the clergy, an increased sense of the awesomeness of the sacrament, notions of personal unworthiness that prescribed sacramental confession before each communion, a preference for ocular rather than gustatory communion, etc. At the beginning of the twentieth century Pope Pius X attempted to restore the sense of the Eucharist as a paschal banquet by lowering the age of "first communion" in the Roman Rite to the age of reason and by his decree on and encouragement of frequent communion. But it was not until the reforms of the Second Vatican Council that the majority of participants at Roman Rite Eucharist would, as a rule, sacramentally commune by receiving consecrated bread and wine.

Three segments of the eucharistic liturgy emphasize its character as a paschal banquet. The first is the blessing prayers associated with placing bread and cup on the altar during the preparation of the gifts:

> Blessed are you, Lord, God of the universe, because from your generosity we have received this bread which we offer to you, fruit of the earth and of the work of human hands: from this it will become for us the bread of life . . .

> Blessed are you, Lord, God of the universe, because from your generosity we have received this wine which we offer to you,

fruit of the vine and of the work of human hands: from this it
will become for us spiritual drink. (MR2002: 514)

These texts intimate how at Eucharist the entire created order is caught
up in the paschal transformation wrought by God. Note that Christians
do not offer nature "raw"; the gifts presented are not wheat and grapes,
but bread and wine, i.e., gifts provided by the Creator through the
world of nature that have been transformed by human intelligence and
will. An entire eco-theology can be developed from this simple ritual,
situating humans as stewards of creation, not exploiters of nature. As
God's deputies for the sustenance of the created order, it is humanity's
responsibility to employ imagination and thought to find ways in which
all God's creatures can "exist together" (*convivium*) in interdependence
and harmony.

A second dimension of the Eucharist as paschal banquet focuses on
the notion of *Pascha* as suffering. The underlying symbolism derives from
a covenant-establishing ceremony in the ancient Near East. After two
kings set the stipulations of an agreement between themselves, they
would have their slaves cut an ox, sheep, or goat in half, hold the bloody
carcasses apart, and walk between the halves of the slaughtered animal,
pointing to it and themselves while declaring: "If ever I break this
covenant with you, may that be done to me." Given this cultural back-
ground, Jews could easily adapt such a covenant-establishing ceremony
in their patriarchal narratives (e.g., Gen 15 where the movement of the
smoking fire pot and flaming torch establish YHWH's covenant with
Abraham) and their ritual behavior (e.g., the slaughtering of animals for
the Passover Seder and at temple worship). One strain of early Christian
theology, in turn, interpreted the torture and death of Jesus as the
slaughtering of the covenant animal by which a new and unsurpassable
covenant was established between God and humanity. While Christian
Eucharist in memorializing the suffering and death of Christ forgoes the
ritual slaughter of animals, the bread used at Mass is not merely gazed
upon but broken and consumed and the wine is not merely hallowed but
poured out and drunk. One might argue that what comes "naturally" to
the bread and wine—a willingness to be torn apart and poured out so
that others might be nourished—is something Christians have to learn
over a lifetime. As the General Instruction of the Roman Missal states:

The Church intends that the faithful not only offer the unspot-
ted victim but also learn to offer themselves and from day to

day be brought to fulfillment, with Christ as mediator, into unity with God and with one another, so that finally God be all in all. (GIRM2002 #79f; MR2002: 37)

A third dimension of the Eucharist as paschal banquet is found in the restoration of communion under both species as an option for lay communicants as well as the clergy. Not only does this remove a ritual-ized status distinction between clergy and laity, as well as promote the fullness of the sacramental sign, but it functions as a parable of the moderate and virtuous use of the world's goods. In the world outside the paschal banquet, some starve while others fill their stomachs to the point of gluttony; around the eucharistic table, however, everyone gets some of the consecrated bread, little though it may be. And in the world outside the paschal banquet, some have only their tears to drink while others drink themselves into insensibility; around the eucharistic table, however, everyone gets a sip of the consecrated wine, little though it may be. Thus is enacted the church's vision of social life: where no one is deprived of necessities, where no one hoards luxuries, but all are decently fed, housed, clothed, and cared for (cf. Joncas, 1996).

## Conclusion: The Eucharist and the liturgy of life

Even though the Latin text for the dismissal dialogue at the conclusion of the eucharistic celebration is simply: "Go, it is sent" (*Ite, missa est*)/ "Thanks be to God" (*Deo gratias*), there is wisdom in the alternative English-language dismissal text: "Go in peace to love and serve the Lord." This alternative text clearly enshrines the ritual function of this element of the liturgy as articulated in the General Instruction of the Roman Missal:

To the Concluding Rite pertains: . . . the dismissal of the people on the part of the deacon or the priest, so that each might re-turn to their good works, praising together and blessing God. (GIRM2002 #90c; MR2002: 39)

It is also an appropriate way to end this examination of how post-Vatican II celebration of the Eucharist highlights the church's vision of human social life. Catholic Christians are reminded that the Eucharist is not an end in itself: it gives participants a foretaste of the kingdom banquet of heaven and it impels worshipers out into the world to do good works. Thus God is praised and blessed not only in liturgical prayer but in communal and individual acts by which God's intention for humanity is acknowledged and enacted. We are back to Bishop Lucker's concern that we not interpret Pope Pius X narrowly on the frequent reception of communion. Liturgical prayer leads to the "liturgy of life."

## References

Guardini, Romano. *The Church and the Catholic and the Spirit of the Liturgy.* New York: Sheed & Ward, 1935.

Huijbers, Bernard J. *The Performing Audience: Six and a Half Essays on Music and Song in the Liturgy,* 2nd ed. Phoenix, Ariz.: North American Liturgy Resources, 1980.

Joncas, Jan Michael. "The Church at Prayer[: Learning to Live for Others]." In *Spirituality and Morality: Integrating Prayer and Action.* Ed. Dennis J. Billy and Donna Lynn Orsuto. New York/Mahwah, N.J.: Paulist Press, 1996. Pp. 80–96.

Joncas, Jan Michael. "Revision, Reform, Renewal: The Impact of *Sacrosanctum Concilium* on Roman Rite Liturgy and Worship." In *Vatican II: The Continuing Agenda.* Ed. Anthony J. Cernera. Fairfield, Conn.: Sacred Heart University Press, 1997. Pp. 25–52.

Joncas, Jan Michael. "Tasting the Kingdom of God: The Meal Ministry of Jesus and Its Implications for Christian Life and Worship." *Worship* 74/4 (July 2000): 329–365.

Jungmann, Joseph A. *The Mass of the Roman Rite: Its Origins and Development* (Missarum Solemnia). 2 vols. New York: Benziger Brothers, 1955.

Ricoeur, Paul. *The Symbolism of Evil.* New York: Harper and Row, 1967.

# 8

# The eucharistic heart of reconciliation and the sacrament of penance in the "order of the faithful"

PAUL FEELA

The Catholic Church is struggling mightily these days to make sense of the mysteries of sin and forgiveness. Awash in a world of brokenness, the church flounders as it tries to find meaning in these mysteries for the life of the faithful. It has become fashionable in ecclesiastical circles to associate the contemporary ills of our culture with the loss of a sense of sin. As early as 1946, Pius XII made this association in a radio address delivered to the eighth annual Congress of the Confraternity of Christian Doctrine in Boston. He said, "Perhaps the greatest sin in the world today is that [men] have begun to lose the sense of sin" (Pius XII, 4). The ethnic wars and documented genocide of the past century, the growth of greed on a global scale that divides the "haves" from the "have nots," and the predictable backlash—desperate acts of indiscriminate terrorism—have turned traditional Catholic notions of sin on their head. Many church observers have noted the trend away from frequent, devotional confession since the Second Vatican Council—even in the face of strong admonitions regularly coming out from the Vatican. Some have attributed this loss of a sense of sin to its privatization, where sin as sin has become a strictly personal matter (Menninger, 25). Others have concluded that the culture's loss of a sense of sin can be more directly associated to the decline in the use of the sacrament of penance.

This "confusion about the confessional" has been compounded in recent months by the public revelation of sexual abuse of minors among the clergy. The irony demonstrated in the way church leadership has attended to this type of brokenness and its response in other areas—

divorced and remarried Catholics, for example—has not been lost on the culture. Many contemporary church-goers have found the confessional to be just too small, too private, and too personal a place in which to frame these mysteries.

Yet, the church continues to insist that an awareness of sin through the regular practice of sacramental penance may help to redress many of society's ills. In the church's response to the dwindling confessional lines, it appears that we have reached a pastoral impasse. The experience found in many parishes seems to indicate that a general or communal form of penance is pastorally more helpful for bringing about a greater awareness of sin, and yet the Vatican continues to forcefully assert the teachings of the Council of Trent that the only ordinary form for sacramental penance is individual, auricular confession.

Throughout his tenure as bishop of the Diocese of New Ulm, Minnesota, Raymond Lucker was aware that the mystery of reconciliation had to be more spacious than its sacramental expressions. In his writings on the topic he seemed convinced that divine forgiveness bathes the world continuously. "Yes, there are many ways that God offers forgiveness to us. We are invited to respond with hearts overflowing with love and gratitude" (Lucker, 439). I believe he instinctively knew there was a eucharistic heart to the mystery of reconciliation. In a pastoral letter to the diocese, Lucker wrote:

> Jesus came to bring the forgiveness of God to all people and to reconcile all of humankind to God. St. Paul said, "In Christ's name be reconciled to God" (2 Cor 5.20). Jesus came not only to forgive each of us, but also to point out that there are sinful structures within society that need to be reconciled. All of us participate in the prejudices, injustices, violence, and oppression of our own society. Jesus came to begin an era where God would reign over all things and called each of us to share in the building up of that reign.
>
> There are different ways of seeking forgiveness. In the Letter to James we read, "Therefore, confess your sins to one another and pray for one another that you might be healed. The fervent prayer of a righteous person is very powerful" (Jas 5, 16). Wouldn't it be a powerful thing if we would turn to a spouse or friend and say, "I feel so guilty for doing what I did. I am sorry. Would you pray with me that God forgives me?" (Lucker, 438)

Bishop Lucker sensed that the sacrament of penance is too small a place from which to live the mystery of reconciliation. But he also understood that in a living tradition only a careful and disciplined study of the past can reveal shifts in the existential and theoretical status of these living truths. Systematic theologies that have linked penance and anointing as "sacraments of healing" have obscured a more basic truth about the nature of these mysteries, a truth that perhaps a liturgical-historical analysis might more readily reveal. In this essay I am pursuing an idea that Bishop Lucker himself pondered: the Eucharist as the primary sacrament of healing. By comparing more carefully the different ways that the sacraments of baptism, Eucharist, and penance have related to one another within the tradition, we can perhaps find a way out of the contemporary pastoral predicament.

In this essay, I do three things. First, I trace the uneven history of the relationship among baptism, Eucharist, and penance in the life of the church. Second, I outline the mandate of the Second Vatican Council and the 1973 revised *Rite of Penance* which it occasioned. Third, I offer a few observations on some possible pastoral implications of the church's renewed understanding of the sacrament of penance in what might be called the "order of the faithful." I end with a brief conclusion on penance and "the eucharistic heart of reconciliation."

## I. Historical background: Shifting relationships among baptism, Eucharist, and penance

From the historical evidence of our tradition, it is clear that an understanding of the early initiation process is fundamental for understanding and shaping any theology of sacramental reconciliation. Baptism was understood to be the primary sacrament for the forgiveness of sins because it inserted people into the paschal mystery of Christ. This process of reconciliation began to happen whenever an unbeliever heard the good news of God's forgiveness in Jesus Christ and responded to it with faith. Through baptism in water and the Holy Spirit, such a person was "added" to the community of "those who were being saved" (Acts 2:47). That is to say: Sinners are "made" into "other Christs" by the action of God. The grace of reconciliation "saves" human beings by forging isolated and alienated individuals into a people. As a consequence of this divine action, individuals are brought into communion with God and with one another. Therefore faith, or the believer's response to God's action, is a matter of allowing God's will to be done—of letting ourselves be fashioned into the body of Christ—as a "holy people" who live for God.

Joseph Favazza has suggested that baptism with water was the *primary* sign of reconciliation with God, while the Eucharist was understood to be the *ordinary* or normative sign (Favazza, 11). We tend to forget that the initiation process did not culminate simply in baptism with water but in the "re-ordered" life of eucharistic living. Participating in this reconciled "order" of those faithfully living in the pattern of Jesus was understood by the early church to be the antidote to a world of sin. The "power of the keys" that is mentioned in the gospel accounts (Mt 16:19, 18:18, Jn 20:23) is essentially the power given to the church to distance itself from the reign of sin. This is why the believer's participation in this ecclesial "ordering" was understood to be crucial for the salvation of the baptized Christian.

The origin of penance as a sacrament distinct from baptism became pastorally necessary when the church began to face the fact that it had within its ranks serious, post-baptismal sinners. These notorious sinners began to be isolated from the ecclesial communion because their scandalous actions made the "communion of saints" into a living lie. As early centuries saw a growing institutionalization of procedures for dealing with the problem of the grievous sinner, a practice of sacramental reconciliation was improvised, modeled on the conversion patterns found within the initiation process itself. Just as a catechumen had to be "fashioned" into one of the faithful, so the serious sinner had to be "re-fashioned." The termination of this penitential process culminated in a formal act of reconciliation and a return to the eucharistic life of the faithful, a process that paralleled the completion of initiation. From the canonical and liturgical legislation evidenced in the penitential controversies of the mid-third century, it is clear that divine forgiveness and being joined to the ecclesial Body of Christ could not be separated.

Only with the reforms carried out in Frankish lands by the emperor Charlemagne (d. 814) and his successors was a compromise reached with the official system of canonical public penance. From that point onward, we see evidence that this sacramental practice was beginning to be used for two related but distinctive purposes. The same procedure was used to reconcile grave sinners *to* the order of the faithful and to foster the continuing conversion of ordinary faithful who were already living *within* the communion of the church. This conflation of purposes led to a blurring of the distinctive sacramental effect of penance. The confusion of meaning began to occur when a return to the eucharistic life lost significance within the process of reconciliation to the church. Forgiveness of sin began to be conceived as something separate from readmission into the order of the faithful. For the grave sinner, reconciliation to the church no longer culminated in a restoration to one's place within the ecclesial order, but only with the right to once again receive Holy Communion. Ordinary faithful as well began to view the forgiveness of sin as something distinct from their participation in the eucharistic life of the church.

Devoted Christians began to pattern their piety not on the continued transformation that would be required for a shared eucharistic life, but by conforming themselves to the penitential obligations imposed on serious sinners. Consequently, a repeatable form of private, individual confession and penance began to emerge in the tradition. This practice was valued by pious Christians as a penitential discipline to promote a more worthy reception of Holy Communion. The Fourth Lateran Council and the Council of Trent affirmed the value of this practice for all baptized Christians and, in effect, made sacramental penance, which initially was a reluctantly embraced pastoral strategy for the conversion of serious sinners, into a normative practice for all Christians (Favazza, 12). In effect, *penitentia secunda* became *penitentia prima*.

This shift of emphasis can be clearly seen in the 1973 *Rite of Penance* which speaks of the distinctive sacramental ways that the Church celebrates Christ's victory over sin. In baptism, the victory over sin "is first brought to light" when the Church proclaims its faith in "one baptism for the forgiveness of sins" (*Rite of Penance*, no. 2). The Eucharist is indicated as the place where Christ's passion is again made present, "'the sacrifice which has made our peace' with God in order that 'we may be brought together in unity' by his Holy Spirit." However, the connection between baptism and the eucharistic life to which it leads is not spelled out. Similarly, the precise relationship between sacramental penance and the forgiveness available through eucharistic participation is not clearly articulated.

In one of the last articles on this topic that he glossed, Bishop Lucker noted the ambiguity of these strained sacramental relationships as they were described in a short editorial by John Garvey:

Unless confession's connection with the idea of baptism is restored, it will seem to be an empty routine for most people . . . Baptism is the sacrament from which the others flow, and it is only through attention to the theology of baptism that our sense of confession—and for that matter all the other sacraments—will be refreshed for us. (Garvey, 7)

Yet, baptism itself concludes in the life of the Eucharist. If that connection is not clearly seen, then it will be difficult to understand how baptism and eucharist can be foundational to the historically lived practice and theology of the sacrament of penance.

## II. Catholic understanding of penance since Vatican II: Sacramental penance is meant to reconcile people *to* the Eucharist

The one consistent thread that ties together the tradition of penance is the belief that the sacrament reconciles serious sinners to God and to the church in order that they might once again participate in the eucharistic life of the faithful. While the sacrament has also been used for devotional purposes throughout much of its tradition, it is clear that recourse to the sacrament when there are no grave sins to confess has never been understood as a necessity for any Christian. In compiled notes from his summer school sessions, Bishop Lucker tried to identify how the church's authoritative teaching on penance has changed through its history. He referred in several instances to decisions reached at the Second Council of Chalon-sur-Saône which met in that city in 813 C.E. The emperor Charlemagne had ordered reform councils throughout his empire, in part, to address the question of forgiveness. One of the concerns was whether Catholics could confess their sins to God alone to receive forgiveness or were obliged rather to approach a priest for divine pardon. The bishops of Gaul declared at Chalon that Catholics were free to choose either way of obtaining forgiveness:

> Confession, consequently, which is made to God forgives sins. That (confession) also, which is made to a priest, we equally affirm brings forgiveness. For God, the author and giver of salvation and health, is wont to display his divine power by invisible action through the former, while through the latter by priestly healing. (cited by MacLaughlin, 24)

Bishop Lucker noted that even the defining canons of the Council of Trent allowed for holding this conviction (see Appendix on "Confession"). While the Council spoke of the necessity of confessing all mortal sins according to kind and number to a priest, it did not deny the possibility of forgiveness by God if a person's contrition is true.

Both of these authoritative convictions about confession are reflected in the current canons governing the celebration of sacramental penance. Following upon the decisions of Trent, the Code of Canon Law affirms:

> Individual and integral confession and absolution constitute the only ordinary means by which a member of the faithful conscious of grave sin (*peccati gravis*) is reconciled with God and the Church. Only physical or moral impossibility excuses from confession of this type; in such a case reconciliation can be obtained by other means. (Canon 960; see Denzinger-Schönmetzer, 1680)

This canon identifies the specific teaching of Trent on the necessity of sacramental penance, namely, a consciousness of grave sin. It also confirms the insight of Chalon that forgiveness—even for grave sin—is possible in some instances by other means.

In *Sacrosanctum Concilium,* the Second Vatican Council called for a reform of the Rite of Penance that seemed to be introduced, according to liturgical scholar James Dallen, as "almost an afterthought" (Dallen, 205). The Council's mandate simply called for a reform of the rites and formulas of penance to express the sacrament's nature and effect more clearly (*SC* 72), but it gave no specific guidelines to direct the reform. The only injunction found in the constitution itself links the baptismal and penitential natures of Lent and emphasizes the church's role in penitential practice (*SC* 109). It seems, therefore, that the revision of the rite has to be understood within a more comprehensive renewal of the church's sacramental life. That intention is most clearly indicated in the Dogmatic Constitution on the Church and expressed in its theological convictions about the nature of sacramental penance: "Those who approach the sacrament of Penance obtain pardon through God's mercy for offense committed against [God], and are, at the same time, reconciled with the church which they have wounded by their sins and which by charity, by example and by prayer labors for their conversion" (*LG* 11). At its deepest level, this passage associates "forgiveness" with "being reconciled with the church" in describing the specific character of sacramental penance. It also describes the fundamental role that the faithful have for reconciling such sinners. Yet, the new rite manifests the same conflicting doctrinal convictions that we have found presented in the historical evolution of the sacrament. Consequently, these were played out in the theological and doctrinal controversies surrounding the new rite's preparation, its implementation, and its procedures. The tension continues to be seen in all subsequent legislation that has followed upon the promulgation of the new rite (see Dallen, 205–249).

Central to Catholic teaching is the belief that God alone forgives sins and readily does so, but only for those who are truly repentant. Since all have sinned, all are in need of redemption. This good news of divine mercy was principally aimed at bringing to human awareness human "dis-order" in the hope that fallen believers might return to the "order" manifested in the community's way of life. This happens in many different ways within the ecclesial community. The sacraments of baptism, Eucharist, penance, and anointing all forgive sins. Yet, throughout the history of the church, what remains consistent within the tradition is the belief that the sacramental source of forgiveness is the Eucharist. As baptismal forgiveness leads to eucharistic participation, so too does sacramental penance culminate in a return to the eucharistic life. What has been less clearly articulated is the manner in which the Eucharist is associated with the remission of sin.

The initial impulse of the tradition was to reserve the formal procedures of public penance for only those extraordinary cases of gospel betrayal. Ordinary sinners "confessed" the efficacy of God's mercy by manifesting it in their communion. This communion consisted in a common life of virtue, of prayer, of mutual correction and forgiveness, of outward acts of bodily mortification or self-giving, and of the everyday struggles to live faithfully with each other in the Lord.

Over the centuries, however, this gradual but hesitant embrace of a post-baptismal reconciliation began to be used not only as a source of reconciliation but also as a means for growing in personal holiness. Thus, the practice of frequent confession often began to substitute for the more costly works of ecclesial living ever-symbolized in the words and actions of the Eucharist itself. Bishop Lucker seemed to understand the implications of this changing emphasis for the tradition:

> Over the centuries the practice of penance has changed. At one time people received the sacrament rarely, perhaps only once in a lifetime. With the influence of the Irish monks, we came to a more frequent reception of the sacrament. For many it later became routine and lifeless. (Lucker, 439)

However, Catholics today realize that there are other ways besides the sacrament for obtaining post-baptismal forgiveness. Bishop Lucker noted many of these quite traditional practices in his pastoral letter: praying to God for forgiveness, praying with one another for forgiveness, and celebrating the sacrament of the anointing of the sick as well.

Nevertheless, he understood that the church is engaged in its truest self when, as the entire community, it prays for forgiveness. "The Mass," he wrote, "is the first sacrament of reconciliation and there are many prayers at the Mass that reflect that teaching" (Lucker, 438). When we pray "Lord have mercy," or "forgive us as . . . we forgive . . ." we are acknowledging our own sinfulness, our need to be reconciled to one another, and our need to be reconciled with God. Eucharist has to be at the heart of any healing.

### III. Some pastoral implications of the church's renewed understanding of the sacrament of penance in the "order of the faithful"

To reflect on the mystery of reconciliation by starting from the eucharistic, ordinary life of the faithful will have profound implications for the contemporary debate over sacramental penance. Could such an approach offer a more fruitful implementation of the 1973 *Rite of Penance*? I offer two observations here that might open up new pastoral possibilities.

First, official instructions on the sacrament of penance since the Second Vatican Council seem to emphasize the more personal, individual aspect of confession as a means to revitalize the sacrament of reconciliation. Much of the legislation to date has focused on defining the "exceptional character" for the use of the third ritual form of the sacrament, general confession of sin with general absolution. Many of the Roman instructions conclude that there is an essential link between the sacramental judgment of the priest and the need for penitents to name their own sins, except where this is not possible. From our examination of the history of the sacrament, we can accept this as true. But the question is: *for whom?* The necessity of confessing individual sins in sacramental penance is required only of the serious sinner. For other sinners, the requirement of confession can be met in other ways. The *Roman Catechism* concludes its section on the necessity of confession by teaching that "the first thing the pastor must teach about confession, [therefore,] is its supreme importance, and in fact its necessity." (*Roman Catechism*, Part II, section 4, number 36). But is there a difference between encouraging the use of sacramental penance for devotional purposes and leaving an impression that it is required in such cases?

What is missing from most current discussions about the state of penance in the church is the straightforward acknowledgment that the eucharistic community itself is the place of forgiveness and reconciliation. The recent legislation surrounding the conditions required for the licit use of general absolution tend to frame the argument as a preference for communal or individual confession. Yet, individual and integral confession is required only for those of the baptized who are conscious that they are in grave sin. If pastoral opportunities are made regularly available for such penitents (and for devotional penitents who wish to make use of the sacrament as well), then clearly parish communal celebrations might be patterned more often in a non-sacramental manner.

The 1973 *Rite of Penance* offers a number of examples for non-sacramental penitential celebrations that foster "the spirit and virtue of penance among individuals and communities" (*Rite of Penance*, Appendix II, 1). These rites were created to accommodate a variety of parish needs, including the seasonal, the thematic, and the celebration of penance for specific groups within the community. The more frequent use of these non-sacramental celebrations throughout the year and especially during Advent and Lent could alleviate some of the burdens imposed on our current pastoral practice. The structure of the new rite itself suggests that the church carries on the ministry of forgiveness and reconciliation in many ways that are both sacramental and non-sacramental.

A second observation follows from our attention to the tradition. Most writings following the implementation of the 1973 *Rite of Penance* have related the contemporary pastoral problems regarding sacramental penance to the declining use of individual penance on the part of Catholics and the misuse of the third form of penance. The question is usually framed in such a way as to imply that individual, auricular confession is the "ordinary" form of forgiveness while the third form is an "extraordinary" rite. But the analysis above suggests it is possible to frame the debate differently.

When the Eucharist is understood as the ordinary or normative sign of sacramental reconciliation in the church, then *all* sacramental penance is "extraordinary" in relationship to it. The third form of sacramental penance is *more* "extraordinary" in character, but only in that it relates to serious sin. All other sins can be forgiven in other ways. Furthermore, the restricted use of general confession for serious sin is due solely to the Council of Trent's claim that the integral confession of serious sins is a constitutive part of the sacrament. This conviction is reflected in the unique obligation imposed only on serious sinners who receive absolution in a general matter. Notice that the person who has serious sins remitted by general absolution is not required to resubmit to absolution but only to subsequently confess individually each grave sin not previously confessed (*Rite of Penance,* no. 34).

## Conclusion:
## Penance and "the eucharistic heart of reconciliation"

In sum, the practice of reconciliation centered on the Eucharist might help to maintain the ancient unity between forgiveness and reconciliation with God and with the church. The history of sacramental penance indicates that these two were allowed to unravel so that the sign of forgiveness at times lived independently of the reality of reconciliation. But, when the Eucharist is understood as the source of forgiveness and reconciliation, then, as William Cavanagh has observed,

> the Eucharist produces forgiveness by demanding a real unity among people now... Participating in the Eucharist does not earn forgiveness nor compel God to forgive sins which God otherwise holds bound. The Lamb of God has already taken away the sins of the world in His sacrifice. The task of the Christian is to live now as if that is in fact the case, to embody redemption by living a reconciled life, and thereby bring the Kingdom, however incompletely, into the present. (Cavanagh, 238–239)

This redemption is to be embodied in persons who are ordered sacramentally by their eucharistic life together. The order into which believers are inserted is capable not only of patterning them after the Risen One, but also of safeguarding them from further shipwreck in their eucharistic living. As Christians, we cannot be built up into God's temple if sacramental penance alone is made to bear the weight of the mysteries of sin and forgiveness. Our understanding of reconciliation has to be established on firmer ground. Only the reconciliation celebrated at the Lord's Supper offers a foundation strong enough from which to live our ordered Christian lives.

Bishop Lucker explored this question throughout his ministry because he knew that the revelation of God's forgiveness is always in danger of becoming a "forgotten truth." And he also understood that this revelation is too important to our lives as human beings to forget.

## References

*Catechismus Romanus.* (English). Trans. Robert I. Bradley and Eugene Kevane. Boston: St. Paul Editions, 1985.

Cavanagh, William. *Torture and Eucharist: Theology, Politics, and the Body of Christ.* Oxford: Blackwell Publishers Ltd., 1998.

*Code of Canon Law.* Trans. Canon Law Society of America. Washington, D.C.: Canon Law Society of America, 1983.

Dallen, James. *The Reconciling Community: The Rite of Penance.* New York: Pueblo Publishing Co., 1986.

Denzinger-Schönmetzer. *Enchiridion Symbolorum.* 36th ed. Frieburg: Herder, 1976.

Favazza, Joseph. "The Future of the Sacrament of Reconciliation." *Ministry & Liturgy* 29/4 (May 2002): 10–13.

Garvey, John. "Sinning and Sorrowing: Taking Confession Seriously." *Commonweal* 13/7 (July 13, 2001): 7.

International Committee on English in the Liturgy. "Rite of Penance." In *The Rites of the Catholic Church: Volume One.* A Pueblo Book. Collegeville, Minn.: The Liturgical Press, 1990.

MacLaughlin, James. "Another View." *National Catholic Reporter* 28/33 (July 3, 1992): 24.

Menninger, Karl, M.D. *Whatever Became of Sin?* New York: Hawthorn Books, Inc., 1973.

Pius XII, Pope. "On Teaching Catholic Doctrine" (text of the radio address delivered to the 8th annual Congress of the Confraternity of Christian Doctrine at Boston, October 26, 1946). *The Catholic Mind* 45/1009 (January, 1947): 1–5.

# 9
# Christ given "for you and for all":
# Vatican II, a theology of sacramental inculturation and its need for further development

SHAWN MADIGAN, C.S.J.

I n the introduction to this book, Bishop Lucker writes: "We do not yet have the fullness of truth. The development of doctrine is ongoing because the ever-given charism of the church as prophet (which is given to the whole church) is ongoing." In claiming this, Bishop Lucker was following Vatican II's insistent grounding of God's revelation in a church made up of women and men: "The holy people of God shares also in Christ's prophetic office: it spreads abroad a living witness to him, especially by a life of faith and love and by offering to God a sacrifice of praise" (*LG* 12).

One application of Bishop Lucker's (and the Council's) deep understanding of revelation for the ways the church lives its life of prayer concerns inculturation. The question of inculturation arises whenever we reflect seriously on the mystery of revelation in the person of Jesus Christ. The incarnation of Jesus Christ and his death and resurrection "for you and for all" have immediate effects on our life of prayer. Christian inculturation, it turns out, is the process of incarnating the presence of the Spirit of Christ "for all people of good will in whose hearts grace is active invisibly" (*GS* 22).

Inculturation in its positive Christian sense realizes and affirms that the love of God surpasses all the limits that culturally conditioned expressions have placed on the Word that continues to take flesh among all people. There is a critical Christian discernment that is part of all authentic Christian inculturation. Ongoing discernment and dialogue within and among the church catholic will always be necessary so that there can be a living tradition in every age and among all peoples.

The Spirit who continues to teach the community of faith all things is heard in many ways by many culturally conditioned believers. To discern what the Spirit is saying to the communities of faith requires true dialogue among the bringers and receivers of the message, the official and unofficial interpreters, and about the critical distinctions between essentials and non-essentials of the Christian tradition. Multiple expressions of what is essential are to be expected.

The present essay will focus on three themes in sacramental inculturation. First, it will summarize the key texts of Vatican II that began a conscious theological understanding of the necessity and meaning of sacramental inculturation. Second, it will systematize the Council's insights by naming three elements inherent in a Christian understanding of inculturation; and it will show that the church has moved further in implementing some elements than others. Third, using the files that Bishop Lucker gathered on this topic, the essay will examine some very particular examples of present and future challenges faced by the church in dealing with sacramental inculturation. A brief conclusion will come back to the connection between inculturation and Bishop Lucker's concern for an adequate understanding of revelation that continues in every age.

## I. Vatican II's *Sacrosanctum Concilium* as the basis of a developing understanding of inculturation

Vatican II's theological description of inculturation began early with the Council's first approved document, *Sacrosanctum Concilium*. The Constitution on the Sacred Liturgy's renewal of liturgy tried to effect a transformative tension among the theological, pastoral, and juridical elements of such a renewal. Four paragraphs of that constitution show the Council's guiding concern for "catholicity" in the liturgy's renewal. They are the paragraphs of the document's Section III D, "Norms for Adapting the Liturgy to the Temperament and Traditions of Peoples" (*SC* 37–40). These few paragraphs hold that, although basic unity was to be maintained, "provision shall be made, when revising the liturgical books, for legitimate variations and adaptations to different groups, regions and peoples, especially in mission countries" (*SC* 38). These few paragraphs began a process of inculturation that carried out in ever new and unforeseen ways the basic hope of the constitution to "encourage whatever can promote the union of all who believe in Christ" and to strengthen whatever expressions can help summon all people into the church's embrace (*SC* 1).

Subsequent documents of Vatican II elaborated upon and clarified a developing theology of inculturation based upon growing understanding of the universality of the paschal mystery. In 1994, the Congregation for Divine Worship and the Discipline of the Sacraments made an official distinction between *adaptation* and *inculturation,* although liturgical theologians had made the distinction soon after the council ended. The official document used *adaptation* to refer to minor changes that make liturgical rites more accessible to the particular community celebrating the liturgy. *Inculturation* proper referred to the dialogue essential to church and culture which is mutually enlightening regarding the complexity that cultural formation involves as the religious imagination of a people, shaped by culture and belief systems, influences understanding and celebration of Christ's presence with and for them and all people (see CDW 1994, 4–6).

It was four paragraphs of *Sacrosanctum Concilium* that began the evolution of theological reflections on the nature of Christian inculturation. The opening words of *Sacrosanctum Concilium* 37 affirm the reality: "Even in the liturgy the church does not wish to impose a rigid uniformity in matters which do not affect the faith or the well-being of the entire community." Respect was shown as the official church encouraged all races and nations to admit elements of their way of life into its liturgy "provided they harmonize with its [the liturgy's] true and authentic spirit." One interesting dimension of inculturation was the decentralization of Roman authority in favor of national collegiality. The territorial ecclesiastical authority (national bishops' conferences) was to decide "which elements from the traditions and cultures of individual peoples might appropriately be admitted into divine worship" (*SC* 40.1). However, adaptations deemed good by bishops' conferences were still to be submitted to the Holy See for approval. That shift of authority to bishops' conferences was altered in the 1994 document which required greater involvement of the Congregation for Divine Worship and the Discipline of the Sacraments (see CDW 1994, 53–65).

Because Vatican II's perspective called for ongoing creativity in the process of adapting and inculturating liturgy, bishops' conferences were strongly encouraged to set up national liturgical commissions of experts in liturgical science, sacred music, art, and pastoral practice and also to create national institutes for pastoral liturgy. Each diocese was to name a liturgical commission of trained, well-informed personnel who would promote the liturgical apostolate in a fitting pastoral manner (*SC* 44, 45).

The Dogmatic Constitution on the Church (*Lumen Gentium*) complemented and furthered the basic theology of inculturation that was grounded in the Mystical Body of Christ and inherent in the paschal mystery. It claimed: "In virtue of this catholicity, each part contributes its own gifts to other parts and to the entire church, so that the whole and each of the parts are strengthened by the common sharing of all things" (*LG* 13).

The Decree on the Catholic Eastern Churches (*Orientalium Ecclesiarum*) affirmed that diverse liturgical practices have always existed, since their liturgical forms have been a traditional part of the Catholic liturgy. Clearly, if historical precedent has any theological authenticity, Catholic liturgy means unity but not uniformity. Vatican II noted that there is liturgically "clear evidence of the great debt owed to the eastern churches by the church universal" (*OE* 5). Variations in worship traditions have been part of the church catholic as long as there have been Christians.

Inculturation was addressed further in the Decree on the Church's Missionary Activity (*Ad Gentes*). "This community of the faithful, endowed with the cultural riches of its own nation, should be deeply rooted in the people" and the "ecumenical spirit should be nourished among neophytes." (*AG* 15). The Christian community should be so organized and developed that "it is able to provide for its own needs as far as possible" (*AG* 15). All Christian communities throughout the world ought to "borrow from the customs, traditions, wisdom, teaching, arts and sciences of their people everything which could be used to praise the glory of the Creator, manifest the grace of the savior, or contribute to the right ordering of christian life" (*AG* 22).

The Pastoral Constitution on the Church in the Modern World (*Gaudium et Spes*) provided a clear theological base for inculturation in its theology of the paschal mystery. Jesus Christ has "in a certain way united himself with each individual . . . the Holy Spirit offers to all the possibility of being made partners, in a way known to God, in the paschal mystery" (*GS* 22). God is manifest in the incarnation of Jesus Christ and this manifestation speaks to all cultures requiring of Christians especially a concern for all humanity (*GS* 54–56).

Other documents addressed the community of all humans, but the earliest challenge for the Council was that of adapting the language of the liturgy: Could the vernacular of the people be used for worship rather than insisting upon Latin as a unifying language? The mystery of Jesus Christ "for you and for all" was the basic unifier, the Council decided, and not the culturally conditioned aspects of one particular unifying language. Indeed, the church had already shifted language from Aramaic to Latin, an early church inculturation. Thus, Latin was not an essential dimension of liturgical prayer, in spite of some who argued for its retention as a "sacred" language (SC 36). In a type of compromise not unlike those made in other Vatican II documents, *Sacrosanctum Concilium*'s early interpreters insisted upon respect for Latin as a liturgical language and adaptation to multiple languages proceeded slowly and carefully. "Translations from the Latin for use in the liturgy must be approved by the competent territorial ecclesiastical authority already mentioned" (SC 36.4). Then these were to be sent to Rome for approval.

Although the Liturgy of the Eucharist was the primary context for use of vernacular in progressive stages, the constitution recognized that the vernacular could be used for sacraments and sacramentals. Bishops from regions speaking the same language were encouraged to consult together on appropriate translations of texts. On October 17, 1963, bishops representing ten conferences of bishops from English-speaking countries decided to formalize meetings that had been occurring among them since the first session of Vatican II. The group that was established would eventually be known as the International Commission on English in the Liturgy (ICEL). Cardinal Giacomo Lecaro encouraged this initiative. He eventually became the president of the Consilium, the group that guided and implemented liturgical reform.

On October 16, 1964, Cardinal Lecaro addressed a letter to all presidents of bishops' conferences (*Documents on the Liturgy*, no. 108, pp. 268–269). Basically, this document advised the presidents to join with bishops of other countries sharing the same or at least similar vernacular to have one version rather than "multiple translations" of liturgical texts. He thought that multiple versions were somehow detrimental to true reform.

In sum, the Council gave the church an understanding of inculturation that reverenced both the particularity and universality of the church. The precise elements of a theology of inculturation became clearer as liturgical adaptation proceeded.

## II. The uneven post-conciliar development
## of a theological understanding of sacramental inculturation

Adaptation and true inculturation have taken on specific meanings as the liturgical theology of inculturation has evolved since Vatican II. Although some liturgical theologians have used a third term, *contextualization,* to clarify meanings, others consider the context that affects ritual adaptation to be a face of adaptation. This essay will follow the latter usage.

*Adaptation* refers to basic and obvious changes that enable believers to have a better understanding of the same rites that have been celebrated for centuries. Early translation of Latin ritual language into the language of the people was considered to be an adaptation. This was inculturation's earliest phase. Then came *contextualizing,* making the particular adaptations that seemed necessary because of a particular community's experience and setting and need. These were not for all people everywhere, but for particular people at prayer. Examples of this proliferated in the post-Vatican II decade. New music fitting for different ages, ethnic groups, and settings was composed. In some groups, standing around the altar was normative. Banners and other forms of participative preparation marked the prayer of many. So-called "children's liturgies," adolescent prayer services, nursing home alterations in the length of liturgical celebrations and forms, and a host of other adaptations for particular communities were tried. Slowly, in some cultures, ministries of laity were called into service as readers. Because the shifts were built on a tradition of earlier practices and present conditions rather than future possibilities, early adaptations tended to be quite non-dramatic, although that judgment might be argued by some.

The deeper or more significant changes growing out of the theology of liturgical inculturation are still in process. True *inculturation* acknowledges that the paschal mystery is always experienced and interpreted through culturally conditioned religious imagination. This is a much deeper reality than translation of language and composition of music, although these two realities can be expressive of inculturation. Cultural conditioning can limit the understanding of the Christian mystery or it can enhance the universality of the expression of the paschal mystery. Because official Roman Catholic Christianity is an inculturated expression of the interpretation of ongoing revelation, there is always need for the universal community of believers to be in discerning dialogue about not only what the Spirit is saying to the churches, but also which symbolic expressions can best mediate that living mystery. Christ is far greater than any cultural expression (see Francis, 2000).

Pope Paul VI seemed to have a good sense of the degrees of inculturation, that is, of adaptation and deeper inculturation. He assumed leadership in translation of rites into the vernacular as an early phase of adaptation. He spoke clearly of pastoral reasons for shifting from the Latin language to the vernacular in order to carry out the hope of Vatican II that people might pray in a manner that encouraged full participation of mind and heart. He was aware that there was some opposition to praying in one's own language on the part of people and clergy. He dealt with the tension between those advocating vernacular prayer and those who called Cardinal Lecaro and the Consilium heretical for not considering Latin the only sacred language.

Paul VI addressed the members and *periti* of the Consilium on April 19, 1967, aware of the tensions between those trying to stop the reform and those who wanted to continue the reform. He stood with the liturgical reforms set in motion by Vatican II and encouraged the Consilium publicly. "The Consilium fully deserves to receive renewed expressions of our high esteem and confidence," he said and added, "Latin is an issue certainly deserving serious attention but . . . liturgical prayer, accommodated to the understanding of the people, is to be intelligible . . . The people's deepest and sincerest sentiments can best be expressed through the vernacular as it is in actual usage" (*Documents on the Liturgy*, no. 86, pp. 228–229).

Between 1965 and 1976 various instructions dealing with the translation of liturgical texts were issued. In 1967, the pope authorized vernacular translations for the Eucharist and Ordination Rites. The Consilium, presided over by Cardinal Lecaro, the Sacred Congregation for Divine Worship, and even the Congregation for the Doctrine of the Faith were all issuing guides and regulations about proper translations from Latin into the vernacular. An instruction from the Consilium in 1969 insisted that the community, the speaker, and the message all affect the inculturated task of doing a "proper translation" (see Chupungco, 1997, 381–397).

In 1974, Cardinal James Knox, Prefect of the Sacred Congregation for the Sacraments and Divine Worship, addressed the Third Synod of

Bishops that gathered in Rome. He reminded the bishops that the translations of worship texts into the vernacular was just the first phase of
liturgical renewal envisioned by Vatican II. The second phase of contextualizing appropriate symbols within each culture was just beginning.
Encouraging new cultural expressions of liturgical prayer meant that
the Roman culture and much of its expression in worship forms and
content were admittedly insufficiently universal. Thus, "the Roman rite
has to give way to new cultural expressions, to reinterpretations, modifications and variations. A universal Roman rite means unity in essentials and diversity in cultural forms" (Chupungco, 1982, 43).

Although initially so-called "missionary lands" were the main object
of liturgical reform and creativity, all bishops were encouraged to assess
which "elements from the traditions and cultures of individual peoples"
are fitting for meaningful worship (*SC* 40). Attempts to put *Sacrosanctum
Concilium* 37–40 into meaningful practice have evolved into a growing
awareness that inculturation is "not primarily a missionary concern but
a cultural exigency" for all people (Chupungo, 1982, 75). That is, in
adapting and contextualizing its worship, the post-conciliar church was
discovering the need for deeper inculturation.

Paul VI showed his theological depth in relating authentic liturgical
inculturation to effective evangelization. His reflections indicated that
he understood culture to be a deeper reality than just extrinsic and ob-
servable practices. He was well aware that "culture" is an entire system
of formative concepts, values, and symbols that express and also shape a
particular people. In 1975 Paul VI urged not just adaptation but true inculturation. Changes should not occur "in a purely decorative way as it
were, by applying a thin veneer, but in a vital way, in depth, and right to
their very roots" (Paul VI, *Evangelii Nuntiandi* 20). This third phase of
creativity had and continues to have a long future.

In spite of the leadership of Paul VI and others—a leadership urging true inculturation that went beyond language—even that basic first
level of adapting the liturgy to the language of the people and finding
"proper translations" for texts continues to be a source of tension. On a
positive note, the incorporation of meaningful cultural and religious
heritage symbols of different peoples into the liturgy is proceeding in
spite of some opposition. The impetus that Vatican II initiated through
*Sacrosanctum Concilium* 37–40 has evolved into a new awareness that Eu-
rocentric worship forms can be enhanced through liturgical dialogue
with non-Western and non-European nations. The vision of the
church's fidelity to itself as a church universal means entering "into

communion with different forms of culture, thereby enriching both it-self and the cultures themselves" (*GS* 58). Under Pope John Paul II the Vatican has addressed the need for continued inculturation so that litur-gical prayer truly fits "the temperament and conditions of different peo-ples" (CDW 1994, 3).

In summary, *Sacrosanctum Concilium* 37–40 awakened a theme that had been dormant for centuries. The theology of inculturation which expanded to include other Vatican II documents has slowly created a more legitimate catholicity of the church. At the same time, resistance to inculturaton has never died. The paschal mystery that somehow touches everyone remains in need of critical dialogue about liturgical celebrations that truly are "for you and for all."

In the last main section of this essay, I take up currently pressing topics in a theology of inculturation. The issues all arise in the clippings that Bishop Raymond Lucker kept. These clippings (and Bishop Lucker's notes on them) provide some foundations for the direction of a lived theology of inculturation in our day.

## III. Directions, tensions, and possibilities in the third phase of liturgical inculturation

Four large subject areas of liturgical inculturation emerge from Bishop Raymond Lucker's files kept between 1963 and 2001. The dom-inant subject areas are the African and Asian Bishops' Synods, transla-tions of the Bible for the Lectionary and of prayer formularies for the Sacramentary, past challenges of inculturation in North American church history, and possibilities and tensions facing the church's future.

Bishop Lucker seemed to admire the African bishops as one group that clearly attempted liturgical inculturation. After twenty years of prayerful study and experimentation guided by the bishops of Zaire, the "Zairean Rite" was officially approved by the Congregation for the Sacraments and Divine Worship in 1987. While this is still a Roman rite for the diocese of Zaire, African images, dance, and some elements new to the Roman rite make this rite one example of the three phases of in-culturation (see Maloney, 433–442).

The African Bishops' Synod that met in Rome in 1994 continued the discussion of ongoing inculturation. The immediate need to trans-late liturgical books into the 150 languages of Africa and the urgent need to allow local customs and symbols into prayer was discussed.

Celebration of a truly African Mass demonstrated one mode of liturgical inculturation, but the bishops also explained how ecumenical relations with their Muslim neighbors as well as non-Roman Catholic Christians expand the context for future expressions of inculturated liturgical prayer. These African bishops have identified the new role of contemporary theologians to be one of critical reflection "in the service of inculturation" ("African Synod," 604).

The incorporation of dance, multiple blessings, and appropriate colors and symbols has assisted the African community's faith. Still, these appropriate manifestations that embody the community's sense of joy and sadness, of ancestor invocation and of multiple blessings, are only a beginning. Each sacrament and its basic symbol system needs critique regarding what is essential and what is not for the particular rite. For example, in eucharistic gatherings, wheat hosts and grape wine are still insisted upon by centralized Roman authorities. Use of locally grown materials for bread and wine has not been allowed, even though wheat bread and grape wine can be afforded only by the wealthiest Africans who can import the products. Wheat bread and grape wine are symbols that separate wealthy people from poor people (Lumbala, 41–56; 60–63; 106–108). The lack of inculturation of these symbols contradicts the sacramental theology of a Christ who is more intimate than the food that becomes us.

Another example of needed inculturation surrounds the ritual of baptism among the Masai of East Africa. The presider pouring water over the head of a woman is troublesome to the Masai. This community believes that a woman who has water poured over the head by another is cursed with infertility (see Schreiter, 1985). The theological challenge that inculturating liturgy demands in Africa is slowly enhancing the richness of dialogue about authentic liturgical catholicity. Knowing what other cultures can do and have done to make the gospel come alive benefits the whole church for "innovations found serviceable in any church provide models for other churches as they endeavor to assess their own developments" (Power, ix).

Certain issues having to do with Asian inculturation also interested Bishop Lucker. He had some notes about the Chinese rites controversies of the sixteenth and seventeenth centuries as well as some jottings about contemporary Asian Bishops' Synods. A link can be constructed by considering the issues surrounding Matteo Ricci (1552–1610). This missionary gained the respect of the Chinese by explaining to them and then demonstrating European scientific instruments like clocks and world maps. Some Chinese were attracted to Christianity through his adaptations of Christianity to Chinese frames of reference and his language facility. His Chinese catechism was a standard manual for generations of missionaries. Matteo Ricci also adapted some actions of the Mass as well as scriptural and worship language to Chinese sensitivities and understanding. He respected local customs, utilizing some of them as a basis for common prayer.

In 1622, Gregory XV created the Congregation of the Propagation of the Faith. That congregation issued an instruction in 1659 that affirmed inculturation efforts. This instruction itself followed on a 1656 decree by Alexander VI that did the same. The 1659 "Instruction to the Vicars Apostolic of the Far East" is worth citing, for it made clear that the Chinese people should not "change their rites, customs and ways unless these are most obviously contrary to the faith . . . What could be more absurd than to carry France, Spain or Italy or any other part of Europe into China? It is not this sort of thing you are to bring, but rather the faith" (cited by Minamiki, 31–32).

But efforts at inculturating worship in Asia were dealt a negative blow by Pope Clement XI in 1704 and again in 1715. A trend toward imposing Roman forms of worship in Asia continued through Benedict XV (who served as pope from 1914 to 1922). Telling this story, George Minamiki says papal actions over two centuries doomed the possibility of the continent of Asia becoming Christianized (Minamiki, 32ff; see especially chapter 3 and its note 54). In a word, lack of inculturation short-circuited the potential of Asian Christianity for centuries.

Today, pastoral Asian bishops are trying to inculturate the liturgy again with respect for the vastly different traditions of Asian peoples. Authentic inculturation of liturgy in Vietnam faces different challenges than the authentic inculturation of liturgy in India or China. The Vietnamese Catholic Church and its long tradition of Eastern symbol systems may be different from the long tradition of symbols in China. A specific example of eucharistic celebration in a Vietnamese village can serve as an example of tensions between Western Roman tradition and Vietnamese meanings.

Vietnamese village society is matriarchal, that is, the head of the house is the mother. When the head of liturgical celebration is a male who comes rarely to the village, the symbol does not resound with the table gatherings of friends led by the woman of the house. In the village, the Catholic pastoral leader is a woman pastoral worker. Although she trains the people, teaches them, and acts as their prayer leader and unifier, she must give way to a traveling male priest who does not know the people or live among them but celebrates the sacrament of unity. This priest wears Western vestments reminiscent of the oppressive colonizers of past history. The beautiful colors and styles that speak to this people of festivities and joyful community gatherings are worn by the woman pastor but not by the visiting male pastor. At the Eucharist, the people gathered do not dance with energetic joy as they would in any other village festive celebration. Yet, they hear of the wonderful works of God and the paschal mystery of life touching all life.

The sacred texts and prayers that have shaped the religious imagination and life of these indigenous peoples for centuries cannot be brought into the celebration in any form. The symbol of wheat bread and grape wine may not convey what is hoped for by Roman law regarding authentic symbols. Here, as in Africa, only the richest people ever have wheat bread or grape wine. The cost of importing these basic materials drives a wedge of symbol interpretation between rich and poor. Is this a church of the poor or the rich? The poor eat bread and drink wine made from their own land, but their sources of bread and wine are evidently not worthy of becoming the Body and Blood of Christ.

The language that is used in the approved texts is no longer the language of the people, because the Roman overseers did not approve the texts reflecting the language of the people. So many changes were made in the texts by Roman overseers that the people at this point are not really praying in their language but rather in a Roman version of what their language should be.

What is essential for unity in celebration of the liturgical life of the church? What is not really essential in mediating the saving presence of Christ to a particular people at a particular time and place in history? There can be no full participation in the liturgy if the people's symbol systems, including their language, are judged inappropriate by a group that knows little about the culture that has shaped the heart of a particular people. The people have been promised full participation in the church through baptism. Do Roman overseers really have the power to deny this? (For further detail on the challenges of inculturation in Asia and elsewhere, see Peter Phan's 1998 article.)

Bishop Lucker was aware that not only "missionary lands," but also North America needs liturgical inculturation. His files include essays on

Bishop John England and on the so-called Americanists. Bishop England seems to have been a hero to Bishop Lucker, a hero of inculturation of the church in North America. England, a native of Cork, Ireland, was appointed Bishop of Charleston, South Carolina, in 1822. On his own, England translated the Latin missal into American English and then had it published so the people could pray in their own tongue. Bishop England did this even though he knew Rome had already condemned the German translation of the Roman missal and placed it on *The Index of Forbidden Books*! For England, it was not only liturgy that needed proper inculturation but also the way church authority was exercised in the new land. According to an essay that Lucker kept in his files, Bishop England held that American Catholics "will never be reconciled to the practice of the bishops and sometimes of the priest alone, giving orders without assigning reasons for the same" (see Swidler, 19).

Lucker's other essays on inculturation attempts in North America center on the 1899 Roman condemnation of the phantom heresy that would become known as "Americanism." This condemnation was a quite subjective condemnation about the views of Isaac Hecker, even though Hecker's views had nothing to do with the religious liberty issues of the Americanists (see Wangler, 13–14). Perhaps in Bishop Lucker's mind, the work of England and of the so-called Americanists provided a foundation for interpreting challenges presented today for the church of the United States. He retained many clippings about the North American bishops and the issues around Lectionary and Sacramentary revisions and translations.

Tensions surrounding Lectionary translations and Sacramentary issues continue as this essay is composed. Readers may be aware that the proposed New American Bible Lectionary and the ICEL Sacramentary texts were overwhelmingly approved by the North American Bishops after a thirteen-year period of genuine scholarly study, composition, and revision. However, the Lectionary texts sat in Rome for four years after their 1992 approval until some bishops went to Rome to inquire. There had been no response from the Congregation for Divine Worship and the Discipline of the Sacraments. At the same time, French, German, Polish, Italian, and Spanish Sacramentaries were approved.

Even though the ICEL translation of Sacramentary texts was more accurate doctrinally than the earlier Sacramentary used in English-speaking countries, and even though the biblical texts in the Lectionary were more biblically accurate than earlier translations, both the Sacramentary and the Lectionary faced problems in Rome. The problems were not doctrinal or liturgical. The two problems were inclusive language and some newly created prayer texts! Inclusive language was doctrinally linked by curial readers to women's ordination and a host of so-called "feminist" issues! New texts seemed to fall out of favor on the principle that older is better (see Trautman, 1997a and 1997b)

The Congregation for Divine Worship and the Discipline of the Sacraments issued *Liturgiam Authenticam* on May 13, 2001. The document seems to conflict with earlier decisions by Vatican II and the magisterium giving the bishops authority over inculturation issues like Bible translations and revisions of texts for worship (see Jensen, 2001). My biblical scholar colleagues, Chris Franke and Vince Skemp, take up the further difficulties with *Liturgiam Authenticam* in their essay for this book. Here it is enough to say that the selective group that wrote the document did not bring a sense of North American context and culture to their task. The writers of the document were a mix of men with little critical knowledge of liturgy or recent biblical theology. One man had a dated graduate degree in scripture. Two others did not speak English as a first language. A fourth was still a Roman graduate student. The two Americans were archbishops well known for their history of inaccurate and biased objections to inclusive language as a "feminist" agenda issue rather than as a catholic issue of gracious language for all.

Fears that guided *Liturgiam Authenticam* and its strong denial of inclusive language and new prayer texts are a step backwards from the intent of *Sacrosanctum Concilium* 37–40 to inculturate liturgy. However, there have been positive things that have happened as well. Inculturation of liturgy in North America since the 1970s has slowly acknowledged the multicultural context of Roman Catholic liturgical prayer. The work of Fr. Clarence Rivers has had a lasting impact on liturgical celebrations for African-American Catholics. Music, dance, and other attempts at liturgical renewal have furthered the theology of liturgy as a work of the people. As their particular stories come into the liturgical story of a Christ for all, inculturation of liturgical life will be enriched (see McGann, 2002).

The Institute of Hispanic Liturgy has served a growing number of Hispanic communities in the United States. Although music and culturally suitable celebrations have emerged, the difficulty today of migration to new communities means that stories of particular Hispanic communities' struggles and triumphs have been compromised or even forgotten. This was a big concern for Bishop Lucker. He was proud of the New Ulm diocesan commitment to staff and support a parish in San Lucas Toliman, Guatemala; but he lamented "the prejudice against migrant workers in our own diocese" (see Lucker, 213–214). As Hispanic people move to areas of the country that are distant from the homes of their parents or grandparents, blending with other groups can mean a loss as well as a gain of traditions.

An issue for the present and future of inculturation of liturgy is that of celebrating with a multicultural community. This is one of the pastoral challenges of the church in the new millennium. Dialogue with the community so that each appreciates the other's cultural gifts is a starting point. Then there is the matter of how much unity and how much diversity the community at prayer can assimilate as it tries to fully participate. Multiple ways to celebrate may be a possible resolution as people grow into the meaning of catholicity (Reza, 1998).

Ecumenical inculturation has yet to be seriously addressed by an official church, but there are at least groups of liturgists from many Christian communions who are in dialogue about liturgical prayer and mutual learning. Organizations like the North American Academy of Liturgy and the National Liturgical Conference have made a point of stressing liturgical prayer among the members of the Body of Christ as a source for greater communion.

## Conclusion:
## Toward a sacramental inculturation "for you and for all"

This essay began by tying the concern for inculturation to Bishop Lucker's focus on the beauty and challenge of Catholicism's understanding of revelation: because our grasp of revelation will never be complete, so we will never finish inculturating the church's liturgy. As the faithful change, so will the expression of the church and liturgical prayer. Today and into the future, liturgical inculturation will be met with many challenges, not only of multicultural communities at prayer, but of private religious sense overshadowing a communal sense, of the varieties of popular religion that color religious imagination, and of the multigenerational issues of meaningful celebrations.

Christianity's encounter with the world through the paschal mystery is "not just with the culture and tradition of European Americans, but with that of the African, Native, Hispanic and Asian Americans as well. This means teaching each other the words to our songs, building church together wherever we are gathered, and growing with each other in each and every way" (Hayes, 83).

The potential for ongoing liturgical inculturation is beyond imagining, but a new catholicity is in progress because of it. Bishop Raymond Lucker knew that the church as prophet will somehow mold a future that continues to inculturate the Christ who is "for you and for all." The Eastern Church has retained a sense that the catholic or universal nature of the Body of Christ will be fully revealed only when the reign of God comes fully. Western Catholicism, at least since the Reformation, has focused on a more narrow, legal understanding of what makes us "catholic." But, at least since the Council made its intentions known in *Sacrosanctum Concilium,* the move toward this more Eastern sense of catholic and the wisdom of inculturation is in process.

With Bishop Lucker we would all do well to admit that, on inculturation as on every other important element of our faith, "we do not yet have the fullness of truth." And if we are frustrated at either the slowness or the speed of liturgical inculturation, we would do well to go back to the Council's words that occasioned Bishop Lucker's openness to change. I quoted those words, from paragraph 12 of the Dogmatic Constitution on the Church, at the beginning of this essay: "the holy people of God shares in Christ's prophetic office." These words insist that revelation continues to be understood in a church of women and men, and of all times and cultures.

While true, this fact alone does not ground the Council's confidence that revelation will continue to be transmitted in the church. That confidence comes from another source, which the same paragraph goes on to name: "The whole body of the faithful who have received an anointing which comes from the holy one cannot be mistaken in belief" (*LG* 12). In a word, we can engage one another more deeply and confidently on the issues surrounding liturgical inculturation because, as Bishop Lucker said in his last homily to the people of New Ulm, "God is here" (see Unsworth, 21).

### References

"African Synod Hailed as 'Historical Event.'" *The Tablet* 248 (May 14, 1994): 603–604.

Chupungco, Anscar. "The Translation of Liturgical Texts." In *Handbook for Liturgical Studies I: Introduction to the Liturgy*. Collegeville, Minn.: The Liturgical Press, 1997.

Chupungco, Anscar. *Cultural Adaptation of the Liturgy*. Mahwah, N.J.: Paulist Press, 1982.

Congregation for Divine Worship and the Discipline of the Sacraments (CDW). Instruction "Inculturation and the Roman Liturgy." *Origins* 23/43 (1994): 745, 747–756.

Congregation for Divine Worship and the Discipline of the Sacraments (CDW). "*Liturgiam Authenticam.*" *Origins* 31/2 (2001): 17, 19–32.

*Documents on the Liturgy, 1963–1979: Conciliar, Papal and Curial Texts*. Ed. International Commission on English in the Liturgy. Collegeville, Minn.: The Liturgical Press, 1982.

Francis, Mark. *Shape a Circle Ever Wider*. Chicago: Liturgy Training Program, 2000.

Hayes, Diana. "Healing the Past, Claiming the Future: Naming and Welcoming the Other." In *The Changing Face of the Church*. Ed. Timothy Fitzgerald and Martin Connell. Chicago: Liturgy Training Program, 1998. Pp. 66–85.

Hillman, Eugene. "Inculturation." In *New Dictionary of Theology*. Ed. Joseph Komonczak, Mary Collins, OSB, Dermot Lane. Wilmington, Del.: Michael Glazier, 1989. Pp. 510–513.

Jensen, Joseph. "*Liturgiam Authenticam* and the New Vulgate." *America* 185 (August 13-20, 2001): 11–13.

Lumbala, F. Kabsele. *Celebrating Jesus Christ in Africa*. Maryknoll: Orbis Books, 1988.

Maloney, R. "The Zairean Mass and Inculturation." *Worship* 62 (1988): 433–442.

McGann, Mary. "Timely Wisdom, Prophetic Challenge: Rediscovering Clarence R. Rivers' Vision of Authentic Worship." *Worship* 76 (2002): 2–24.

Minamiki, George. *The Chinese Rites Controversy from Its Beginnings to Modern Times*. Chicago: Loyola University Press, 1985.

Paul VI, Pope. Apostolic exhortation *Evangelii nuntiandi*. *Origins* 5/28 (1976): 459–468.

Phan, Peter. "How Much Uniformity Can We Stand? How Much Do We Want? Church and Worship in the New Millennium." *Worship* 72 (1998): 194–209.

Power, David. *Celebrating Jesus Christ in Africa*. Maryknoll, New York: Orbis Books, 1998.

Reza, Mary Frances. "Cultural Diversity in Worship: Will We Survive?" In *The Changing Face of the Church*. Chicago: Liturgy Training Program, 1998. Pp. 148–158.

Schreiter, Robert. *Constructing Local Theologies*. New York: Orbis Books, 1985.

Swidler, Leonard. "An Americanist Hero, John England: Still Ahead of His Time." *Commonweal* 122/7 (April 7, 1995): 18–20.

Trautman, Bishop Donald (1997a). "Texts for the Third Millennium: The Revised Sacramentary." *Liturgy* 90 (August-September, 1997): 4–7.

Trautman, Bishop Donald (1997b). "Texts for the Third Millennium: The Revised Lectionary." *Liturgy* 90 (October, 1997): 5–10.

Unsworth, Tim. "A Man Who Was Filled with God." *National Catholic Reporter* 37/42 (October 5, 2001): 21.

Wangler, Thomas. "Americanism." *The New Dictionary of Theology*. Ed. Joseph Komonczak, Mary Collins, OSB, Dermot Lane. Wilmington, Del.: Michael Glazier, 1989. Pp. 13–14.

# IV

# Guarding Human Dignity

## Re-reading *Gaudium et Spes* for what it is asking of the church in our day

*Vatican II:"In reality it is only in the mystery of the Word made flesh that the mystery of humanity truly becomes clear... The Christian is certainly bound both by need and by duty to struggle with evil through many afflictions and to suffer death; but, as one who has been made a partner in the paschal mystery, and as one who has been configured to the death of Christ, will go forward, strengthened by hope, to the resurrection. All this holds true not only for Christians but also for all people of good will in whose hearts grace is active invisibly... In Christ, light is thrown on the mystery of suffering and death which, apart from his gospel, overwhelms us. Christ has risen again, destroying death by his death, and has given life abundantly to us so that, becoming [children] in the Son, we may cry out in the Spirit: Abba, Father!"(GS 22).*

*Bishop Lucker:"As I get older, as I read and reflect on the Gospel message, as I teach and share my experience with others, as I pray, my faith becomes much simpler, less complicated... God's plan centered in Christ is to share divine life with us... God unconditionally, faithfully loves us and just wants us to love him in return with our total being, and then love one another as Jesus did. Jesus is our head, we are all members of the body, the church which is on pilgrimage. Poor, sinful human beings, we are united with Christ to change the world."(Lucker, 350, 352)*

*Alcoholics Anonymous:"Just because it is simple doesn't mean it will be easy."*

Paul Wojda's essay "A Gift Abundantly Given: The Conciliar Roots of a Consistent Ethic of Life" begins this section. He claims that the consistent life ethic articulated by Cardinal Bernardin and by Pope John Paul

II has its roots in *Gaudium et Spes*'s radical shift of focus in Catholic morality. Vatican II turned the church's moral attention from timeless rules about "human nature" to solidarity with persons. The church, says Wojda, decided to look for signs of the authentically human in the "joys and the hopes, the griefs and anguish" of real human beings in the real world. This means two things: the church acknowledges that it is never easy to discern what God's love is asking from us, here and now in our own lives; and the church promises to be in the midst of life's struggles helping us discern what we are being asked. A "consistent ethic of life" is a response to the God who has given us everything we have and are.

Russell Connors's essay, "*Gaudium et Spes* on Marriage: What 'Went Forward'? What Might Be 'Going Forward' Now?," borrows a phrase from Jesuit theologian Bernard Lonergan to say theology is always looking to see what is "going forward" in church understanding. Connors shows how Catholic thought "went forward" at Vatican II to understand marriage as a fully human reality that is also sacramental of God's presence in the world. He also says more might be "going forward" now in our day as we ask more precisely what in human love is sacramental of God.

In this book's concluding essay, "Peace and Justifiable War: Catholic Social Thought and Its Call to Us Today," Amata Miller reflects on what is surely the most timely topic of this volume, peace and justifiable war. She reviews the church's historical movement between more pacifist and "just war" approaches on these questions, and says that a third and deeper approach may be emerging in our day. Her essay points out how personally challenging this approach will be in the lives of believers: we will need to examine and strengthen our own practices of forgiveness and reconciliation in order to effect forgiveness and reconciliation in the world.

# 10
# A gift abundantly given:
# The conciliar roots of a consistent ethic of life

PAUL J. WOJDA

That Vatican II witnessed a radical change in Catholic life is not vigorously disputed. Though some romanticizing of pre-conciliar Catholicism still raises itself up from time to time, most of us accept the view articulated by Bishop Lucker (1927–2001), who lived precisely half his life before and half his life after the Council. Lucker wrote the following in a 1989 pastoral letter: "Some people see the 1940s and 1950s as 'good old days.' Everything was clear. We knew where we stood . . . Looking back I can now see the other side. With the wisdom of hindsight I also recognize in those days signs of real decline and apathy" (Lucker, 321).

So we accept that the Council changed much for Catholics. But where debate rages is over the nature of the changes implemented by the Council and the implications of those changes for our understanding of Catholic moral doctrine as a whole. In its Declaration on Religious Liberty (*Dignitatis Humanae*), to take but the best-known example, the church accepted its juridical disestablishment by the state as valid in principle and not merely as a concession to the circumstances of secular modernity. After centuries of teaching to the contrary (for example, that "error has no rights"), does such a change constitute an authentic development of church doctrine? Or is it simply an inexplicable and by implication unwarranted "about-face"?

What if *Dignitatis Humanae* does represent a moment of genuine development? Might the same be true of church teaching elsewhere, perhaps on the neuralgic issues of artificial contraception, divorce, and women's ordination? More to the point, do recent papal and bishops' statements to the effect that capital punishment ought to be abolished, or its use at least severely curtailed, constitute a substantive change of centuries of ecclesial approbation of the death penalty? Or are these statements just so much tinkering at the rough edges of doctrine? Indeed, when it comes to Catholic moral doctrine, is there anything *but* rough edge?

There is no better context for examining these questions, and thus for observing the reformation of Catholic moral teaching instigated by Vatican II, than official church teaching around the (literally) life-and-death issues of abortion, euthanasia, and capital punishment. There are, of course, other life-and-death issues to which the church's magisterium has addressed itself since the Council. Nuclear war and poverty come immediately to mind, as do the many recent developments in bio-medical ethics (organ transplantation, embryo research, genetic engineering, etc.). However, where proclaiming and protecting the inviolable dignity of human life is concerned, official church teaching over the past forty years has coalesced around these three forms of killing in particular. Together they constitute the foundational practical issues within the "consistent ethic of life," the quasi-official approach to life issues that first emerged in the early 1980s in the work of Cardinal Joseph Bernardin of Chicago and that informs John Paul II's call, in *Evangelium Vitae* (1995), to build a "culture of life." The consistent ethic of life remains the church's most provocative, though still underdeveloped, contribution to the ongoing public debate over each of these issues.

To understand how these three issues came to be connected in church teaching as the preeminent threats to human life and dignity in our day is to learn a good deal about where Vatican II took Catholic moral doctrine on "the dignity of human life," where it has come since, and, with all due respect for the freedom of the Holy Spirit, where it might be going from here. Such is the basic aim of this essay, the three sections of which correspond roughly to this temporal sequence. My central claim is that the fundamental change in perspective articulated in the opening sections of *Gaudium et Spes*—widely described as a shift from a scholastic preoccupation with a static "human nature" to a more dynamic theological personalism—is less the transition from a purportedly "classicist" to a "historically minded" mentality, as many have argued, than the rediscovery and *repossession* of an ancient wisdom about the reckless generosity of God, the fragility of the good, and the fundamentally tragic character of entire cultures grown blind to their own blindness about the transcendent origin of human life. The consistent ethic of life extends and deepens two foundational insights that *Gaudium et Spes* repossessed from the ancient church: first, that our very life is the gift of a prodigal God ("He has given life abundantly to us"); and, second, that our capacity to both recognize this and respond in kind ("crying out in the Spirit: Abba, Father!"—both texts are from *GS* 22) is fatally compromised first by our tolerance and then further by our ratification of the lethal practices of abortion, euthanasia, and capital punishment.

This repossession distinguishes post-conciliar from pre-conciliar moral teaching more than any other single factor; and its most important consequence is an increasing appreciation in church teaching (above all on "life-issues") that the church itself is possessed by the Spirit who, together with the Father and the Son, constitutes its very life. One might say that, as official church teaching has "repossessed" an ancient wisdom, so too has the church been "repossessed" by the Spirit. Such a claim would be the height of arrogance—the worst of what many suspect governs the official Catholic approach to morality—were it not that understanding Catholic moral doctrine in these terms demands, for good trinitarian reasons, a conception of the church as journeying along what St. John of the Cross calls the way in which one "possesses not." The consistent ethic of life is from this perspective an ethic by and for those along this way: it is the *via crucis*, a way of dispossession. Its future, and the future of Catholic moral doctrine, will likely depend on its ability to bring life to the church, and thus bring the church to life.

## I.  Pre-conciliar church teaching on abortion, euthanasia, and capital punishment

Prior to Vatican II, magisterial statements on moral issues such as abortion, euthanasia, and capital punishment were very much the reflection of the more detailed treatment of these topics in the moral "manuals" that had dominated seminary instruction in moral theology for the past two centuries, and where, of course, popes and bishops had received their own training in the discipline. That approach, sometimes referred to as "scholastic," or "neo-scholastic," had the following major characteristics. Its principal concern was with the analysis of discrete *acts* (in contrast to character), understood as the results of the free and deliberate choices by which individuals realized both their proximate natural (happiness) and ultimate final good (beatitude). This meant, of course, that abortion and euthanasia were considered separately from capital punishment; for, among other things, the latter is not the act of a single individual, but of legitimate political authority, the state, acting through its representative.

The manuals were not unaware that human acts are performed by human beings, and thus not ultimately separable from questions of character and virtue. In some ways, questions about whether a particular act was fully voluntary (freely willed) or performed in full knowledge of the law were central to this entire approach, which was very much geared toward training priests to administer the sacrament of penance. Nevertheless, subjective issues such as individual culpability and the erring conscience took a clear back-seat to the main "objective" issue, namely, whether a particular act or kind of act was right or wrong, where right meant conformity to a principle or precept of natural, positive, or church *law*. When it came to the standard examples of abortion and euthanasia, the matter was clear and precise. As the deliberate taking of innocent human life, abortion and euthanasia contradicted the natural law precept that forbids killing (because it is contrary to the good of life), as well as the fifth commandment (which is but a divinely revealed articulation of the natural law), and were thus absolutely prohibited.

As with virtually all law-based approaches to morality, the moral manuals sidled slowly toward a sin-obsessed minimalism, that is, toward a preoccupation with the diverse ways in which the law might be transgressed, as well as with the possible exceptions to that law, the so-called "hard cases." Capital punishment, along with killing in war, was one of the better-known exceptions to the prohibition of direct killing. Indeed, more than simply exceptions, both capital punishment and war were actually justified on the grounds that the state was divinely mandated, for the sake of the common good, both to protect innocent life from unjust aggression, and to "execute wrath on the wrongdoer" (Rom 13:4). Few bishops challenged the practice, much less called for its abolition.

Questions about the nature and destiny of the human person were implicitly addressed by the structure of the twofold end of the human being assumed throughout the manuals; to the extent that they understand the ultimate end to be eternal beatitude with God, the manuals contain an at least implicitly theological view of human beings. But this broad theological canopy did little real work on such issues as killing, since the principles and norms of the natural law, and the natural virtue of justice, were sufficient to arrive at concrete determinations of right and wrong in all but the most extreme cases. On these issues, moral theology looked very much like moral *philosophy*: the Sermon on the Mount played a supporting role, at best.

Finally, it should be said that in this approach the language of human *nature* predominated over that of the human *person*. Much has been made of this distinction in post-conciliar moral theology, though the differences are often more apparent than real. Both terms are equally abstract, and to that extent equally polyvalent. The term "nature" has by and large been taken to connote a deductive or static anthropology, in which the *humanum* is defined ahead of time in terms of certain immutable "givens" (for example, the human being is defined as rational, free, possessing certain fixed inclinations, etc.). "Person," on the other hand, tends to connote an anthropology open to the ongoing empirical study of human nature and to that extent less focused on what is "given." Understood in this way, the distinction certainly does capture some important characteristics of both pre- and post-conciliar moral teaching.

The strength of Catholic moral doctrine informed by these various elements should not be lightly dismissed, especially where the issues revolve around the taking of life. The broadly *philosophical* approach before the Council allowed popes and bishops to address church, state, and society with a supreme confidence that what the church teaches is nothing other than what is universally confirmed by natural reason. The focus on *acts*, and their evaluation in terms of *law*, gave Catholic teaching a logical precision that enabled it to arrive at very specific conclusions regarding particular sorts of actions, and clearly to distinguish these from a range of analogous, but not identical types of action. Lynch mobs did not constitute legitimate authority; their murderous deeds were in fact unjustifiable killings. Not every removal or refusal of life-prolonging medical treatment was tantamount to killing the patient; under well-defined circumstances, forgoing such medical care could well be understood as charitable. Similarly, not every surgical intervention that foreseeably resulted in the death of the unborn child (for example, the removal of a cancerous uterus) constituted a direct abortion; so, not all such actions were always wrong. Finally, the confidence in an *unchanging human nature* was instrumental in consolidating the church's image as a bulwark against the rising tide of moral skepticism and relativism in Western intellectual and, increasingly, popular culture.

The power of this approach is very well illustrated by the August 3, 1941, sermon of Bishop Clemens August Graf von Galen, of Münster,

Germany, in which he spoke out vehemently against the by then not-so-secret Nazi "euthanasia program" (*Aktion T-4*), which had been implemented in 1939 to further cleanse Hitler's *Volk* of its mentally disabled and otherwise undesired members. (Earlier German episcopal conferences had likewise spoken strongly against the involuntary sterilization laws of 1933.) The British RAF even air-dropped copies of von Galen's sermon over Germany. The bishop's words effectively halted the program, though tragically the Nazis simply took the methods, and much of the equipment (gas chambers, furnaces, etc.) to the east, where they played a decisive role in the "Final Solution." Despite the fact that von Galen's sermon did nothing to prevent *that* abomination—and in this respect it is instructive to compare the clarity and vigor of church teaching on abortion and euthanasia with the centuries of its equivocation on anti-Semitism—it still can be appreciated as what official moral doctrine in the pre-conciliar mode was capable of achieving. Michael Burleigh puts it more bluntly: "The authoritarian and totalitarian aspects of Roman Catholicism proved its saving grace" (Burleigh, 42).

But von Galen was an exception. More typical is the story of Cardinal William O'Connell, Archbishop of Boston, who throughout the 1920s persistently maintained his position of public neutrality on one of the most troubling political events of that decade, the capital trial and eventual execution in Massachusetts (August 23, 1927) of Sacco and Vanzetti. Serious questions about the justice of the trial proceedings had been raised, and an anti-Italian, anti-Catholic gloom hung over everything. Privately, O'Connell appealed to Governor Fuller for clemency. Anything beyond that, however, he seemed to fear would be taken as unwarranted church interference in secular affairs: "always distasteful here," as he explained to Cardinal Hayes of New York (Toseillo, 53). Ironically, then, just as official church teaching on the absolute prohibition of direct killing of the innocent had empowered von Galen's very public opposition to the Nazis, so too official church teaching on the permissibility of capital punishment allowed O'Connell only a weak public statement, just days before the execution—and immediately following a personal audience with the condemned men's sisters—to the effect that human judgments are imperfect but nevertheless indispensable for the good order of society. And this on the case that did more to undermine public confidence in judicial procedure than perhaps any other in the United States prior to *Gore* v. *Bush*.

It might be argued that Cardinal O'Connell made poor use of the tradition at his disposal; after all, he *might* have spoken out more decisively, one way or the other. However, it is perhaps closer to the truth to say that the tradition of the moral manuals in which he had been formed was, by the 1920s, already showing how ill prepared it was to meet the challenges of contemporary politics, morality, and culture. Von Galen's heroics notwithstanding, the inability of the Vatican to avoid Hitler's cynical manipulation of it in 1933 is only the most startling illustration of this sad fact. As further evidence we have the remarkable admission of Bernard Häring (who would go on to play a major role in the revision of moral theology before, during, and after Vatican II) that during his seminary formation in the early 1930s (in Germany) the only course he truly detested was the one in moral theology! The primary text was Aertnys-Damen's *Theologia Moralis*, a well-known manual, which Häring disparages as an "incredibly legalistic" treatment of Christian morality. He and his fellow seminarians were able to master its lessons rather easily through rote memorization, using the lecture periods to catch up on sleep (Häring, 18).

What Häring, Lucker (in the text that opens this essay), and many others were noticing was that the dominant form of Catholic moral teaching had long since ceased to inspire the church. A recumbent people are in no position to receive life, much less give it. Vatican II, and specifically *Gaudium et Spes*, promised to change that.

## II. Vatican II on abortion, euthanasia, and capital punishment

Where then did the Council take official church teaching on abortion, euthanasia, and capital punishment? A quick read of *Gaudium et Spes* might suggest not very far at all. Abortion is mentioned only twice, euthanasia once, and capital punishment seems not to be addressed at all. (The only possible exception entails reading the statements referring to enemy-love in *GS* 28 to include condemned criminals among those to be loved: "We must distinguish between the error [which must always be rejected] and the people in error, who never lose their dignity.") Moreover, the references to abortion and euthanasia are slight. A first occurs within the often-cited list of "crimes" in *Gaudium et Spes* 27, where abortion appears alongside euthanasia, in the only instance where the two are mentioned together; a second, to abortion only, occurs in *Gaudium et Spes* 51, in the chapter on the "The Dignity of Marriage and Family," where it is quickly eclipsed by the issue of the "responsible transmission of life."

First appearances are deceiving, however, for a closer examination reveals that *Gaudium et Spes* addresses very few practical issues with any degree of detail. The long second part, "Some Problems of Special Urgency," which takes up five rather broad moral issues (marriage and family; the development of culture; economic and social life; political community; war and peace), comes closest to doing so, but could not be mistaken for a treatise in applied moral theology. Indeed, on at least one set of vexing practical issues ("population, family, and births"), the document explicitly defers to the expertise of the special papal commission that had been formed to give these topics "further and more careful investigation" (GS 51, note 14). In other words, the relative silence of *Gaudium et Spes* on these three issues should not be taken as evidence that the Council was unwilling to reconsider them, or their relationship to each other, within official church teaching.

In fact, given the sort of concerns raised in the first part of the document—especially the challenge of modern atheism (GS 19–21)—*Gaudium et Spes* is unmistakably involved in the revision of Catholic moral doctrine at its fundamental levels. And because the "tectonic" movements of these deeper strata of moral doctrine invariably affect *all* the more specific practical issues at the surface, it is more accurate to say that not even the smallest pebble of Catholic moral doctrine was left untouched by the Council. With respect to church teaching on abortion, euthanasia, and capital punishment, these deeper shifts eventually led to narrowing the "divides" that had separated their individual treatment in pre-conciliar moral teaching. That is to say, these foundational shifts led to the emergence of a "consistent ethic of life."

The single most important and widely acknowledged shift in this regard is the one that brings the question regarding the human person ("But what is humanity?," GS 12) to the center of all moral inquiry, and which makes the *integral* good of the human person the measure of all moral action and political policy. This "personalist" approach is the most familiar post-conciliar characteristic not only of Catholic moral doctrine but of most moral theology as well. At its heart is the conviction that no genuinely human response to moral and political problems can avoid entering into the mystery that is the human person, and confronting there the profound questions about the human person: "Who are we?"; "Where did we come from?"; "Where are we going?" Though post-conciliar morality still seeks what pre-conciliar morality had called the human good *as such,* its focus on the "person" does capture a much different understanding of how, and where, we actually discern the humanly good *as such.*

What *Gaudium et Spes* presupposes by the concept "person" is not a timeless human essence encountered in clear and distinct propositions, which can never be touched or harmed, but a striving, historical, embodied subject. We are French Catholic philosopher Pascal's (1623–1662) "reed," simultaneously the most fragile and most glorious of creatures. What results is a concept of goodness that is itself both glorious and fragile, captured well in the title of contemporary American moral philosopher Martha Nussbaum's book *The Fragility of Goodness*. The human *longing* to know and enjoy the truly good, to be free to do so, without fear, in community with others, with at least the minimum of material conditions necessary for the pursuit, is *itself* an integral aspect of that good. To conceive of it as such is immediately to be reminded of how delicate this good is, how much the modern world, while giving lip service to it, actually fails in its various practices to respect it, or more often than not subverts it in the service of power for its own sake. Here, then, is how to read the catalogue of "crimes" in *Gaudium et Spes* 27: as the set of contemporary (and in some cases *ancient*) practices that threaten the fragile good of human persons.

*Gaudium et Spes* has been mistakenly criticized for its overly optimistic assessment of the human person, for not taking sin seriously enough, as well as for a somewhat Pollyannaish attitude toward contemporary culture. What such criticisms fail to grasp is that its account of the human good as perennially fragile means that *Gaudium et Spes* must take sin, attacks upon that good, *more* seriously, not less. The forms of wickedness listed in *Gaudium et Spes* 27 could be described, in the language of the manuals, as transgressions of a law or command, that is, as so many models of disobedience. *Gaudium et Spes* prefers another idiom, one which raises the stakes of moral behavior much higher: these are deeds that "poison civilization . . . [that] debase the perpetrators more than the victims and militate against the honor of the creator." Those who perform these deeds, as well as cultures and regimes that countenance them, shrivel. Such are the truly disabled, who steadily lose their ability to abandon themselves for their neighbor's sake and who ultimately lose sight not only of their neighbor in need, but of God. There is something dreadful contemplated here; switching metaphors slightly, we might describe it as the prospect of entire cultures beset by a moral asthma: choked not by an inability to inhale, but rather by an inability to exhale, to "cry out in the Spirit, 'Abba, Father,'" and to that extent unable to recognize a sister and brother in the face of every neighbor.

The list of misdeeds in *Gaudium et Spes* 27 also discloses another consequence of the shift that brought the integral good of the human person into the center of Catholic moral life and thought: a new *synoptic* approach to morality, in which a variety of issues, once treated disparately, are now brought together in a more unified and *poetic* mode of analysis. One might bemoan the loss of the precision and logical rigor that had been the hallmark of the moral manuals. Many have. On the other hand, what is lost in precision is more than made up for by the opening of what might be called the "analogical moral imagination." That the otherwise disparate crimes in *Gaudium et Spes* 27 are but different forms of assault on the good of human persons forces one to reconsider the underlying unity of these crimes, and, more important, the underlying unity of the moral life as a whole. Abortion is not exactly like unfair labor practices (or war, or capital punishment), but the similarities are sufficient to require one to check the centrifugal forces that separate the immediate unity of moral experience into often artificial categories. As is by now perhaps obvious, *Gaudium et Spes* 27 ought to be seen in this light as the precursor of the "consistent ethic of life."

It is worth noting, finally, that this analogical approach to moral issues is not new at all. It is in fact characteristic of the most important theologians of the early church (above all Augustine, who never met a tangent he didn't pursue), the Hebrew prophets, whose minds were brimming with metaphor, and, not least, Jesus himself, whose parables opened more than a few ears and brought many to life.

If the integral good of the human being is the measure of all things moral, the measure of the human being is Jesus, the incarnate *logos* and wisdom of God. *Gaudium et Spes* is unequivocal about this. The personalism it propounds is not simply the highest of high humanisms, but a deeply *theological* personalism. The true height and depth of human dignity, which from a worldly promontory can only be guessed at, is fully disclosed in the trinitarian light of the one creator God made manifest in the life, death, and resurrection of Jesus. As *Gaudium et Spes* puts it:

> Further, the Lord Jesus, when praying to the Father, "that they may all be one . . . even as we are one" (Jn 17:21-22), has opened up new horizons closed to human reason by indicating that there is a certain similarity between the union existing among the divine persons and the union of God's children in truth and love. It follows, then, that if human beings are the only creatures on earth that God has wanted for their own sake, they can fully discover their true selves only through a sincere gift of self. (*GS* 24, slightly amended)

The key word here is, of course, *gift*. *Gaudium et Spes* invites its reader to ponder the astonishing dignity of every human life as nothing less than a divine truth freely *given*, and in its light to realign one's relationships with neighbor, self, and, above all, with God. Thus, what in the manuals had been merely backdrop—the Spirit-led journey into God's own life—becomes the foreground of Catholic moral thought. Appropriately, *Gaudium et Spes* closes its first chapter, in good evangelical fashion, with a (Byzantine) liturgical hymn to life: "It is therefore through Christ, and in Christ, that light is thrown on the mystery of suffering and death which, apart from his Gospel, overwhelms us. Christ has risen again, destroying death by his death, and has given life abundantly to us so that becoming sons in the Son, we may cry out in the Spirit: Abba, Father!" (*GS* 22).

In summary, then, while it might appear that Vatican II left official teaching on such issues as abortion, euthanasia, and capital punishment untouched, in actuality the Council dramatically shifted the foundations on which all moral issues, but especially those concerning the dignity of human life, would henceforth be understood to rest. By bringing the question about the human person into the center of Catholic moral inquiry, it opened the way for a richer understanding of the human good, and for a more serious appreciation of its fragility in the face of modern threats to it. At the same time, it also provided a new point of unity and restored an imaginative method for investigating the relationship between a wide range of both life-giving and life-taking actions within the moral life as a whole. Finally, it restored to Catholic moral doctrine its evangelical and doxological flavor by bringing its latent theological context forward. Particularly in light of this final achievement, we might say that Vatican II was the occasion for the repossession of the church's moral doctrine, and itself, as *gift*. What the church teaches is but what it has heard, seen, and touched with its hands (1 Jn 1:1-3). It follows, then, that ceaseless giving, endless dispossession, is the inner logic of church teaching. One would be hard-pressed to find this lived and living teaching on the pages of a pre-conciliar moral manual.

## III.  Official teaching since Vatican II

What did the conciliar reformation of Catholic moral doctrine accomplish, especially on the questions of abortion, euthanasia, and capital punishment? Through its recovery of the evangelical and doxological sources of both the content and form of Catholic moral wisdom, the

Council liberated church teaching on these issues from the irrelevance to which it had all but succumbed by the early 1960s. It might be thought strange to claim that it is through an *emphasis* on the scriptural and liturgical foundations of Catholic moral life that the church's teaching on abortion, euthanasia, and capital punishment was rescued from irrelevance, because it is often assumed that the church purchases its relevance at the cost of its particular identity. However, this assumption overlooks the fact that pre-conciliar Catholic moral doctrine was both generic (by design) *and* irrelevant, not only for much of contemporary culture, but for many Catholics as well (recall Häring's unfriendly remarks about his seminary training in moral theology).

In short, the Council gave the church something worth saying to contemporary culture, and within the church, something worth arguing about. In doing so, the church hardly abandoned its high estimation of natural reason; on the contrary, the church takes natural reason seriously enough to debate its requirements—*Should capital punishment really be the law of the land?*—precisely because of and not despite the church's theological convictions. Consequently, in an odd-seeming but perfectly logical corollary to all this, the Council's liberation of moral doctrine has rendered that doctrine more capable of forming a particular people. To be drawn into contemporary debates among Catholics about abortion, euthanasia, and capital punishment is to be made part of a tradition of moral inquiry in which one is trained to appreciate what matters morally and why.

Accordingly, the years since Vatican II have seen a flurry of official statements and declarations on each of the three issues. To name only the most significant, on abortion: *Humanae Vitae* (Paul VI, 1968), "Declaration on Procured Abortion" (Congregation for the Doctrine of the Faith [CDF], 1974), "*Donum Vitae*" (CDF, 1987), "Faithful for Life" (National Conference of Catholic Bishops [NCCB], 1995); on euthanasia: "Declaration on Euthanasia" (CDF, 1980), "Nutrition and Hydration: Moral and Pastoral Reflections" (NCCB, 1992); on capital punishment: "Statement on Capital Punishment" (NCCB, 1980); "Responsibility, Rehabilitation, and Restoration: A Catholic Perspective on Crime and Criminal Justice" (United States Conference of Catholic Bishops [USCCB], 2000). Each of these documents reflects the influence of Vatican II, and *Gaudium et Spes* in particular, to varying degrees. All quite clearly adopt an evaluative framework in which the integral good of the person is the fundamental measure of individual action, public morality, and civil legislation. A theological, indeed scriptural framework is explicitly invoked (for example,

Jesus' words and deeds as a model for assessing proper care of the un-born and vulnerable aged, penal policy, etc.).

Far more important than any of these statements taken individually, however, is the emergence of abortion, euthanasia, and capital punishment as the foundational "linked" issues in what is without doubt the most important post-conciliar development in official doctrine regarding human life: the "consistent ethic of life" and the magisterial document that in many ways embodies that ethic, John Paul II's encyclical *Evangelium Vitae* (1995). As noted above, the consistent ethic of life was already anticipated by *Gaudium et Spes*, in particular in the list of crimes against human life in *Gaudium et Spes* 27. However, it was only in the early 1980s that the ethic came to articulation as a potentially coherent approach to moral issues touching on the protection and promotion of life. Cardinal Joseph Bernardin, Archbishop of Chicago, who as president of the United States Conference of Catholic Bishops had just recently shepherded to its publication that body's document on U.S. nuclear policy ("The Challenge of Peace: God's Promise and Our Response," 1983), delivered a series of lectures reflecting on how in the process of drafting that statement he had come to appreciate the interconnection between a variety of contemporary assaults on the dignity of human life: war, poverty, abortion, euthanasia, and capital punishment. He proposed that there was, or at least ought to be, a "link" between these issues in Catholic moral doctrine. He saw the link as resting on two fundamental principles: that all human life is sacred and all human life is social. Together, he argued, these two principles constitute the warp and woof of the "seamless garment" of Catholic moral doctrine about human life. (See Bernardin's lectures in Feuchtman, 1988.)

The idea that these five issues could be coherently addressed on the basis of these two principles alone was quickly criticized by a variety of Catholic moral theologians, and since then the consistent ethic of life has not undergone any appreciable development in those quarters. Despite this, it continues to inform the U.S. bishops' approach to virtually all moral issues and has even become the platform of a secular movement advocating non-violent social change (see www.seamless-garment.org). Further development awaits the outcome of current debates over the meaning of magisterial opposition to capital punishment. The key issue, as noted at the very outset of this essay, is whether such opposition represents a genuine development of official church teaching or only its adjustment in light of present circumstance. While these debates are important on their own terms, it is equally important not to forget how they arose in the first place, and here it is necessary to see the massive influence of *Gaudium et Spes* on *Evangelium Vitae*, whose promulgation in 1995 touched off the contemporary furor. Among other things, it made it necessary to revise the *Catechism of the Catholic Church* to reflect John Paul II's statement that the execution of criminals is morally legitimate in only the most exceptional of cases, namely, when there would be no other way of protecting society. According to the pope such cases are today "rare, if not practically nonexistent" (*EV* 56; see *Catechism of the Catholic Church,* 2267).

It is puzzling that *Evangelium Vitae* considers capital punishment to be on the same page as abortion and euthanasia in the catalogue of significant contemporary threats to human life and its dignity. It wasn't there in *Gaudium et Spes* 27; nor, as noted above, has the tradition considered it a matter of individual morality, like abortion and euthanasia. It is the infliction of punishment by the state on justly convicted criminals, that is, on the guilty, not the innocent, which according to long-standing Catholic tradition is not only the right but the duty of political authority to inflict. However, a careful reading of *Evangelium Vitae*'s first chapter dispels the confusion. That chapter describes a situation that had already been warned of: "Often refusing to acknowledge God as their source, men and women have also upset the relationship which should link them to their final destiny" (*GS* 13; see also the treatment of atheism in *GS* 19–22). Three decades later, the pope sees an application of the Council's words in the growing number of the world's "democracies" in which abortion, euthanasia, and capital punishment are sanctioned in both public morality and law.

At the risk of oversimplification, the unifying theme is "culture," an issue already espied by *Gaudium et Spes* (53–62) in its assertion that the true and full development of the human person occurs only "through culture." For the Council, "culture" means "the cultivation of the goods and values of nature . . . all those things which go to the refining and developing of humanity's diverse mental and physical endowments" (*GS* 53).

Attacks on the good of human life in contemporary culture differ from those of predecessor cultures, argues John Paul II, in that they are often "scientifically and systematically programmed," claimed in public morality as integral to the exercise of a distorted concept of individual liberty, and, ominously, protected by the laws of the very institution—the State—responsible for defending life. Nowhere in *Evangelium Vitae* is the question explicitly put, but it fairly cries out on every page: how can a State whose concept of justice permits the deliberate destruction of *innocent* human life be entrusted to employ the gravest of human punishments? Can a State that forswears a transcendent order of justice through its commitment to an ever more expansive definition of individual liberty long conceal its true character as what Augustine called a "large robbery"? John Paul II has, in effect, diagnosed how morally "asthmatic" contemporary liberal democracies have become.

This is, in short, the provocative issue at the heart of current Catholic moral doctrine on human life. It is an issue that takes us directly back to the pages of *Gaudium et Spes*, not only those concerned with the issue of culture or even with the various crimes against life, but to those concerned with the challenge of modern atheism. And to this extent *Evangelium Vitae*, with its stark opposition between a "culture of life" and a "culture of death," takes us back even further to the early, prophetic roots of Christian morality. From this perspective, choosing the "way of life" means more than committing to a set of "pro-life" socio-economic programs and political policies. It means radically revising one's concept of life itself. In what is partly an exegesis of *Gaudium et Spes* 24 ("that human beings . . . can fully discover their true selves only in sincere self-giving") John Paul II proposes that this revision ultimately brings us to contemplate the cross, from which Jesus, who died loving those who were killing him, proclaims that "*life finds its center, its meaning and its fulfillment when it is given up*" (*EV* 51, emphasis in original). "At this point," the Pope immediately concludes, "our meditation becomes *praise* and *thanksgiving,* and at the same time urges us to imitate Christ and follow in his footsteps" (emphasis added). It may well be that the chief "pro-life" work of the church is to help its surrounding culture learn to breathe once more, precisely by both singing out and living its commitment to a "culture of life."

## Conclusion:
## Whither church teaching on "life"?

Where the church's moral doctrine on the dignity of human life—the consistent ethic of life—will go from here is in part a question of the ongoing "reception" of *Evangelium Vitae*. Among theologians the main questions, at least in the short run, will be two: whether its teaching on capital punishment constitutes a genuine "development" in moral doctrine and, second, what structured account of Catholic moral theology best captures the reformations in Catholic morality begun at Vatican II (including whether the consistent ethic of life represents a more coherent approach than any of its alternatives to the moral questions regarding the protection and promotion of human life). For the church as a whole, the people of God, the issues are far weightier. The crucial question is whether the trajectory of church doctrine on human life from *Gaudium et Spes* to *Evangelium Vitae* will continue to have the power of forming a people capable of traversing the way in which one "possesses not," of looking upon the cross as its fulfillment and only hope. A spate of interest, both popular and scholarly (for example, see Robert Royal's recent book), suggests that the most significant voices in answer to this question will not be theological, at least not in the narrow academic sense. Rather, if the character of that trajectory is indeed one of responding to God's "abundant gift" by our own giving, then the answer to this question will be found where it always has been: in the lives of the saints and, especially, the martyrs. Bishop Lucker understood this:

> A teacher is effective to the extent that he or she is a witness. Pope Paul VI said one time that "Modern men and women listen more willingly to witnesses than to teachers, and if they do listen to teachers it is because they are witnesses." A witness is one who shows by his or her life what they believe, what they stand for. (Lucker, 433)

## References

Burleigh, Michael. *Death and Deliverance: Euthanasia in Germany, 1900–1945.* Cambridge: Cambridge University Press, 1994.

Feuchtman, Thomas, ed. *The Consistent Ethic of Life.* Kansas City: Sheed & Ward, 1988.

Häring, Bernard. *Free and Faithful: My Life in the Catholic Church.* Liguori, Mo.: Liguori/Triumph, 1997.

Royal, Robert. *The Catholic Martyrs of the Twentieth Century.* New York: Crossroad Publishing Co., 2000.

Toseillo, Rosario Joseph. "'Requests I Cannot Ignore'—A New Perspective on the Role of Cardinal O'Connell in the Sacco-Vanzetti Case." *The Catholic Historical Review* 68/1 (January, 1982): 46–53.

# 11
## *Gaudium et Spes* on marriage:
## What "went forward"?
## What might be "going forward" now?

RUSSELL B. CONNORS, JR.

In his brief pastoral letter "Sexual Responsibility," Bishop Lucker wrote the following about sex:

> Sex, our human sexuality, is holy. It makes us God-like ... We are like God not only in that we can think and choose—that is, in our spirit. We are also like God in our bodies, in our sexuality. We share with God himself the power to create, to give life. Men and women are given the awesome gift of bringing into the world other human beings who are also called to eternal life.
>
> Sexual union is holy, beautiful, life giving and joyful in marriage where two people have freely committed themselves to one another for life. Intercourse is a sign of total human giving. Sexual union outside a permanent total commitment is not responsible. It becomes recreational sex, selfish sex, sex for fun. (Lucker, 225)

These words display that Bishop Lucker was a man of the Second Vatican Council. He knew the teachings and convictions of the Council well. This is certainly the case in regard to the Council's teaching on marriage as it was briefly but significantly stated in the Pastoral Constitution on the Church in the Modern World *(Gaudium et Spes)* in paragraphs 47–52. To use a phrase of the late Jesuit theologian Bernard Lonergan, one of the tasks of theology—and particularly the historian of theology—is to try to discern what might be "going forward" in the

191

church's theology and teaching at any given time (Lonergan, 178, 189, 319–326). Nearly forty years after *Gaudium et Spes,* Bishop Lucker's words help us see that something (actually several things) "went forward" in the Council's teaching on marriage.

At the risk of reducing (and oversimplifying) Vatican II's important teaching on marriage to a few sentences, I offer the following paragraph as an attempt to display some of the key elements of that teaching. I will use many of *Gaudium et Spes*'s own words to do so. Paragraph numbers from the Council's text are in parentheses.

> Marriage is first and foremost a most special form of friendship (par. 49), an "intimate partnership of life and love" (par. 48), the type of love that in its center is a love that is "eminently human" (par. 49) in that it involves the mutual self-giving of one's whole being—body, affections, mind and spirit— to another (par. 49). Because of the nature of this type of authentic human love and also because it is a mirror of divine love (par. 50), married love moves creatively beyond itself in the way it is "ordered to the procreation and education of children" (par. 50). This intimate covenant (par. 48) of life and love and this form of mutual self-bestowal (pars. 48, 49) reveal, in a particularly dramatic way, something of the nature of God and of God's love. Married love wells up "from the spring of divine love"; (par. 48) it is "caught up" (Latin: *assumitur*) into divine love (par. 48), and is a marvelous sign or sacrament of God's love for humankind and Christ's love for the Church (pars. 48, 49). In a word, authentic married love—both as fully human reality and as sacrament of the divine—is marked by *fruitfulness,* as parents receive the "supreme gift" (par. 50) of children. Although marriage is "not instituted solely for procreation" (par. 50), the fruitfulness of married life and love is manifested in a preeminent (but not exclusive) way in its openness to new life.

Three convictions in the Council's teaching on marriage stand out. First, and most fundamental, is an appreciation that the special partnership that is marriage and the special form of love that is at its center are first and foremost *human realities.* Second, one of the essential marks of the intimate and loving partnership of marriage is its *fruitfulness.* Third, both as a special form of friendship and as an intimate and loving partnership marked by fruitfulness, married love is "caught up" (*assumitur*) into divine love; that is, it is a magnificent sign or sacrament of the love of God and of God's partnership with humankind. The three parts of this article that follow will reflect, in turn, on each of these three convictions in the teaching of *Gaudium et Spes* on marriage. Emphasis will be on the first conviction—the Council's recognition of marriage and marital love (in all its dimensions) as fully human realities—because in my view this is the most significant "accomplishment" of the document's teaching on marriage. To be sure, the three convictions are intimately connected to one another, so there is something difficult about discussing them separately. Along the way, therefore, I will try to do justice to the way in which the Council's teachings on marriage are woven together so well.

The thesis here is that these three convictions regarding marriage "went forward" at Vatican II. The Council's teaching was an accomplishment in that it went a long way to leave certain old and stubborn ideas behind as it articulated its positive understanding of the intimate and loving partnership that is marriage. At the same time, as the phrase "going forward" suggests, the Council's teaching was not the last word. Since the Council, the teaching on marriage (by both theologians and bishops) has developed further. At the very least, a number of important questions seem to continue to "go forward" today—perhaps as "unfinished business"—in light of the teaching of *Gaudium et Spes* on marriage. I will note and reflect briefly on some of those questions as we proceed.

## I. Marriage as human reality:
## An "intimate partnership of life and love"

After an introductory paragraph (*GS* 47) that describes first some of the ways marriage and family life are "esteemed" and supported in the modern world and then some of the ways in which marriage and the family are threatened, *Gaudium et Spes* (in par. 48) begins its own theological discussion of marriage by describing it as an "intimate partnership of life and love." This is the first and perhaps most important thing the Council fathers said about the nature of marriage.

In the Latin text, the phrase under examination here is *intima communitas vitae et amoris coniugalis*. Married partners form an intimate *community*, a special partnership (as *communitas* is most frequently translated). Elsewhere (par. 49) the word "friendship" is used. In that context married love is described as "eminently human" (par. 49) particularly in regard to the physical expressions of affection and love that are manifestations of the friendship (*amicitiae*) proper to marriage (par. 49). Whatever else marriage is, it is a *human reality*, a most special and important interpersonal partnership.

What could be more basic, more obvious, than this? And yet it is important to recognize that in 1965 this emphasis on marriage as *first and foremost* a human partnership, an interpersonal relationship, and a special form of friendship constituted something "going forward" in the church's teaching. Indeed this new emphasis "went forward" with something less than complete consistency; the same paragraphs of *Gaudium et Spes* also describe marriage in less personal, less relational categories; the text sometimes refers to "the married state" and to marriage as an institution (48).

Although these differences in the description of marriage are not irreconcilable, the difference in emphasis is dramatic. This is partly explained by the stunning differences between the texts submitted in 1962 to the "Preparatory Commission" (under the leadership of Cardinal Alfredo Ottaviani from what was then known as the "Holy Office," the Vatican office concerned with Catholic doctrine) and the final text of *Gaudium et Spes* in 1965. Theologian Theodore Mackin described this fascinating and important historical "moment" extremely well in his *What Is Marriage? Marriage in the Catholic Church*.

In Mackin's view, the text that captures best what the Holy Office *hoped* the Council would say about marriage is the following:

> It is most opportune to recall, clarify and reconfirm the main headings on the doctrine of marriage: its origin, its end, its essential properties, its use. Then it should examine and define in the matters of birth control, periodic continence, *amplexus reservatus* [withdrawal after intercourse, without ejaculation], artificial insemination, consummation (penetration and semination), impotency, therapeutic abortion, mixed marriages, and the Petrine privilege, so called. There should be a careful examination of the validity of marriages in general of the baptized, and of the conditions of this validity. (Mackin, 249)

As this text indicates, if Cardinal Ottaviani had gotten his way, what the Council would have done regarding marriage would have been to provide a concise and careful canonical definition of marriage, stating precisely—in traditional categories—what is necessary for a valid marriage to exist between baptized persons. Included would have been a catalogue of the church's teachings on a host of moral issues, most notably about the sexual practices that are right and wrong for married couples. In Mackin's view, those behind the proposed text of the Holy Office hoped that the bishops would "condemn the new errors" that had gained popularity in the decades before the Council, especially the *increased* emphasis on love in marriage and the *decreased* satisfaction with describing marriage by reference to its primary and secondary ends: procreation and the mutual aid of the spouses. In a reply to several cardinals who had criticized the text, particularly for the way it left virtually unrecognized the significance of love in marriage, Ottaviani replied that talk about marital love "must all be taken with a grain of salt (*cum mica salis*)" (Mackin, 256).

As history would have it, of course, Ottaviani did *not* get his way. The bishops rejected the juridical, technical, and moralistic approach to Christian marriage proposed by the Holy Office and instead, under the leadership of Cardinals Doepfner, Frings, Alfrink, Leger, and Bea, opted for an approach that would be, as Bea put it, "less juridical—more positive and constructive" (Mackin, 257). What "went forward," then, was a description of marriage that is based on the conviction that marriage is first and foremost a *human reality*, that sees the intimate partnership of marriage as a special form of *love and friendship*, and that presumes that *sexual intimacy* in marriage is important for the life of the marriage relationship. Let us examine briefly each of these three elements of the teaching in *Gaudium et Spes*.

### Marriage as a human reality

What is so important about emphasizing that marriage—the sacrament of marriage—is first and foremost a human reality? The answer to that question connects us to one of the primary themes of this book—the nature of divine revelation. To say that the sacrament of marriage is first of all a human reality is to recognize that human experience itself is *capable of* being a "doorway to the sacred." As theologian Richard McBrien has explained so well, God's presence in the world, God's revelation to humankind, is a *mediated* reality. God's loving presence is made known to us *in and through* human experience (McBrien, 11–12). Human experience, in all its concrete, historical, evolving, and diverse "messiness," is *capable of* disclosing God's loving presence. This is perhaps the most fundamental "methodological" conviction of *Gaudium et Spes*. Followers of Christ should pay close attention to "the joys and hopes, the grief and anguish" (par. 1) of human beings; we must seek to read carefully "the signs of the times" (par. 4) because it is in and through our experiences as human beings that God's presence and God's will can be made known to us. What the Council fathers wrote about marriage—emphasizing that it is first of all a human reality—is very much in keeping with this central theme of *Gaudium et Spes*.

In the previous paragraph I have placed the phrase *capable of* in italics in order to note something important: human experience is *capable of* being a "doorway to the sacred," but there is nothing automatic about it. Human beings are *capable of* all sorts of other things as well: deception (most insidious, I think, is self-deception), selfishness, injustice, and of course violence—in a word, sin. Our daily newspapers—on virtually any day—remind us all too well of this sobering fact. So, even though it remains the case that human experience is *capable of* being a means of God's revelation to us—a claim that might be called "Catholic optimism"—we ought not be naïve about this. Perhaps this is why the Council fathers began *Gaudium et Spes* (par. 4) by telling us that we must read carefully the "signs of the times," sifting through the ups and downs of human experience in order to discern the presence of the spirit of God at work within us. Catholic tradition urges us to be optimistic in regard to what humankind is *capable of* being and doing; but we must be wise as well.

An important implication of this emphasis on experience, and one of the things that continues to "go forward" in Catholic theology since the Council, is a renewed emphasis on human experience as a source of theological reflection, indeed a source of God's revelation. From liberation theology's call to attend to the concrete experience of the poor as a "privileged place" of God's care and compassion, to feminist scholars urging us to include the experiences and voices of women in what "counts" as human experience through which God's Spirit may be revealed, to the challenging voices of gay and lesbian persons asking that their experiences of friendship and love "count" as human experiences that might "open up" to the sacred, theology today is marked by a dramatic turn to experience. What "went forward" at Vatican II—with the recognition that marriage is first and foremost a *human reality* being an example—is the conviction that theology must give an adequate account of concrete human experience in order for its theological conclusions to make any real sense to believers.

### Marriage as a form of love and friendship

What is so important about emphasizing that marriage is a special form of *love and friendship*? Again, who does not know this? What could be more basic? Sadly, however, Catholicism seemed to have lost a firm grip on this fundamental truth. In its desire to bolster the social *institution* of marriage and perhaps to protect it from the apparent vagaries and fragility associated with love, Catholic teaching had emphasized with increasing rigor that marriage is fundamentally an institution that is meant to serve its primary end: the procreation and education of children. Surely, the love and mutual support of the spouses is to be encouraged, but the nature of marriage itself, recent Catholic teaching had insisted, should not be founded on something as fragile as human love.

It is nothing less than a breakthrough, then, that *Gaudium et Spes* returned to such a basic human reality—the gift and mystery of human love and friendship—as the centerpiece of its reflections on Christian marriage. Although the bishops did not seek to define the nature of marriage with the precision that church lawyers desire, their description of marriage gave great emphasis to the centrality of human love. Marriage is a special form of friendship, an intimate partnership of life and love, a covenant that involves the loving and mutual gift of self to another. The Council fathers could not have disagreed more with Cardinal Ottaviani in concluding that the reality of love in marriage must be taken very seriously, and not at all with a grain of salt.

The influence of this renewed emphasis on human love in marriage has been significant; but in some ways, perhaps, the full truth of this conviction is still "sinking in." When Pope Paul VI reaffirmed traditional Catholic teaching's opposition to artificial means of birth control, for example, he knew that it would not do simply to say that the wrongness of contraception is that it interferes with the primary end of marriage, namely procreation (as Pope Pius XI had been able to say in 1930). Rather, he needed to show that birth control is incompatible with the true meaning of marital love (*Humanae Vitae*, pars. 7–9). That, quite obviously, is a subtler and frankly more difficult argument to make than Pius XI's argument. As we know, the argument in Paul VI's 1968 encyclical convinced many Catholics, but certainly not all. Many others have understood love in marriage in a way that insists that although the loving marital *relationship* should be open to new life, each and every expression of love in intercourse need not be. John Paul II took up where Paul VI left off, and has spent much of his papacy emphasizing the beauty and sacredness of marital love, arguing that it calls for a total gift of self that is rendered incomplete and less-than-truthful by the use of contraception (*Familiaris Consortio*, pars. 11, 32). The point here is simply this: Catholic teaching about marriage and about a host of important moral issues has been significantly different—indeed more complex—because of what "went forward" in *Gaudium et Spes*.

Canon lawyers—church lawyers—have likewise been challenged by the church's new emphasis on love in marriage. As canonist Charles Guarino has explained, in the past when the church was asked to consider the possibility of declaring the annulment of a marriage, it did so by considering the nature of marriage in somewhat narrow, but clear categories: "procreative rights and obligations" (Guarino, 369). More expansive considerations, such as whether or not a person was capable of a mutually loving and supportive interpersonal relationship, or whether or not he or she was capable of a total gift of self to another, were not considered. Today, however, in light of the Council's teaching that marriage involves human friendship, an "intimate partnership of life and love," canonists have had to (been allowed to) consider a much wider range of issues in considering whether or not a genuine marital covenant had been established. And so the grounds for annulment have expanded, and the arguments and conclusions of tribunal judges have become more subtle, more complex, and, to be sure, more controversial.

The Council's teaching on the centrality of love in marriage could hardly have been more central in the mind of Bishop Lucker. His pastoral letters display a consistent, steadfast effort to emphasize the centrality of love and friendship in marriage. What is also evident in his writings is the conviction that love and friendship are central ingredients of human flourishing *for all people*, married or not. In one of his pastoral letters, Bishop Lucker acknowledged that this is an insight he came to somewhat late in his life: in order for his own life, including his spiritual life, to flourish he had to attend to his need for friendship and love. This humble reflection of his gives us a glimpse of Raymond Lucker as a "work-in-progress" (Lucker, 324–325).

### Marriage and sexual intimacy

As we have seen, *Gaudium et Spes* described marriage as "eminently human" (par. 49). Married love, the bishops taught, involves a special affection that "can enrich the sentiments of the spirit and their physical expression with a unique dignity and ennoble them as the special features and manifestations of the friendship proper to marriage" (par. 49). Later on the bishops emphasized the importance of sexual intimacy in marriage by noting that when "the intimacy of married life is broken, it often happens that faithfulness is imperiled and the good of the children suffers" (par. 51). Circumstances that break off such intimacy are deeply regrettable and, one would presume, ought to be avoided if at all possible.

Once again, we might ask, who does not know this? Nonetheless, such acknowledgment of the importance of sexual relations for the welfare of the marital relationship is something of a break-through in *Gaudium et Spes*. In the decades prior to the Council, Catholic teaching had emphasized that sex in marriage was primarily for the purpose of procreation and only secondarily for the mutual benefit of the spouses. Though *Gaudium et Spes* does not disavow that conviction explicitly, its emphasis is very different. Sexual relations are seen as part and parcel of the human reality of marriage itself, as fundamentally good, and as an important source of affective and spiritual nourishment for the marital relationship itself. These convictions are very different, for example, from the ones that Cardinal Ottaviani and the Holy Office had hoped the bishops at the Council would make their own.

If it is the case—and it is—that the emphasis on love in marriage and on the importance of sexual intimacy in marriage are part of what "went forward" in *Gaudium et Spes*, it is also the case that these emphases seemed to make the task of Paul VI more difficult in *Humanae Vitae*. The pope reaffirmed the church's traditional opposition to artificial means of birth control and called for couples who need to limit the size of their family to forgo sexual relations, restricting sexual intercourse to natural periods of infertility. Depending upon a variety of circumstances, that can mean that for some couples the intimate manifestations of love proper to marriage—deemed very important for the well-being of the marital relationship in *Gaudium et Spes* three years earlier —may in fact be possible only rarely. That, of course, is part of what the controversy concerning Catholic teaching on birth control has been about for the past thirty-five years. On one hand, as part of its recognition of the human reality of marriage, recent Catholic teaching emphasizes the importance of sexual intimacy in the marriage relationship. On the other hand, Catholic moral teaching calls for married couples to forgo sexual intimacy in order to live in accord with the requirements of the natural moral law. As did Paul VI, Pope John Paul II has recognized that this teaching would create situations for some couples that would be "arduous," and that some would be "tormented by difficulties" as they tried to live faithfully in accord with the church's teaching, especially in regard to periodic abstinence from sexual intercourse, perhaps for long periods of time. And the pope has acknowledged that "many couples would encounter difficulties not only in the concrete fulfillment of the moral norm but even in understanding its inherent values" (*Familiaris Consortio* 33). No one disagrees that on these matters he is surely right.

## II. The "fruitfulness" of married life and love

As we have seen, prior to the Second Vatican Council—more precisely, since the promulgation of the Revised Code of Canon Law in 1917—Catholic teaching had understood marriage in terms of its *ends*, that is, relative to the purposes of marriage, what is it *for*. Canon 1013.1 stated the dual ends of marriage as follows:

> The primary end of marriage is the procreation and nurture of children; its secondary end is mutual help and the remedying of concupiscence. (Mackin, 209)

As Mackin explains, this was the first time in the church's history the categories "primary and secondary" were used to describe the ends of marriage. The framers of the 1917 Code used those categories to describe what marriage is *for*, but the description was received by canonists, bishops, and theologians as a precise definition of marriage itself, that is, what marriage *is*. Moreover, in the decades that followed, church law and theology interpreted these categories to mean that the "end" of the mutual aid of the spouses was subordinate to the "end" of procreation, and in fact not even part of the essential end of marriage (procreation), but distinct and separable from it. It should be noted that although the language of "primary" and "secondary" was new, the fundamental conviction was not; for centuries Catholic tradition had understood marriage—and sexual intercourse within marriage—to be directed essentially toward procreation. From the church's embrace (especially St. Augustine's embrace) of many of the tenets of Stoic philosophy in the early centuries of the church's life, the conviction was that sexual intercourse in marriage was "justified" (it requires justification) by its potential for procreation (Mackin, 136–142). Until Vatican II this was the view of marriage and of sexual expression within marriage in the official teaching of the Catholic Church.

Not surprisingly, there was a good deal of dissatisfaction with this juridical, restricted, and minimalistic way of thinking. Led by Herbert Doms and Dietrich von Hildebrand, in the years following the 1917 Code a number of Catholic scholars questioned the appropriateness of speaking at all of the "ends" of marriage. It is better, they proposed, to focus on what marriage *is* rather than what it is *for*, and what marriage *is*, above all, is a community of persons. Mackin summarizes Doms's proposal this way:

> But it is a community of persons with a meaning and therefore a value within itself. This is the becoming-one of two persons (Doms called this *Zweieinigkeit*, two-in-oneness), the creating of the I-Thou in which the man and woman can be brought to completion as human beings. Again this is not to deny that a marriage can serve ends outside of itself, nor that among those ends procreation may be primary. But the first intelligible, the first value in marriage is this meaning, this person-completing union—a meaning and a value which are there and give a "reason" for marriage distinct and even separable from procreation. (Mackin, 226)

From the 1920s until the eve of the Second Vatican Council there was a lively debate on this matter. Dissatisfaction mounted with the adequacy of describing or defining marriage by referring to its primary and secondary ends, and there was particular dissatisfaction with the relatively insignificant place given to love in marriage. But a corresponding insistence also mounted on the part of church officials that marriage should be described in such primary/secondary categories. For example, in his 1930 encyclical letter on marriage, *Casti Connubii*, Pope Pius XI used these categories as his fundamental way of discussing the nature of marriage, even though he also tried to stress the importance of love in marriage. And in the early 1940s Doms's book, by order of the Holy Office, was taken out of publication and circulation in Catholic circles. Even so, his ideas did not go away. All this serves as the context of the 1962 document the Holy Office submitted to the Preparatory Commission of the Council that has been referred to earlier. What the Holy Office wanted was a strong reaffirmation that marriage is an institution with primary and secondary ends.

As we know now, the Holy Office did not get what it wanted. Nowhere in the text of *Gaudium et Spes* are the primary and secondary

ends even referred to. That is not an oversight, but a deliberate choice
by the majority of the bishops at the Council, one that came only after
"long and again bitter debate" (Mackin, 262). Rather than speak of marriage using such juridical and minimalistic categories, *Gaudium et Spes*
discusses marriage in a personalistic and "maximalistic" way by emphasizing, as we have seen, the centrality of the love of the spouses for one
another in the marital relationship.

But what about procreation? The Latin title of paragraph 50 is *De
matrimonii fecunditate* and this is very significant. The phrase means "concerning the fecundity of marriage," or more simply, the "fruitfulness of
marriage." What marriage *is*, the bishops' teaching emphasizes, is an
eminently human form of love and friendship, an "intimate partnership
of life and love." A *characteristic* of this partnership is that it is meant to
be "fecund" or fruitful. Paragraph 50 states it this way:

> Marriage *and married love* are by nature ordered to ["ordinan-
> tur"] the procreation and education of children. Indeed chil-
> dren are the supreme gift of marriage and greatly contribute to
> the well being of the parents themselves . . . Without intending
> to underestimate the other ends of marriage, it must be said
> that true *married love and the family life which flows from it* have
> this end in view: that the spouses would cooperate generously
> with the love of the Creator and Savior, who through them will
> in due time increase and enrich his family. (GS 50, emphasis
> added)

The phrases I have emphasized are part of what "went forward" at
Vatican II. Rather than speak of marriage as an institution whose primary end is procreation, the bishops chose to keep love in marriage as
the central reality and speak of children as the fruit of the love of the
spouses. Put differently, marital love is meant to be fruitful, particularly
in the way it is "ordered to" the procreation and nurture of children.
This was a much more personalistic and positive way of expressing
what "the intimate partnership of life and love" is all about. Marriage
and married love are meant to be—are mature to the extent that they
become—fruitful.

Just three years later when Paul VI addressed the question of birth
control in *Humanae Vitae,* he did so by first talking about what he called
"the two great realities of married life," marital love and responsible
parenthood. He spoke of sexual expression, sexual love, in marriage

this way: "By means of the reciprocal personal gift of self, proper and exclusive to them, husband and wife tend toward the communion of their beings in view of mutual perfection, to collaborate with God in the generation and education of new lives" (*Humanae Vitae* 8). Pushing the Council's ideas even further, Paul VI saw love in marriage—including the couple's sexual expression of that love—to be directed both toward the communion of the spouses and to the procreation of new life. Marital love, he went on to say, is meant to be *human, total, faithful and exclusive, and fruitful* (par. 9). Catholic teaching has come to understand the fruitfulness of marriage not as an end of the institution of marriage, but as one of its essential characteristics.

Lisa Sowle Cahill is among many Catholic theologians—and married laypersons—who have welcomed this more personalistic and holistic way of thinking about married love and parenthood. She writes that "physical satisfaction or pleasure, interpersonal intimacy, and parenthood are not three separate 'variables,' or *possible* meanings of sex which we are morally free to combine or omit in different ways. Sex and love as fully *embodied* realities have an intrinsic moral connection to procreativity and to the shared creation and nurturing of new lives and new loves" (Cahill, 212). Like many Catholic scholars, Cahill does not go so far as to say, as did Paul VI, that *every act of intercourse* in marriage must retain its procreative potential. Her interest, instead, is on *marital relationships*. Such *spousal relationships*, she argues, are essentially linked to procreativity. As she puts it, "spousehood and parenthood are linked in the long-term commitment of the couple, sexually expressed" (Cahill, 212–213).

Cahill's reflections are indicative of two of the things that continue to "go forward" today in Catholic theology after the Second Vatican Council: an effort to understand more fully the link between sex, love, and parenthood, and an effort to explore more carefully just what "fruitfulness" might mean. As we have seen, many scholars, like Cahill, prefer to speak of the fruitfulness of the marriage *relationship*, if not necessarily every act of intercourse. Others, such as pastoral theologians (and married couple) Evelyn Eaton Whitehead and James D. Whitehead, have suggested that "fruitfulness" should not be understood as a reality that refers exclusively to the procreation of children, but that it includes the many different ways that mature marital love is capable of going "beyond itself," with or without children (Whitehead and Whitehead, 144). Moreover, they have written, "we also recognize that every adult life, whether one is married or not, must necessarily be fruitful" (144). If the Whiteheads are right—and I believe they are—then it is important not to limit "fruitfulness" to married love, but to acknowledge that other forms of friendship and love (e.g., the love of single persons and, some propose, the love present in gay or lesbian partnerships) might likewise be capable of "fruitfulness."

The argument here is not that all of these ideas about "fruitfulness" are those of the bishops at the Second Vatican Council. Indeed, many of them are not. Rather, the suggestion is that among the things that went forward from *Gaudium et Spes* is a new way of thinking about the fruitfulness of marriage, a way of thinking that has prompted new reflections on the nature of marital love, as well as new and (for some) challenging reflections on the nature of human love in all its forms.

## III.  Married love as a "sacrament of divine love"

Brennan R. Hill is among many Catholic theologians who believe we are in a time of transition in understanding the sacramental nature of marriage, a transition prompted largely by the teaching of *Gaudium et Spes* on marriage. To appreciate what "went forward" in this regard it is important to consider briefly how the sacrament of marriage was understood prior to the Council. It is worth quoting Hill's account of this at some length.

> Central to the Christian view of marriage is the belief that marriage is a sacred symbol of Christ's presence and power. Traditional theology, however, has tended to describe this symbol more as a static reality. Marriage in fact has often been looked at as a "state," a reality created by God and then instituted or raised to the level of sacramentality by Jesus. This traditional view seems to have been built largely on the thinking of Augustine, who first described marriage as a *sacramentum*, or an indelible sign or sealing of an irreversible commitment. This commitment, in Augustine's view, is not primarily of the spouses to each other, but rather it is a joint commitment of the couple to God . . . The traditional point of view has taken the position that marriage is a pre-ordained "state" that is irrevocably "entered into" by the vows of marriage and that the agreement is finally "sealed" through sexual intercourse. (Hill, 4)

The emphasis in this view of the sacrament of marriage is much more on the activity of God than on the activity of the spouses. The married "state" has been established by God and the sacrament of marriage has been established by Christ. The couple "enters in" to this pre-ordained "state" and their irreversible commitment is a sacrament or sign of God's irrevocable commitment to be present with and to love humankind. Hill calls this a "static" perspective on the sacrament of marriage (Hill, 4).

As we have seen in regard to other matters, *Gaudium et Spes* makes no effort to disavow this view of the sacrament of marriage. Catholic tradition does not work that way. Instead, along with some remnants of what Hill described as the traditional view, the Council's teaching on the sacrament of marriage—provided only in glimpses—displays a different emphasis on what it means to say that marriage is a sacrament.

As we have seen, the emphasis in the Council's teaching is on the special and "eminently human" form of friendship and love that is marriage. This carries over into its perspective on the *sacramental* nature of marriage. "Authentic married love is caught up (*assumitur*) into divine love and is directed and enriched by the redemptive power of Christ and the salvific action of the church . . . spouses are penetrated with the spirit of Christ and their whole life is suffused by faith, hope, and charity; thus they increasingly further their own perfection and their mutual sanctification, and together they render glory to God" (*SC* 48). Later on, elaborating on what the phrase "eminently human" means, the bishops say that it involves an "affection" that embraces the entire shared life of the spouses, including the intimate, physical expressions of love in intercourse. Concerning such love, the bishops taught the following: "The Lord, wishing to bestow special gifts of grace and divine love on married love, has restored, perfected, and elevated it. A love like that, bringing together the human and the divine, leads the partners to a free and mutual self-giving, experienced in tenderness and action, and permeating their entire lives" (par. 49).

The "eminently human" reality of love in marriage is "caught up" in divine love in such a way that marital love is "more than" human. In all of its manifestations and dimensions—physical, affective, intellectual, and spiritual—love in marriage is "more than" human love. It is permeated with the Spirit of Christ, the Spirit of God, so that spouses are a sign of God's loving presence with humanity and, more specifically, a sacrament of Christ's loving and abiding presence with the church, his body.

While this "sacramental theology" of the Council seems to emphasize what the human reality of married life and love is *capable of*, it also
makes it clear that the sacramental nature of marriage results, at the
same time, from the grace and activity of God. That is what is meant by
the phrase "caught up," or "taken up"; through nothing less than the
grace of the Spirit of God, the human reality of love in marriage is "assumed" into divine love. Married love remains a human reality, *and at
the same time* is able to display nothing less than the loving presence of
God. As Hill puts it, what the Council's teaching signals is a much more
dynamic view of the sacrament of marriage (Hill, 5–7).

To say that the approach of *Gaudium et Spes* to the sacrament of
marriage—the ability of the human reality of marital love to be "caught
up" in divine love—"went forward" after Vatican II is an understate-
ment. Bishops, pastors, preachers, retreat directors, spiritual directors,
theologians, and of course married couples themselves saw in the
Council's teaching a powerful and overdue affirmation of the goodness
and holiness of love in marriage, in all its manifestations. Perhaps no
one has seen this more clearly and expressed this more eloquently than
sacramental theologian Bernard Cooke, who proposed that Christian
marriage be seen as the most basic sacrament. Cook describes the
sacramental significance of human relationships as follows:

> In our love and concern for one another, in our friendships and
> in the human community that results, we can gain some insight
> into what "God being for us" really means. These human rela-
> tionships are truly insights into God, but not just in the sense
> that they are an analogue by which we can gain some meta-
> phorical understanding of the divine. Rather, humans and their
> relationships to one another are a "word" that is being con-
> stantly created by God. In this word God is made present to us,
> revealing divine selfhood through the sacramentality of our
> human experience of one another. (Cooke, 75)

Cooke goes on to say that marriage is the paradigm of the kind of
friendship and love that are *capable of* being a sacrament of, or a revelation of the divine. And that is why he proposes that marriage is the
most basic of the sacraments. The loving marital relationship discloses
something of the mystery of God in a concrete and enfleshed way that
no other sacrament does. The sacrament of marriage is a revelatory

"word": God is love, God's nature is to be in loving relationship with all that is.

But for Cooke it is significant that it is not only the special form of love and friendship we call marriage that is sacramental. All forms of genuine human friendship are *capable of* being such "revelatory words" of God and about God. This insight into the sacramental significance of the human realities of friendship and love is part of what "went forward" in *Gaudium et Spes*.

## Conclusion:
## What is still "going forward"?

What continues to "go forward" in the life of the church is our reflection on the Council's insight into the sacramental significance of human life. As evidenced in his 1992 pastoral letter on "The Cycle of Love," Bishop Lucker was marvelously aware of this. Drawing on a description of love given by Anne Wilson Schaef, Lucker described love as a "continuous flow of energy from the lover to the loved and from the one who is now loved to the lover" (Lucker, 381). This way of viewing love, Lucker thought, was also a marvelous way of describing humanity's relationship with God: "God first loves us totally, unconditionally. Such love calls for us to respond and to love God in return 'with all our mind, all our heart and all our strength'" (Lucker, 381). Surely the fully human love of married persons for one another displays this "cycle of love" in a dramatic manner; such love also manifests the fact that human love can "open up" to God's love and, at the same time, "be taken up" into divine love by the grace of God. For Raymond Lucker, and for many others as well, among the things that seem to have "gone forward" and that continue to "go forward" in light of the Second Vatican Council is the conviction that human love is centrally important *for all people* and an important "place" where humanity's relationship with God is revealed.

## *References*

Cahill, Lisa Sowle. "Can We Get Real about Sex?" In *Perspectives on Marriage: A Reader.* Ed. Kieran Scott and Michael Warren. New York: Oxford University Press, 1993. Pp. 207–214.

Cooke, Bernard. "Christian Marriage: Basic Sacrament." In *Perspectives on Marriage: A Reader*. Ed. Kieran Scott and Michael Warren. New York: Oxford University Press, 1993. Pp. 71–81.

Guarino, Charles. "Canonical and Theological Perspectives on Divorce and Remarriage." In *Perspectives on Marriage: A Reader*. Ed. Kieran Scott and Michael Warren. New York: Oxford University Press, 1993. Pp. 361–376.

Hill, Brennan R. "Reformulating the Sacramental Theology of Marriage." In *Christian Marriage and Family*. Ed. Michael G. Lawler and William P. Roberts. Collegeville, Minn.: The Liturgical Press, 1996. Pp. 3–21.

John Paul II, Pope. Apostolic exhortation *Familiaris Consortio*. *Origins* 11/28 (1981): 437, 439–468.

Lonergan, Bernard. *Method in Theology*. New York: The Seabury Press, 1972.

Mackin, Theodore. *What Is Marriage? Marriage in the Catholic Church*. Mahwah, N.J.: Paulist Press, 1982.

McBrien, Richard P. "Mediation." In *Catholicism*, rev. ed. San Francisco, Calif.: Harper San Francisco, 1994. Pp. 11–12.

Whitehead, Evelyn Eaton, and James D. Whitehead. "The Passage into Marriage." In *Perspectives on Marriage: A Reader*. Ed. Kieran Scott and Michael Warren. New York: Oxford University Press, 1993. Pp 136–145.

# 12
# Peace and justifiable war:
# Catholic social thought and its call to us today

AMATA MILLER, I.H.M.

D eliberations about peace and war have a long history in Catholic
social thought, with a revival since Vatican II. Bishop Lucker was
one of those rare individuals who continually pondered new developments while seeking to remain true to the fundamental traditions
of the church, and he led his people in ways that drew out the practical
implications of church teaching on social issues. He served as Minnesota President of Pax Christi and was active in Call to Action, the
Catholic organization for reform in the church and in society. In 1998
he joined a group of bishops writing a joint pastoral on the morality of
nuclear deterrence, moving beyond the conditional acceptance of deterrence found in the 1983 pastoral of the bishops in light of continued
research, development, and testing by the U.S. He said clearly to his
people in June, 1998:

> The United States shows no intention of moving forward with
> progress to disarm and certainly no commitment to eliminate
> these weapons entirely. We believe we need to raise a clear, unam-
> biguous voice in opposition to the continued reliance on nuclear
> deterrence. I am convinced that possessing nuclear weapons is
> evil and we must do everything possible to change our govern-
> ment policy. (Lucker, 510)

That he came to this active participation in the deliberations late in
his own life reflects the long, very human struggle of the church over
the centuries both to reflect Christian principles in its teaching on
peace and justifiable war and to discern appropriate actions, given

moral and socio-cultural-political realities. This essay will do three things: first, it will briefly overview the history of Catholic thinking on peace and war up to Vatican II; second, it will describe basic elements of the "completely fresh appraisal of war" called for in *Gaudium et Spes* (par. 80) and in ensuing papal and episcopal documents; and, third, it will suggest some particular challenges we face in our day. The essay ends with a brief conclusion.

## I.  History of church teaching on war and peace up to Vatican II

The teaching of the church on peace and justifiable war over the centuries clearly reflects the varied societal conditions in each era of Western history. Based on scriptural traditions that sought to link the Old and New Testaments, church teaching confronted images of the warrior/defender God as well as of the nonviolent Jesus. The peace tradition recognized changes in the image of God and in Israel's messianic hopes for peace and justice after the exile as part of the evolution of human understanding of God's intent (Lammers, 1994, 718). However, the varying priority given to just war teachings and the call to peace-making over the years reflects the ongoing creative tension between these images of God as well as changing world conditions, as will be evident in what follows.

Early Christian communities were minority groups within their societies. As followers of Christ, they witnessed to his peacemaking and nonviolence. By the fourth century, however, the church had become influential in society and had to grapple with issues of war and peace in a warlike world. So Augustine developed the rudiments of what became the just war theory. Given the reality of predatory invasions, Christians had to wrestle with the questions of when Christians and Christian nations could justifiably go to war and by what rules moral behavior in warfare was to be governed. These two basic questions evolved over time into the still-used aspects of just war ethics and international law: *jus ad bellum* and *jus in bello*. The question was always one of restraints on war so that justice could be maintained (see Johnson's book-length treatment).

During what are called the "Middle Ages," when church and state were united in Christendom and battles for property and power were fought under codes of chivalry, the thinking of canon lawyers and secular scholars came together in the development of rules for justifiable war (Johnson, 121–171). Social and cultural realities required that a priority be put on order and deference for authority, and these prevailed within the church's teaching on peace and justifiable war over the long centuries before Vatican II.

Through the work of medieval scholars, Thomas Aquinas and the later scholastics, especially Grotius and Victoria in the globalizing world of the fifteenth century, the just war tradition took shape. As developed, the basic criteria for declaring a war justifiable (*jus ad bellum*) include: (1) waged by a legitimate authority; (2) a just cause; (3) war as the last resort; (4) need for a formal declaration of war; (5) reasonable hope of success; (6) proportionality between what is to be gained and lost in the war; and (7) right intention. The criteria for conduct of a justifiable war (*jus in bello*) include: (1) immunity of noncombatants from direct attack; (2) proportionality of specific tactics. Though changing conditions in society and in weapons technology dictated modifications in specific applications of the criteria, these still form the basis of the analytical framework in terms of which Catholic teaching has used the ethic of justifiable war (NCCB, 1983, pars. 80–110; and Hehir, 1980, 19).

Reflecting the realities of a Western world divided into nation states, Leo XIII in *Rerum Novarum* limited the common good to that of the nation and reaffirmed the priority of order and adherence to the decisions of national leaders, assuming them to be seeking justice and the common good of their people (*RN* 34). His views prevailed until deadly weapons technology, the magnified scope of wars, and evidence of governmental injustice necessitated new moral attention to issues of war and peace. Though there are signs of church inaction during World War II, Pius XII again addressed the moral issues involved. He presaged Vatican II by making the motto of his pontificate "*Opus justitiae pax: peace as the fruit of justice*" (cited by John Paul II, *SRS* 39). In light of the destructiveness of nuclear technology, though he did not outlaw war, he reduced the theory's just causes for war from the three previously allowed (defense, avenging evil, and restoring rights that had been violated) to one. All wars of aggression were prohibited. The only allowable cause for war was self-defense (Himes, 1991, 331). At the same time, he outlawed for Catholics pacifism in the form of conscientious objection (Hehir, 1980, 17). Thus, whatever history reveals as his role during World War II, he did raise up again and add new dimensions to papal teaching on peace and justifiable war issues.

John XXIII, already in his 1961 encyclical, *Mater et Magistra,* had recognized that what Leo XIII had called the "social question" had become international (*MM* 37). John XXIII would develop in his 1963 world-heralded encyclical, *Pacem in Terris,* themes of human dignity and rights. In that letter he raised the issues of the international common good, which for him clearly included economic justice and peace; a new emphasis on women; the necessity of some form of world government; and the plight of the world's poor (*PT* 84, 135ff.). His insight, foresight, and courage in "opening the windows" of the Church to see the world anew led him to convoke Vatican II. Calling for new moral teaching in light of "the signs of the times,"Vatican II led to a new era of reflection and official church teaching on war and peace (*GS* 4).

## II. Vatican II and ensuing church teachings

In the opening of its fifth chapter, *Gaudium et Spes* evidences the elements of the "fresh appraisal" (*GS* 80) of peace and war for which it called:

> In our generation, which has been marked by the persistent and severe hardships and anxiety resulting from the ravages of war and the threat of war, the whole human race faces a moment of supreme crisis in its advance towards maturity. Humanity has gradually come closer together and is everywhere more conscious of its own unity; but it will not succeed in accomplishing the task awaiting it, that is, the establishment of a truly human world for all over the entire earth, unless all devote themselves to the cause of true peace with renewed vigor. . . Accordingly, the council proposes to set down the true and noble nature of peace, to condemn the savagery of war, and to encourage Christians to cooperate with all in securing a peace based on justice and charity and in promoting the means necessary to attain it. (*GS* 77)

Visible here is a new priority of peace, human dignity, and economic justice; also visible is a recognition of the strategy of deterrence and of the complexity of determining just means toward peace, as well as a condemnation of the brutality of modern war. All of these are evident in what many scholars have observed to be the ambiguity and others have seen as politically motivated compromises in church teaching about peace and justifiable war during Vatican II and since. Perhaps this is not surprising, since popes and bishops have attempted, as in the historic teaching on peace and war, to be faithful to the teachings of Christ by giving guidance for conscience formation in the world as it is. And the teaching has stressed that this is a world of widespread abysmal poverty, more and more sophisticated weapons of mass destruction, growing and diverse tensions between and within nations, and the absence of international political institutions to deal with conflicts and injustices. Each of these has been addressed in various encyclicals and letters from episcopal conferences as well as in local advocacy work and the education of the people of God stemming from them. For example, these are evident themes in the thinking and the pastoral letters of Bishop Lucker.

Scholars of both peace and justifiable war seem to agree on the major contributions of Vatican II teaching to their thought. *Gaudium et Spes* newly emphasized peace as more than the absence of war, as something that has to be built up continually, both within individuals and by governments, and also through justice and mutual love which attends to human rights (*GS* 78). Reversing the teaching of Pius XII, the Council gave approval to conscientious objection as long as it does not violate the common good or the rights of others and includes alternative forms of community service. It also called for legalization of conscientious objection (*GS* 78–79). In the Council's only anathema, genocide and "indiscriminate destruction of whole cities or vast areas with their inhabitants" were condemned (*GS* 79, 80). Thus, Vatican II condemned total war but, unwilling to judge the *intent* of authorities, made no clear moral statement about deterrence (Hehir, 1980, 27). The ambiguity of this and other statements necessitated further development of the teachings in light of world realities.

Focusing on the ways to peace, Vatican II stressed the need for economic justice. It noted the material and human costs of the arms race, calling it "one of the greatest curses on the human race" and saying that "the harm it inflicts on the poor is more than can be endured" (*GS* 81). It also spoke of "excessive economic inequalities and delays in correcting them" as the roots of wars between peoples (*GS* 83). In addition, it called for greater international cooperation to discover ways better than war to achieve common security; for "a real beginning of disarmament" through negotiations and "effective guarantees" (*GS* 82); and for the establishment of institutions to promote peace (*GS* 83). The Council also called for setting up a new kind of international order, "a community of nations" exhibiting greater international cooperation in economic matters to ensure the universal common good and address the "intolerable want" of many areas of the world (*GS* 84–86). These calls continue to recur from church leaders and others.

Paul VI developed Vatican II themes of economic justice in his encyclical *Populorum Progressio* ("On the Development of Peoples") in 1967. In 1971, the third synod of the world's bishops following Vatican II took place in Rome; that synod's document, *Justice in the World*, further developed this aspect of the movement toward peace. In his 1971 encyclical, *Octogesima Adveniens* ("A Call to Action") Paul VI explored the links between economic justice, human dignity, and the political order, emphasizing that action for justice and peace was a personal responsibility for every Christian individual and organization (*OA* 48–50). He repeatedly spoke about the need for disarmament. In a 1965 speech before the United Nations General Assembly, he called for disarmament as the first path to peace, saying in oft-quoted words, "No more war, war never again!" (see Bernardin, 1991, 279). In 1978, near the end of his papacy and at the first special United Nations session on disarmament, Paul VI said: "It would be a tragic illusion to believe that the arms race might continue indefinitely without causing a catastrophe" (see Langendorfer, 294). In 1968 Paul VI had already drawn attention to the priority of peace by initiating observance of a World Day of Peace. The destructiveness of nuclear weapons themselves and of their accumulation, as well as the links between peace and economic justice made by his predecessor and by Vatican II were continually being pondered and put before public authorities and people of faith.

The impact of the Vietnam War, especially in the United States, has to be noted in this reflection on Catholic teaching about peace and justifiable war. The war generated dramatically new kinds of responses by Americans, particularly the young, and shaped the context for the later pastoral letter on peace by the U.S. bishops. Strong anti-communism operated among American Catholics and affected objectivity of judgment about causes, even though many Catholic papers and journals engaged in intellectually stimulating discussions of the issues involved (O'Brien, 121–122). Since *Gaudium et Spes* contained certain sections that could be used to criticize U.S. action in Vietnam as well as other sections that legitimized just war thinking, it contributed to American confusion and reluctance to challenge national policy (O'Brien, 124). Conflicting actions by U.S. Catholic bishops during the period also contributed; in 1971 fourteen New England bishops issued a pastoral that condemned massive use of airpower in Vietnam, but at the bishops' meeting that year strong propositions against the war were defeated. However, gradually, the bishops had begun to apply the just war criteria to the situation in Vietnam. By 1971 they at least had war on the agenda of their meeting and recognized that they had to consider whether or not this war met the justifiable war criteria (O'Brien, 125–131). Meanwhile, Catholic as well as other church leaders had begun to play an important part in opposition to the war and the Catholic Resistance movement grew in size and influence, developing thought and acting to influence public policy (O'Brien, 136–144). O'Brien ends his comprehensive history of the developments of the Vietnam era with some words about the vibrancy of the church as a people of God, words reminiscent of the kind of pastoral ministry Bishop Lucker practiced among the laity:

> So, while the debate about a theology of peace would go on, the thrust of Catholic action would be toward developing awareness of the moral dimensions of social and political life, educating for peace and justice, and forming lay leaders and ministerial representatives capable of carrying the Christian message into everyday life. (O'Brien, 144)

In 1983 the National Conference of Catholic Bishops issued its pastoral letter, "The Challenge of Peace: God's Promise and Our Response" (NCCB, 1983). The letter was written under the chairmanship of (then archbishop) Joseph Bernardin, and involved a process of consultation with diverse experts and the preparation of several drafts which were widely circulated for comments from the laity. Later reflections by participants in the process testify both to the openness of the process and to the tensions inherent in the complexities and in the variety of points of view on both the socio-economic-political situation and on Catholic social thought on peace and justifiable war since Vatican II.

In a 1991 article, Cardinal Bernardin summarized the state of Catholic teaching on war and peace, explaining what "The Challenge of Peace" had tried to do. First, the drafters wanted to speak out strongly against the nuclear arms race "because of the threat it poses to the world as well as the cost it exacts even if the weapons are never used" (Bernardin, 1991, 280). In this they followed the papal approach to arms control and disarmament and made statements that were "cautious and carefully drawn" (Bernardin, 1991, 280). They applied the criteria of the just war tradition to the use of nuclear weapons and stated that counter-population warfare was categorically ruled out and that there could never be a just cause for initiating a nuclear war; further, they questioned whether or not a limited nuclear war could ever be possible (NCCB, 1983, pars. 146–161). They considered the policy of deterrence and concluded, like John Paul II, that only a conditional moral acceptance could be given to it, because it could be justified only as an intermediate step on the way to progressive disarmament (NCCB, 1983, pars.162–187). Looking at specific U.S. public policies of the time, the bishops recommended: halting the development of new nuclear weapons systems; supporting deep bilateral reductions in nuclear arsenals and enhancing the degree of control over existing deployed weapons; and moving gradually toward disarmament—bilaterally and with guarantees (NCCB, 1983, pars. 188–192).

"The Challenge of Peace" also carefully addressed the other strand of Catholic teaching—the pacifist one which had been dominant in the earliest days of Christianity, but had been relatively neglected until Vatican II. As Bernardin put it: "Change, both in the church and in the world, precipitated a new appraisal not only of war itself, but also of our manner of reflecting on it" (Bernardin, 1991, 281). So they began with a section titled "The New Moment" in which they laid out the nature and the dangers of the new situation (NCCB, 1983, pars. 126–138). They concluded with a statement of their own perplexity about how to prevent the use of nuclear weapons, how to assess the strategy of deterrence, and how to spell out moral responsibility in a nuclear age. But they ended with a ringing reaffirmation of their certainty that the "no" to nuclear war was "definitive and decisive" (NCCB, 1983, pars. 126–138).

In this letter the bishops stated that just war and pacifism (in the sense of nonviolence) are "distinct but interdependent methods of evaluating warfare." The bishops noted that both strands of the church's teaching share a common presumption against the use of force as a way to settle disputes though they differ on some specifics (NCCB, 1983, par. 120). Bernardin believed that both strands are needed in order to morally judge the current realities in which we find ourselves; both have the intent of moving toward peace, but they differ in method. He thought that in this time of ever more sophisticated weapons the two strands come together in the sense that partisans of both views agree that now human beings *have* to find nonviolent means to resolve our conflicts (Bernardin, 1991, 281–282). "The Challenge of Peace" stresses as practical measures the use of diplomacy, the establishment of a U.S. Academy of Peace, deeper study of nonviolence as a way to resist evil, and the development of a theology of peace (NCCB, 1983, pars. 200–230).

Differences persist. Moral theologian Kenneth Himes points out that the bishops said that pacifism may be an individual choice "for persons committed to a genuine peace but who cannot accept that violent means may restore the peace"(Himes, 1994, 708; see NCCB, 1983, par. 224). He indicates that the bishops clearly affirm that a state has the right of self-defense in war, even though they just as clearly say that immoral means cannot be used (NCCB, 1983, par. 221). Pacifists like Eileen Egan and Bishop Thomas Gumbleton and others write of nonviolence and peacemaking as a way of life incumbent on all followers of Jesus (see Egan and Gumbleton). And so the creative tension continues.

In the period since 1983, bishops, both in the United States and elsewhere, and others have continued to address questions of peace and when and what kind of war could be justifiable given the context of our times. (For example, our times are marked by changes in Cold War tensions, the continuing arms race, the ongoing strategy of deterrence, new developments in weapons technology, the progress of globalization, new awareness of pandemics such as AIDs, ecological devastation, and the spread of international terrorism.)

In 1991 Cardinal Bernardin looked back to the peace pastoral of 1983 and noted that there had been a special committee of bishops appointed in 1985 to assess the teachings of the pastoral in light of changed conditions. By the time the report of the committee was issued in 1988, such changes included the Intermediate Nuclear Forces Treaty which resulted in a small reduction in nuclear weapons and thus accorded with the pastoral's challenge on arms control and bilateral negotiations. Regarding Reagan's Strategic Defense Initiative, the bishops concluded that the risks outweighed the benefits and so that initiative did not meet the moral criteria of the 1983 pastoral. The 1988 report continued to stress that the bishops had given only "strictly conditioned moral acceptance" to the strategy of deterrence and it argued that the pastoral's moral criteria required that stronger steps toward arms control and disarmament be taken (Bernardin, 1991, 283).

The previous year Bernardin had addressed a conference at the University of South Carolina on the political, strategic, and ethical dimensions of nuclear deterrence. His topic was how nuclear policy in the post–Cold War world of the 1990s had to be adapted to the new realities of what he called a second phase of the nuclear age, when the superpower relationship had changed drastically. He noted that certain characteristics had set the 1980s apart from the rest of the nuclear age. The general public had become aware of elements of what had been a debate among experts about nuclear weapons and nuclear policy. In the nuclear freeze movement the public had demanded more arms control and pushed U.S. policy toward arms control negotiations.

On the changes brought about during the 1980s, one political scholar emphasizes the importance of the 1989 revolutions overturning communism in Eastern Europe, because they contributed "the idea of transnational civil society that emerged from the intensive dialogue between Western European peace movements and the developing peace and human rights groups in Eastern Europe" (Kaldor, 1995, 60). For his part, Bernardin concluded, in words that may prove prescient, that the electorate is now "more capable of entering the nuclear discussion when it believes the elite is either too complacent or too adventurous" (Bernardin, 1990, 633). He also noted that there were two poles in the ethical aspects of an increasingly central nuclear debate by 1990. Those at one pole of the debate over deterrence believed that a morally justifiable deterrent was possible because moral limits of means and ends could be maintained. Those at the other pole saw an inevitable contradiction between credible deterrence and the prohibition against killing the innocent. Bernardin concluded that both positions were "internally coherent" and detailed, and that they both "conveyed a sense of confidence that the move from ethical assessment to policy conclusions was both possible and evidently imperative" (Bernardin, 1990, 632–633).

He restated the fact that the bishops had actually taken a third position, which gave only conditional acceptance to deterrence and called for restrictions in targeting, deployment, and declaration as well as for work for transformation of the political setting within which deterrence operated. This view was developed, he noted, at a time when no one thought a fundamental change in superpower relationships was possible. In the 1990s, he said, priority should be given to the political aspects of the change that actually took place, emphasizing the transformation of relationships in the new setting which changed the ethics of nuclear strategy (Bernardin, 1990, 633). Thus, he moved ideas of the morality of deterrence closer to focus on the end—peace in justice for all (Bernardin, 1990, 633–634).

In 1993, the U.S. bishops issued a statement to commemorate the ten-year anniversary of their peace pastoral, reminding Catholics of the continuing urgency of the nuclear threat and of the challenge of peace.

Among the new questions and concerns to be addressed they mentioned new developments in nonviolence, noting that

> Although nonviolence has often been regarded as simply a personal option or vocation, recent history suggests that in some circumstances it can be an effective public undertaking as well . . . These nonviolent revolutions challenge us to find ways to take into full account the power of organized, active nonviolence. (NCCB, 1993, 453–454)

In a move that takes pacifism in the sense of nonviolence to a new place in Catholic social teaching, the bishops called for further study of the ethical implications of this kind of alternative public policy. Though they again restated a nation's right to self-defense, they noted the possibility that in some future situations of conflict "strikes and people power could be more effective than guns and bullets" (NCCB, 1993, 454). Making this the first of the new issues to be addressed, the bishops' conference took some new steps in the recognition of peaceful means as well as peace as end.

In what seems to be a further change in priorities, the bishops only secondarily treated the new just war questions that required attention in the early 1990s, calling for moral consideration of contemporary strategies in light of previously articulated standards on moral uses of force. They expressed skepticism that any modern war could meet the just war criteria and called for work on "refining, clarifying and applying" that tradition. They treated conscientious objection at greater length than previously (NCCB, 1993, 455). They concluded with a statement of their hopes that their anniversary reflections would help to engender new dialogue within the Catholic community and with the broader community on the moral dimensions of foreign affairs. They reminded Catholics that the vocation of peacemaking is an "essential part of our mission to proclaim the Gospel and renew the earth" (NCCB, 1993, 464).

In the response to the terrorist destructions of September 11, 2001, the U.S. bishops again spoke out on war and peace, using both strands of the tradition in what they characterized as "a balanced approach." Though those who wished for a condemnation of a military response were disappointed, the increasing priority given to themes of human dignity and economic justice as necessary elements of peace and of nonviolence as a recognized means to peace was evident. The bishops clearly indicated that the criteria of just war theory should be used in this case, saying that "the traditional moral norms governing use of force still apply even in the face of terrorism on this scale." In another place they indicated again their affirmation of those criteria, but added that the use of force had to be a last resort. They recognized that some hold the just war theory and are justified in doing so. After indicating that the preference for nonviolence is a "valid Christian response" they noted that:

> the church has sanctioned the use of the moral criteria for a just war to allow the use of force by legitimate authority in self-defense and as a last resort. Those who subscribe to the just war tradition can differ in their prudential judgments about its interpretation or its application. (USCCB, 2001, 917)

It seems that, by this time, just war theory and the claims of peacemaking are on equal footing, and that those who hold just war theory also must defend their views. Commenting on this statement, theologian and counselor on international affairs for the U.S. bishops Drew Christiansen has noted: "The appeal to just war reasoning in the statement was notably cautious and not the least bit jingoistic" (Christiansen, 2002a, 39). Especially under the circumstances, this reflected a marked shift of emphasis by church leaders.

Since the beginning of his papacy in the late 1970s, John Paul II has continued to focus on the links between peace and justice. He has issued social encyclicals such as *Sollicitudo Rei Socialis* in 1987 and *Centesimus Annus* in 1994 and given many speeches on the dominant influence today of "sinful social structures" resulting from the perennial human thirst for material possessions and power and giving rise to wars down the centuries (see *SRS* 36, 39). In fact, he mentioned this concept and his concern about its causative role in "the continuing chasm in living standards" between groups of nations in his first encyclical, *Redemptor Hominis* (*RH* 16; cited in NCCB, 1983, par. 259). He has continued the theme of *Gaudium et Spes*, which saw the roots of war in situations of human poverty. In his continued emphasis on the priority which must be given to the needs of the poor and vulnerable and on the virtue of solidarity as the "moral response to the reality of our interdependence," a virtue that demands our ongoing dedication to the common good, he has stressed the underlying moral elements of peacemaking (*SRS* 36–39). In his various writings and speeches he has continued to address the tragedies of modern warfare in terms of human carnage, diversion of material resources away from basic human needs, and ecological damage.

And in his 2002 World Peace Day message, after noting world realities "in which the power of evil seems once again to have taken the upper hand," he lifted up again the church's conviction that evil "does not have the final word in human affairs" and the hope for world peace which he characterized as evidence of the triumph of "the noblest aspirations of the human heart." He developed this theme of peace by beginning with his own conviction based on his experience and confirmed in scripture, that "shattered order cannot be fully restored except by a response that combines justice with forgiveness. The pillars of true peace are justice and that form of love which is forgiveness." In what could be an allusion to pre-Pius XII just war theories, he reminded his hearers that prior understandings of what made war justifiable no longer hold. He went on to say that "forgiveness is the opposite of resentment and revenge, not of justice" and is required for true peace. He cited the continuity of both Augustinian and Vatican II definitions of peace as justice (meaning "right order") and re-emphasized the fact that it is forgiveness which "heals and rebuilds troubled human relations from their foundations" (John Paul II, 2002, 8).

Along with this stress on peace and forgiveness, he reaffirmed the right to self-defense in situations of terrorism, seeing this also as a dimension of justice, one which must be exercised within "moral and legal limits on choices of ends and means." He called especially for correct identification of the perpetrators; for holding guilty individuals and not nations, ethnic groups, or religions responsible; and for multifaceted international cooperation to relieve conditions of oppression and marginalization that engender terrorism (John Paul II, 2002, 8–9). But, in confirmation of the current priorities, he devoteed the bulk of his message to addressing forgiveness, not justifiable violence, as the means to true peace: "No peace without justice, no justice without forgiveness" (John Paul II, 2002,11). This emphasis on forgiveness seems to be the heart of the pope's message today, one that breaks new ground in the church's long tradition of teaching on peace and justifiable war (see Christiansen, 2002b).

In sum, this overview of the long history of church teaching on peace and justifiable war evidences the development of the "completely fresh appraisal of war" called for by Vatican II (*GS* 80). As with other developments in this area of teaching over the centuries, this "fresh appraisal" was engendered by both changes in conditions of society and of warfare and also by a greater emphasis on principles of peacemaking in the church's moral tradition. From a primary focus on restraints on war in order to reach the goal of peace, the teaching has come to a primary focus on the goal of peacemaking itself. In particular, the teaching is increasingly focusing on our need to develop nonviolent means of peacemaking. While still maintaining the right and duty of nations to use force in self defense, and continuing to apply the just war criteria in moral analysis, popes, bishops, and the laity are putting much greater emphasis, as in the early years of Christianity, on peace and nonviolence as the way of the gospel.

## III. The challenges before us in our day

Much remains and will always remain to be done. Vatican II's call for a whole new way of thinking about peace and war still challenges Catholics as well as other people of faith. We are in the midst of a sea-change in our views of the world and of relationships to self, to God, to neighbor, and to all of creation. The world seeks for modes of international relations that will bring order in the midst of a new period of globalization. Global affairs specialist Mary Kaldor recently noted that a "new cosmopolitan politics, based on goals such as peace, human rights or environmentalism, is emerging side by side with the politics of particularism." She titled her 1999 book, New and Old Wars, and wondered whether we can conceive of a different kind of world, one where violence is controlled on a transnational basis. (Kaldor, 1999, 139). People wonder what can make the use of force justifiable in a time of weapons of mass destruction. Scholars and leaders grapple with what order and justice mean in an era of new hunger for true peace. Especially necessary are both realism about the world as it actually is today and hope in the God who writes straight with crooked lines.

The goal has to be to develop guidelines that are both realistic and visionary, and are for both the short term and the long term. This is the challenge as it has been all through the ages—to keep the ultimate vision of a peaceful world clear and to provide moral principles to guide actions in the here and now. But today the moral presumptions toward life, toward justice, toward nonviolence, toward forgiveness are growing stronger from both the vision and the reality. And so, as we strive toward the vision of a world characterized by true peace, the agenda for action is multifaceted.

This article is too short to cover all of the directions for action treated in detail by the scholars whose writings are listed at the end of this article. But in the spirit of Bishop Lucker's pastoral style, there seems to be an urgency about the need to speak in private and public forums, and to act for peace and justice as individuals and as church now. Let us consider just a few of the most critical challenges addressed in Catholic social teaching about peace and justifiable war. I frame those challenges in a traditionally Catholic, threefold way here: we face challenges to our speaking, to our thinking, and to our acting.

First, there are areas where changes in personal attitudes and public policy demand more vocal action; we must speak. Those who value life must oppose once again nuclear escalation and possible aggressive use of weapons of mass destruction by all powers. The horrors of nuclear warfare and the demonstrated "mistakes" of even those weapons we deem accurate have to be faced. The American habit of strategies of annihilation and "unconditional surrender" (Johnson, 259) must be modified, and our leaders must be held accountable for the morality of their decisions.

People of faith are also called to name the cycle of violence that feeds on itself in domestic and international strife in many areas of the world. This is all too evident in civil and ethnic tensions, as well as in international terrorism and wars. Governmental status measured by arms stocks, by arms trade, and by arms budgets diverts resources badly needed to meet basic human needs and eliminate the poverty and marginalization in which wars and terror are bred. This kind of diversion happens in both rich and poor countries, though it is most severe among the poorest. As members of the same human family as the world's poor, we need to speak loudly for comprehensive disarmament.

In addition, as people called to create community, we must advocate for increased international collaboration in dealing with threats such as international terrorism, global climate change, the AIDS pandemic, and excessively unequal benefits and sacrifices resulting from globalization. To deal with each of these transcends the ability of any single nation acting alone. We have to be part of creating and strengthening international institutions and an international rule of law to maintain a global social order of peace and justice. The founders of the United States saw the power of collaboration over conflict, and developed a pattern of both federal and states' rights and responsibilities. So too, in this era, as citizens of our country and of the world, we have to learn how to collaborate for the universal common good.

In recent decades, Catholic teaching has increasingly emphasized the connections between commitment to the economic development of the poorer nations and commitment to world peace. We have become aware that burdens of poverty and exclusion from participation in world affairs adversely affect the basic ability to live. We now see on our TV screens how the lack of access to basic resources engenders cycles of violence. We have to learn to live more simply so that others may simply live. And we need to speak out with and on behalf of the world's poor, to advocate for increased public and private assistance in ways that enable people to help themselves.

We face a whole second area of challenges; that is, we are challenged to new and deepened ways of thinking. We must develop a full theology of peace rooted in biblical tradition and in the experience of the world's people over the centuries. This will include our probing John Paul II's conviction that the "pillars of true peace are justice and that form of love which is forgiveness" (John Paul II, 2002, 8). It is new and strange for us to think that forgiveness must underlie any lasting peace—new for us in our personal lives, to say nothing of in international relations. We have just begun to understand the ramifications of things like "truth commissions." Also, in addition to the scholarly pursuit of the theology of peace and forgiveness we need new tools to disseminate this theology in educational practice. We must render our theology in forms more usable to people of all ages, educational backgrounds, and languages.

Catholicism insists that our thinking is changed by the way we pray. As at other times in history, our petitions will have to include prayer for peace in its fullest sense in both liturgical and non-liturgical rituals. This will both open our hearts to the ways of peace and allow the God of surprises in whom we believe and hope to act through us as we work for peace. This kind of prayer will also strengthen us for the struggle for social structures that will enable all people to live as God intended—in the tranquillity of the order of a world that is just, peaceful, and sustainable.

Last, people of faith face the challenge of finding new and deepened ways of acting. John Paul II's call for "serious and mature thinking" about forgiveness as essential to peace may be the most difficult challenge of all for us (see Christiansen, 2002b). Living out the kind of other-centered ethic required for forgiveness will be strange and hard for us who live in increasingly individualistic cultures. The pope has witnessed to this theme and spoken about it, yet we are surely only at the beginning of making connections between our own practices of forgiveness and justice and peace in the world.

Nonviolence has to be explored as a real alternative to conflict on interpersonal and societal levels. Examples of nonviolent social action are becoming better known: Gandhi's liberation of India, Martin Luther King's campaign for civil rights, Mandela's resolution of apartheid issues, and Czechoslovakia's Velvet Revolution are at least known to us—if not yet deeply understood. Parents and teachers are especially important in helping foster the development of skills for nonviolent conflict resolution. Embodying nonviolence in all of our spheres of influence will demonstrate its power and spread its influence.

## Conclusion

The topic of peace and the question of when the use of force could be considered morally justifiable have once again become urgent. As this chapter has shown, the ultimate goal has always been peace, but now peace is understood as embracing the fullness of economic justice for all and forgiveness born of love for the other and a sense of human solidarity. The nature of war, of the use of force, has also changed as weapons technology has developed into means of mass destruction. Humanity has seen the realities of the cycle of violence in previously unbelievable forms of torture, genocide, suicide bombers, and international terrorism. Unilateralism endangers the universal common good which requires collaboration and new ways of dealing with the inevitable conflicts that arise among human beings.

In short, we are in one of those periods during which new ways of speaking, thinking, and acting are absolutely essential. That we live out Jesus' call to be peacemakers is more necessary than ever. This means living out of a vision of a peaceful world intended for all by the God in whom we believe. And it also means daily action in the spirit of the kind of peace of which Paul VI spoke when he wrote in *Populorum Progressio*: "Peace cannot be limited to a mere absence of war, the result of an ever precarious balance of forces. No, peace is something that is built up day after day, in the pursuit of an order intended by God, which implies a more perfect form of justice" among all people (*PP* 76).

## References

Bernardin, Joseph Cardinal. "The Changing Nuclear Debate in the 1990s." *Origins* 19/39 (March 1, 1990): 629, 631–634.

Bernardin, Joseph Cardinal. "*The Challenge of Peace* Revisited." In *One Hundred Years of Catholic Social Thought*. Ed. John Coleman. Maryknoll, N.Y.: Orbis Books, 1991. Pp. 273–285.

Christiansen, Drew (2002a). "After Sept. 11: Catholic Teaching on Peace and War." *Origins* 32/3 (May 30, 2002): 33, 35–40.

Christiansen, Drew (2002b). "Hawks, Doves and Pope John Paul II." *America* 187/4 (August 12-19, 2002): 9–11.

Egan, Eileen. *Peace Be with You: Justified Warfare or the Way of Nonviolence*. Maryknoll, N.Y.: Orbis Books, 1999.

Gumbleton, Bishop Thomas. "Peacemaking as a Way of Life." In *One Hundred Years of Catholic Social Thought*. Ed. John Coleman. Maryknoll, N.Y.: Orbis Books, 1991. Pp. 303–316.

Hehir, J. Bryan. "The Just War Ethic and Catholic Theology: Dynamics of Change and Continuity" In *War or Peace? The Search for New Answers*. Ed. Thomas Shannon. Maryknoll, N.Y.: Orbis Books, 1980. Pp. 15–39.

Hehir, J. Bryan. "Catholic Teaching on War and Peace: The Decade 1979–89." *Theology: Challenges for the Future*. Ed. Charles Curran. New York: Paulist Press, 1990. Pp. 355–384.

Himes, Kenneth M. "Pacifism and the Just War Tradition in Roman Catholic Social Teaching." In *One Hundred Years of Catholic Social Thought*. Ed. John Coleman. Maryknoll, N.Y.: Orbis Books, 1991. Pp. 329–344.

Himes, Kenneth M. "Pacifism." In *The New Dictionary of Catholic Social Thought*. Ed. Judith Dwyer. Collegeville, Minn.: The Liturgical Press, 1994. Pp. 707–708.

John Paul II, Pope. "Message for World Peace Day." *America* 186/1 (January 7-14, 2002): 7–11.

Johnson, James Turner. *Just War Tradition and the Restraint of War: A Moral and Historical Inquiry*. Princeton, N.J.: Princeton University Press, 1981.

Kaldor, Mary. "Who Killed the Cold War?" *Bulletin of Atomic Scientists* 51/4 (July/August, 1995): 57–60.

Kaldor, Mary. *New and Old Wars: Organized Violence in a Global Era*. Stanford, California: Stanford University Press, 1999.

Lammers Stephen. "Roman Catholic Social Ethics and Pacifism." In *War or Peace? The Search for New Answers.* Ed. Thomas Shannon. Maryknoll, N.Y.: Orbis Books, 1980. Pp. 93–103.

Lammers, Stephen. "Peace." In *The New Dictionary of Catholic Social Thought.* Ed. Judith Dwyer. Collegeville, Minn.: The Liturgical Press, 1994. Pp. 717–721.

Langendorfer, Hans. "Disarmament." In *The New Dictionary of Catholic Social Thought.* Ed. Judith Dwyer. Collegeville, Minn.: The Liturgical Press, 1994. Pp. 292–294.

National Conference of Catholic Bishops (NCCB). "The Challenge of Peace: God's Promise and Our Response." *Origins* 13/1 (1983): 1, 3–32.

National Conference of Catholic Bishops (NCCB). "The Harvest of Justice Is Sown in Peace." *Origins* 23/26 (December 9, 1993): 449, 451–464.

O'Brien, David. "The American Catholic Opposition to the Vietnam War." In *War or Peace? The Search for New Answers.* Ed. Thomas Shannon. Maryknoll, N.Y.: Orbis Books, 1980. Pp. 119–150.

United States Conference of Catholic Bishops (USCCB). "Living with Faith and Hope after September 11." *Origins* 31/25 (2001): 413, 415–420.

# Conclusion:
# Revelation, church, and "eucharistic living"
# as the legacy of Vatican II

WILLIAM MCDONOUGH

> . . . Order is the only possibility of rest.
>
> The made order must seek the given order, and find its place
>> in it . . .
>
> The scattered members must be brought together. . .
>
> Rest and rejoicing belong to the task, and are its grace.
>
> Let tomorrow come tomorrow. Not by your will is the house
>> carried through the night.
>
> Order is only the possibility of rest.
>
> —Wendell Berry, "Healing"

In this book's introduction, Bishop Lucker noted that the usual way of listing the Second Vatican Council's documents is church first, and revelation second. But, then he gave his blessing to ordering our book differently: revelation first, and church second. It did not much matter to him.

At this book's end, I come back to Bishop Lucker's openness on this question as help for our grasping the legacy of Vatican II. Revelation and church; or, church and revelation? Maybe it does not much matter. Maybe what does matter deeply—maybe what the legacy of Vatican II above all else is—is that we learn to keep revelation and church together; that we come to see and live their connection; that we learn how overplaying one is (already has been) harmful for our life of faith.

Wendell Berry's words above illumine the challenge we face. The poet speaks of "order" in two senses. Or, he speaks of one order that has two dimensions: the made order and the given order. Order both is *the only* possibility of rest, and it is *only the* possibility of rest. The one order on which our lives depend is both a task and a gift. Order as task and as gift illumines the relationship of church and revelation. Are they not the two sides of the one order Berry describes?

Bishop Lucker wanted this book to focus on church, that is, on order as a task for us, on order as *the only* possibility of rest. His introduction to this book speaks of his desire, not for some new church, but for us to learn together "how to be a good church, how to be a renewed church, and how to touch the hearts of people." He was engaged until his death with this concern. The renewal seeker's order is a made one, continually worked on.

Bishop Lucker also wanted this book to focus on revelation; that is, on order as a gift for us, on order as *only the* possibility of rest. He quoted Psalm 116 in almost every conversation I had with him at the end of his life:

> What shall I return to the LORD for all his bounty to me?
> I will lift up the cup of salvation and call on the name of the LORD,
> I will pay my vows to the LORD in the presence of all his people.
> Precious in the sight of the LORD is the death of his faithful ones. (Psalm 116:12–15)

The psalmist's order—that even his dying is safe in God—is not a made order, but one accepted as a gift. Bishop Lucker concerned himself at the end of his life with keeping these two senses of order together.

Our book, *Revelation and the Church,* is about order, both as given and made. Church, Berry's made order, insists that whatever we claim to know of God either leads us toward life shared with others or it is deception. Church is self-critical order that keeps seeking to become more responsible. Revelation, Berry's given order, insists that whatever order we have established is provisional—part of a final, full order hidden in God. This order does not make too much of itself; it rests and trusts.

Vatican II actually gave a third set of names to our twin pairs of revelation-church and the given-made orders. It spoke of the heavenly and earthly churches. *Lumen Gentium* emphasized the unity between the two: "The earthly church and the church endowed with heavenly riches are not to be thought of as two realities. On the contrary, they form one complex reality comprising a human and a divine element" (*LG* 8).

Our book addresses the believer's need—that is, the need of every one of us—to keep together the made and given orders, church and revelation, the visible and the invisible churches. Our first and primary conclusion is that it does not much matter whether we talk first about revelation or first about church, only that we always talk about and try more and more to live them together.

If the primary legacy of Vatican II is a challenge to keep church and revelation together in our common life, then Catholic theologian Peter Drilling outlines what we face:

> We have to be careful not to separate the invisible from the visible church. That has been one possible solution to the corruption found in the visible church. Since there is corruption, that isn't really the church at all. The real church is the invisible church. But, no, we would say that the visible and the invisible are the same church, and that is why we fret (sometimes too much, in my view) about who is in the church and to what extent. But to the point is the fact that Jesus quite clearly chose very flawed disciples. Which would we say is an inviting figure if one is looking for a pure, unsullied character to represent Christ? Peter, Thomas, any of them? Yet, Jesus loved them and welcomed them to be apostles despite their rejection of him before his executioners and others. In other words, for reasons too mysterious for me to fathom, the triune God seems content with a messy church that goes through terrible contortions to try to get it right. Indeed, what does getting it right mean? Your view? My view? Whose view? One thing we can at least do is pay attention to all the church's members, whether in Rome or in any/every local church, whether pope or bishop or presbyter or deacon or every interested member of the baptized faithful. We are all in this together. Is that what the church universal means? It's not about a location, but about the whole People of God. And here we are again, back at the priestly, prophetic and royal People of God. (Drilling, personal correspondence; see also Drilling, 1988)

So, the primary legacy of Vatican II is a challenge to keep revelation and church together. A brief second thing can be said, and it arises from Drilling's words about our "messy contortions" as we try to "get it right" in the church. While this book was conceived as one about changes in the church, it has become one about order in its two dimensions. Change is certainly connected to both parts of order. And so the appendix of this book reprints large portions of Bishop Lucker's lists about changes in church teachings that have already occurred and about changes that may someday occur.

Change, though, particularly the question of what particular changes should now happen, is a corollary concern to our main task of keeping revelation and church together. Whatever changes occur must themselves serve the goal of keeping revelation and church together. As Drilling suggests, what changes need to be made is less central than is a process of "paying attention to all the church's members." The process is more important than the product. It is not only Drilling's words that indicate this; so did the words and actions of Bishop Lucker.

There is a third and last conclusion, also corollary, but this one to be outlined at greater length. Our book turns out to be an at least partial description of what the process of keeping revelation and church, the two orders, together will entail. Not only Wendell Berry's poem, but also one of this book's essays spoke directly to the question of order. Paul Feela's essay asks what the place of the sacrament of penance is in the "order of the faithful." The order of the faithful, he writes, comprises the *ordinary* life of believers. And then he defines this ordinary life as "eucharistic living, embodying redemption by living a reconciled life" (see chapter 8 above).

Eucharistic living summarizes the order achieved by keeping revelation and church together. Is such living not what results when revelation is authenticated in the communal lives of human beings, and when the church does not make an idol of its own ordering function? Each of this book's twelve essays adds something to a description of eucharistic living, of revelation and church ordered to each other.

Let us look back, then, a last time at what we have learned from our twelve essays about Vatican II's legacy of order, of its vision for our ordinary, eucharistic lives.

First, Terence Nichols's essay claims evolution and revelation share the view that human beings are involved in a journey that is bigger than any of us reckoned with when we began it. Revelation, he says, does not add specific content to scientific descriptions about how the journey of evolution happens; it adds only trust that this journey is leading somewhere. His essay gives at least this content to eucharistic living:

because of its confidence that truth will set us free (see Jn 8:32), it seeks and listens to truth wherever it arises and never closes itself down in the search for truth.

Catherine Cory and Corrine Patton's essay on a scriptural under-standing of revelation emphasizes revelation as the personal insertion of God's own self into human history. God's initiative of love supports what is truest about human beings and prophetically challenges human beings to become more human. From this essay we learn that revelation is transformative knowledge that leads to different living. Eucharistic living is transformed living.

Chris Franke and Vincent Skemp's essay emphasizes how much the official Catholic Church has grown in its approach to the Bible in the last century. The church reads the Bible now as a pilgrim, not searching for final answers but for help and confidence on its journey. Eucharis-tic, ordinary living for believers meditates on the scriptures and on its "great cloud of witnesses" (Heb 12:1) as it makes its own way.

For J. Michael Byron, the church is a community of communities in which unity is measured more by engagement than by uniformity. Here is Byron's contribution to our description of eucharistic living: ". . . one cannot understand the gospel without living it concretely in a local communion of love."

Byron speaks of the "great urgency" of ecumenism for any church —that is, for our Vatican II church—that understands its identity as communion. From Byron's wonderful start, this book could have gone on to engage the urgent ecumenical and interfaith challenges we face. That this book is missing specific attention to these challenges is a weakness. But the ecumenical and interfaith challenges are not different in kind from the one already clear from Byron's essay (as well as from Terence Nichols's essay): eucharistic living seeks communion wherever there are openings to it.

Susan Wood's essay on bishops as teachers gives a further element to our description of eucharistic living. The present scandals of church leadership notwithstanding, hierarchy (literally "sacred or holy rule") is not opposed to eucharistic living. Indeed, Vatican II's understanding of bishops as prophetic leaders underlines a further element of eucharistic living. What matters first is holiness. What Wood calls the "communal and dialogical" authority of bishops is an authority that only holiness can carry into the world.

Catherine Michaud's and my essay on the papal apologies further specifies Wood's point. Leading by holiness in this life has repentance as its primary form. Repentance, willingness to change directions and start again, is at the heart of eucharistic living. The recent papal apologies clarify that our biggest failures in eucharistic living have been failures of love, even more than failures of intelligence.

J. Michael Joncas's essay addresses five aspects of the mystery of the eucharist: memorial, sacrament, sign, bond, and banquet. Joncas writes: "The Eucharist is not an end in itself: it gives participants a foretaste of the kingdom banquet of heaven and it impels worshipers out into the world to do good works." It is the Eucharist that brings the made and given orders, the orders of task and gift, together. Eucharistic living is a life of good works fed by God.

Paul Feela's essay gave us the term "eucharistic living." That he shows sacramental penance as an "extraordinary" form of forgiveness in the church suggests just how radical "ordinary" eucharistic living is. Such living accepts that working toward personal and communal reconciliation is the ordinary task of a believer. Eucharistic living forgives "seven times seventy times" (Mt 18:22).

Shawn Madigan's essay on inculturation underlines the messiness and spaciousness of the order that comprises ordinary eucharistic living. We have barely begun to live the vision of adapting and inculturating the life of prayer that Madigan develops in this essay.

Paul Wojda's essay—and the deep consistent ethic of life he describes—implies that eucharistic living may never be content with entrenched name-calling on the so-called "life issues" of abortion, euthanasia, and capital punishment. If it is a "culture of life" that the church is seeking to build up, then eucharistic living is the never-ending search to make connections with the other, or finally to see the deep connections with the other that are already there.

Russell Connors's essay on marriage says Vatican II makes clear that something is "going forward" in our understanding of human love. Eucharistic living is willing to live itself into a deeper understanding of love. It acknowledges that it does not yet know how to love. By such living, we will ourselves become better able to discern the forms that love takes in our world. Eucharistic living, we could come to understand from Connors's essay, accepts that it will know more the more it loves. It redoubles its efforts to love in order to scan the horizon to see more clearly where love is emerging in the world.

Finally, Amata Miller's essay on peace and justifiable war could not be more timely. Sent with the rest of this book to the publisher just a year after the attacks of September 11, 2001, it goes to print as talk of further war is in the air. This essay—and eucharistic living—does not pretend to know in advance when war is justified. But it makes clear that our own eucharistic living is what makes us able even to begin to know a practical way toward peace in the world. Miller claims that Catholic teaching is more and more insistent that good judgments about peace in the world will come only from people working on forgiveness in their own lives. Eucharistic living, it again comes clear, takes the plank out of its own eye before it messes with specks in the eyes of others (Mt 7:3).

The legacy of Vatican II is that we must keep revelation and church together. Its corollary legacy is to show us that this happens only in the fragile dying and rising of eucharistic living. We do well to close here with the episcopal motto of Bishop Lucker, for it contains and holds together both parts of order. Like the father of the epileptic boy in Mark's Gospel, Bishop Lucker asked for a deeper sense of the given order, of revelation; and he pledged his dedication to the made order, to church. With both the father of that boy in the gospel and with Bishop Lucker, we would do well to say: "Lord, I do believe. But help my lack of trust" (Mk 9:24). (This is a paraphrase from several different translations of the verse. Bishop Lucker brought a wood carving of these words into his retirement.)

## References

Berry, Wendell. "Healing." In *What Are People For?* San Francisco, Calif.: North Point Press, 1990. Pp. 9–13.

Drilling, Peter. "The Priest, Prophet and King Trilogy: Elements of Its Meaning in *Lumen Gentium* and for Today." *Eglise et Théologie* 19 (1988): 179–206.

# Appendix:
# Some notes by Bishop Lucker
# on change in the church

Beginning sometime in the late 1980s, Bishop Lucker began preparing two documents detailing changes and possible future changes in authoritative church teaching. These documents were meant for classroom use and are very informal. We are reproducing parts of each of the documents. In each case, we have edited out material that was not immediately relevant to the topic of this book.

The first part of this appendix (ONE: CHANGES) reproduces Bishop Lucker's notes on thirty-seven of an original list of sixty-four topics on which church teaching has changed over the years. The second part of this appendix (TWO: TEACHINGS THAT COULD CHANGE) reproduces Bishop Lucker's notes on fifteen of an original list of twenty-two topics on which church teaching could someday change.

Both parts of this appendix are in exactly the same (informal) order of Bishop Lucker's original notes. We have not added additional or explanatory references. Each part of the appendix begins with a listing of the topics to be treated. Then each topic on the list is taken up singly. After the topic is named, Bishop Lucker's notes are divided into an "A" section (which details church teaching as it has been historically) and a "B" section (which details either how the teaching has already changed or may one day change). It should be noted particularly in the second part of this appendix (on teachings that might change in the future) that Bishop Lucker includes arguments for change proposed by various theological sources without indicating whether he agrees with the proposed change or not.

---

Note: Throughout the appendix Bishop Lucker cites conciliar documents according to the translation of Walter Abbott, ed. *The Documents of Vatican II*. New York: Guild Press, 1966.

## I. CHANGES IN AUTHORITATIVE CHURCH TEACHINGS

1. Authority
2. Biblical Criticism
3. Bishops—Election
4. Church and State
5. Church Can Err
6. Confession
7. Creation in Six Days
8. Democracy
9. Development of Doctrine
10. Dissent
11. Eastern Schism
12. Ecclesiology
13. Ecumenism
14. Ensoulment
15. Error Has No Rights
16. Galileo
17. Gospels—Authorship of the Gospels
18. Inculturation
19. Infallibility of Encyclicals
20. Jews
21. Justice in the Church
22. Laity—Participation in the Church
23. Local Church
24. Marriage—Definition of
25. Membership in the Church
26. Modernism
27. Moses—Author of the Pentateuch
28. Religious Freedom
29. Revelation
30. Sacramental Theology
31. Salvation
32. Sexuality
33. Slavery
34. Social Teaching
35. Teaching Role of Bishops
36. Women
37. Worship—Changes

*Key*:
**Teaching**
**A.** Description and Source
**B.** Teaching as changed, developed, expressed differently, or denied

## 1. Authority

**A.**  1.  For one pope to appear to go against another is seen as unacceptable because it would undermine papal authority. Emphasizes status, hierarchic, uniformity, centralization, authoritarianism.

2.  Boniface VIII taught that no one can be saved except in obedient subjection to the Roman Pontiff—necessary for salvation—all people are subject to the pope: "We declare, state and define that it is absolutely necessary to salvation for every human creature to be subject to the Roman Pontiff"—Boniface VIII, 13th century (Denzinger-Schönmetzer, 875).

3.  *Humani Generis* (1950s) said that whenever a pope goes out of his way to speak on a controverted issue, the subject is no longer a matter of free debate among theologians.

**B.**  1.  Vatican II expressly rejected the teaching of *Humani Generis*.

2.  Pope John XXIII said the substance of church teaching is one thing, the way that it is taught another. John XXIII said we convince more by the argumentation than by force (speech at beginning of Vatican II). See also Vatican II, *GS* 62.

3.  Pope Gregory the Great, in the commentary on the Book of Job, reproved those "who do not seek to correct their subjects by calmly reasoning with them, but rather hasten domineeringly to compel their assent." Elsewhere he writes, "Holy Church says: Do not consent to my statements because I am in a position of authority, but aim rather through reasoning to determine their truth" (*The Tablet*, 25 June 1994).

## 2. Biblical Criticism

**A.**  1.  *Testem Benevolentiae*—Leo XIII
    a)  Exegetes could not apply mere natural criticism to the sacred books.
    b)  Bible is unique and could not be compared with other near Eastern literature.

          c)   Inspiration restricted to the author whose name was known by tradition and not to the editors.

          d)   Several sources theory unaccepted.

    2.   Leo XII (*Ubi Primum*,1824) and Pius IX (*Qui Pluribus*, 1846) wrote against translating the Bible into the vernacular.

**B.**   1.   Pius XII: *Divino Afflante Spiritu,* 1943

          a)   Not just Vulgate

          b)   Go back to original languages.

          c)   Use historical method.

          d)   Study the literary forms.

    2.   Vatican II: "In order to get at what the biblical writers intended, attention should be paid (among other things) to literary genres . . . historical and cultural context" *DV* 12.

    3.   John Paul II on 25th anniversary of the Constitution on Divine Revelation: "To claim, as fundamentalists do, that the Word of God can be grasped without taking into account the human aspects of its expression leads to all kinds of errors and illusions."

    4.   Pontifical Biblical Commission, "The Interpretation of the Bible in the Church" (*Origins*, 10 January 1994).

## 3. Bishops—Election

**A.**   1.   The Council of Nicea established once and for all that bishops must be elected by all the bishops of a province with final confirmation by the metropolitan and that no bishop can be transferred to another diocese (McBrien column, 24 August 1989).

    2.   At Vatican I there was not a single black bishop.

    3.   The Second Lateran Council (Canon 28) in 1139 prescribed that all bishops were to be elected by the appropriate cathedral chapter.

    4.   It was a custom for centuries in many European countries that rulers had the authority to nominate bishops.

**B.**   1.   All bishops are now appointed by the pope.

    2.   At Vatican II there were perhaps 500 black bishops.

    3.   Today (1988) there are seven or eight black cardinals (Lauret, *50 Years*).

    4.   "What history does tell us is that the episcopal selection system we now have and the relative roles in it of Rome and the local

church are products of the 19th century and its needs. The system is not absolute. It has changed in the past. It can change again." (James Hennesy, *America*, 8 November 1986, p. 292).

## 4. Church and State

**A.**   1.   Gregory XVI in 1832 encyclical *Mirari Vos* condemned Lamennais's notion of religious liberty and the separation of church and state.
2.   Pius IX (in *Syllabus of Errors*, 1864) condemned the statement: "The Church is to be separated from the state and the state from the Church."
3.   That document also condemned the view that "in the present day, it is no longer necessary that the Catholic religion be held as the only religion of the state to the exclusion of all other modes of worship."
4.   Bishop Felix Dupanlop of Orleans developed distinction between thesis and hypothesis regarded by Connell of Catholic University as official Catholic teaching.
5. Leo XIII, *Longinque Oceani.*

**B.**   1.   Vatican II

## 5. Church Can Err

**A.**   1.   Church as a divine institution without spot or wrinkle: Church itself as pure and holy.
2.   Perfect society—complete institution
3.   Communio

**B.**   1.   *Ecclesia semper reformanda*
2.   Pilgrim Church—Church of sinners
3.   People of God—sometimes unfaithful
4.   "The Church, holding sinners in its embrace, is at the same time holy and always in need of being purified and incessantly pursues the path of penance and renewal" (*LG* 8, *UR* 6).
5.   The church itself in its official actions has committed errors and sins.
   a)   Burning heretics
   b)   Persecuting Jews
   c)   Excesses of Holy Wars
6.   Statement of John Paul II calling for recognition of errors and mistakes in preparation for the year 2000—apostolic letter *Ter-*

*tio Millennio Adveniente* (1994) called on the church to repent for serious historic offenses. "Acknowledging the weakness of the past is an act of honesty and courage which helps us strengthen our faith, alerts us to face today's temptations, and challenges and prepares us to meet them."

## 6. Confession

**A.** 1.  In 813 the bishops of Gaul assembled to address the pressing concerns of the day. One of these was whether Catholics could confess their sins to God alone to receive forgiveness from him or were obliged rather to approach a priest for divine pardon. The bishops of Gaul declared that Catholics were free to choose either way of obtaining forgiveness. "Confession, consequently, which is made to God forgives sins. That (confession) also, which is made to a priest, we equally affirm brings forgiveness. For God, the author and giver of salvation and health, is wont to display his power by invisible action through the former, while through the latter by priestly healing" (Second Council of Chalon, 813) quoted by James MacLaughlin in *NCR,* July 3, 1992.

**B.** 1.  Council of Trent spoke of the necessity of confessing all mortal sins according to kind and number to a priest. It did not, however, deny the possibility of forgiveness by God if a person has the right kind of contrition. "The first thing the pastor must teach about confession, therefore, is its supreme importance, and in fact its necessity" (*Roman Catechism,* Kevane translation, Pt. 2, sec. 4, Penance, n. 36).

   2.  Rite of Penance gives three forms.

## 7. Creation in Six Days

**A.** 1.  Common teaching was that according to Genesis the world was created in six days.

**B.** 1.  1948—Biblical Commission characterized the creation account: "relates in simple and figurative language, adapted to the understanding of a less developed people, the fundamental truth presupposed for the economy of salvation, as well as the popular description of the origin of the human race" (McBrien, 11 February, 1982).

## 8. Democracy

**A.** 1. *Syllabus of Errors,* 1864, condemned democracy.

 2. For many centuries up until 1870 popes had set a most undemocratic example when they ruled the papal states as absolute monarchs.

**B.** 1. Leo XIII encyclical *Libertas* (20 June 1888) said that it was official teaching that "the church observes no form of government that is not *per se* adapted to preserving the good of its citizens."

 2. Pope John XXIII was the first pope in Catholic history to endorse democracy. He said in the encyclical *Pacem in Terris*, "It must not be concluded, however, that because authority comes from God, therefore men have no right to choose those who are to rule the state, to decide the form of government, and to determine both the way in which authority is to be exercised and its limits. It is thus clear that the doctrine which we have set forth is fully consonant with any truly democratic regime."

## 9. Development of Doctrine

**A.** 1. Pope John XXIII opening speech at Vatican II: The substance of the ancient deposit of faith is one thing and the way in which it is presented is another.

**B.** 1. Vatican II, *DV* 8, says, "This tradition which comes from the apostles develops in the church with the help of the Holy Spirit. For there is a growth in the understanding of the realities and the words which have been handed down. This happens through the contemplation and study made by believers, who treasure these things in their hearts (cf. Lk 2:19, 51), through the intimate understanding of spiritual things they experience and through the preaching of those who have received through episcopal succession the sure gift of truth. For as the centuries succeed one another the church constantly moves forward toward the fullness of divine truth until the words of God reach their complete fulfillment in her."

## 10. Dissent

**A.** 1. Prior to Vatican Council II many theologians were silenced because they dissented from accepted Catholic teaching.

    2.  Pius XII in *Humani Generis* stated that there is "no possibility of dissent" after a pope "goes out of his way" to speak on a controverted matter.

**B.**  1.  Dissent is good for the church. "Dissent is not a threat but an invigorating contribution to continued life and growth." "Whatever its name, whatever opposition, dissent, disagreement, critical evaluation—a community without it is a community in comfortable stagnation" (McCormick, *America*, 8 November 1986, pp. 279–280).

    2.  The bishops of the United States laid out conditions under which dissent is legitimate in their statement, "Human Life in Our Day," 1968.

    3.  "Dissent"—"questioning" or "reflection" might be better words—is essential for theological enterprise. If everyone accepted the status quo, there would of course be no questioning. If there is no questioning, however, there can be no development of doctrine. If there is no development of doctrine, then the church and its teaching are no longer alive" (Fogarty, *America*, 11 October 1986, p. 184).

    4.  Vatican II, *GS* 62: "Let it be recognized that all the faithful, clerical and lay, possess a lawful freedom of inquiry and thought and the freedom to express their minds humbly and courageously about those matters in which they enjoy competence."

## 11. Eastern Schism

**A.**  1.  It is an error to say that "The Roman pontiffs, by their too arbitrary conduct, have contributed to the division of the Church into Eastern and Western" (*Syllabus of Errors*, n. 38, 1864, Pius IX). It was thought that the Papal States were essential to the independence of the pope.

**B.**  1.  "Pope John XXIII was perfectly happy to admit on several occasions that papal policy *vis a vis* the eastern Churches had not always, in earlier centuries, been wise, during the developing quarrel with Constantinople" (E. Y. Hales, *Pope John*, pp. 31–32).

    2.  Paul VI also.

## 12. Ecclesiology

**A.**  1.  The Church of Christ is the Catholic Church.

2. The Church is a perfect society.
3. The Church is considered primarily as hierarchy.
4. The Church is a spiritual organization concerned with preaching the word and celebrating the sacraments.

**B.**  1. The Church of Jesus Christ subsists in the Catholic Church.
2. The Church is a mystery, human as well as divine.
3. The Church is the whole people of God.
4. The mission of the Church includes service to human needs in the social, economic, and political order.

## 13. Ecumenism

**A.**  1. Pius XI—*Mortalium Animos,* 1928—condemnation of the ecumenical movement
   a) Congresses open to all who invoke the name of Christ cannot lead to unity but are "subversive of the foundations of the Catholic faith."
   b) There is but one way . . . by furthering the return to the one true Church of Christ, "for from that one true Church they have in the past fallen away."
2. Pius XII did not relax this ban, *Humani Generis.*
3. Leo XIII also—see Fogarty, *The Vatican and American Hierarchy,* p. 140.
4. Association for the promotion of the Unity of Christendom condemned by Holy Office in 1864.
5. Solemn declaration of the Council of Florence 1438 on relation of Holy Roman Church to other Christian Churches. This council restored unity, "but in subsequent centuries much more extensive dissensions made their appearance and large communities came to be separated from the full communion of the Catholic Church."
6. Pius XI, "The crafty enemies of the Church and human society attempt to seduce the people in many ways."
7. "Under the protection of the Bible Societies which have long since been condemned by this Holy See, they distribute to the faithful under the pretext of religion, the Holy Bible in vernacular translations" (*Nostis et Nobiscum,* 14).

**B.**  1. Pope John XXIII invited Protestants to the Council and gave them choice seats—copies of the documents in their own language—created Secretariat for Christian Unity.

2. Accepting blame (on both sides) for separation and disunity in the Church (Vatican II Decree on Ecumenism).

3. Decree on Ecumenism reversed condemnation of common prayer for unity and urged cooperation.

## 14. Ensoulment

**A.** 1. For many centuries it was common church teaching that some period of time was required before ensoulment would take place, 40 days for male and 80 days for female fetuses.

**B.** 1. The present standard Roman Catholic position is that a complete human person arises at the time of fertilization. A departure from what was held by Church teachers for centuries. "This new position is backed by reference to recent scientific discoveries. It is argued that the complete genetic code for a new individual is present from the very moment of fertilization and that the genome is what constitutes a human individual" (Hansen, *America*, 22 October 1994, p. 15).

## 15. Error Has No Rights

**A.** 1. It was commonly taught that "error has no rights." Cardinal Ottaviani, prefect of the Holy Office, was a champion of this position.

2. Augustine wrote a treatise on the right of the state to suppress non-Catholics. Augustine's treatise was used to justify the Inquisition. The basic premise was that error has no rights (see article by Tim Unsworth on the Inquisition in *Salt*, July-August 1991).

**B.** 1. John XXIII—*Pacem in Terris,* 1963—discarded the axiom that error has no rights. Used by the inquisitors and heresy hunters down to modern times to torture if not burn dissenters such as: Joan of Arc, Savanarola, and Jan Hus among others. He likewise distinguished between communism as an atheistic creed to be condemned and a political system to be contended with.

## 16. Galileo

**A.** 1. Galileo was condemned in 1633 because he denied that the earth was the center of the universe and that the earth revolves about the sun. The issue was that Galileo taught something which seemed to go contrary to the teaching of the scriptures which say that the sun rises and sets. Cardinal Bellarmine said that "the Council of Trent forbids the interpretation of the scriptures in a way contrary to the common opinion of the Holy Fathers . . . all agree in interpreting them literally as teaching that the sun is in the heavens and revolves around the earth with immense speed, and that the earth is very distant from the heavens, at the center of the universe and motionless." Galileo was sentenced to abjure his "heresy" and to keep silent on the subject for the rest of his life.

**B.**  1.  In 1992 Pope John Paul II received a report from a special commission to study the issue which formed the basis for Galileo's trial, and the pope admitted the error of the church's condemnation. The pope termed the situation a "tragic, mutual, incomprehension." *Time* magazine said, "Galileo contended that the scriptures cannot err but are often misunderstood." "This insight," said Pope John Paul, "made the scientist a wiser theologian than his accusers" (*Time*, 28 December 1992).

## 17. Gospels—Authorship of the Gospels

**A.**  1.  Severe restrictions on this by Biblical Commission 1905–1915: for example, that the apostle Matthew wrote the first gospel before the others and before the destruction of Jerusalem. Scholars are not free to advance the two-source theory. The Apostle John wrote the fourth gospel.
   2.  *Pascendi,* Pius X, September 8, 1907, n. 34.
   3.  Rome around 1910 affirmed that the letter to the Hebrews was written by Paul (Rahner, *Faith in a Wintery Season*, p. 144).

**B.**  1.  Pontifical Biblical Commission issued an "Instruction on the Historical Truth of the Gospels" (1964) that gives three stages in gospel development: (1) Jesus, (2) apostolic preachers, (3) sacred authors. The evangelists "selected some things, reduced others to a synthesis, and still others they explicated, keeping in mind the situation of the churches."

## 18. Inculturation

**A.**  1.  Up until shortly before Vatican Council II, church teaching was expressed through Greek philosophical concepts, Roman organizational structures, Germanic tribal customs, and European social and political forms.

**B.** 1.    Through advances in the historical critical method, new theological methodologies. Through liberation theology and feminist theology new efforts were made to express the teachings of the church in language and forms understandable to the people of the present day. For example, the biblical message has to be translated from its Aramaic, Greek, or Hebrew expression into modern modes enabling it to be used in prayer, work, social life, customs, legislation, science, and art in diverse locales and cultures.

    2.    Theology is the science of understanding the truths of faith using human experience, human language, human philosophy and other studies. The African Synod especially stressed the importance of inculturation.

## 19. Infallibility of Encyclicals

**A.** 1.    "Generally what is expounded and inculcated in Encyclical Letters already for other reasons appertains to Catholic doctrine. But if the Supreme Pontiffs in their official documents purposely pass judgment on a matter up to that time under dispute, it is obvious that that matter, according to the mind of the same Pontiffs, cannot be any longer considered a question "open to free debate among theologians." Pope Pius XII *Humani Genesis: Concerning some false opinions threatening to undermine the foundations of Catholic doctrine* (August 12, 1950).

**B.** 1.    Changed in pre-Vatican II document to "public debate."
      a)    Does not appear in final Constitution on the Church.
    2.    John XXIII, opening speech at Vatican II: "The substance of the ancient deposit of faith is one thing and the way in which it is presented is another" (Peter Hebblethwaite, *Pope John XXIII, Shepherd of the Modern World,* 432; Abbott, 715). "Today the Spouse of Christ prefers to use the medicine of mercy rather than severity. She considers that she meets the needs of the present age by showing the validity of her teaching rather than by condemnations" (Abbott, 716).
    3.    See Sullivan, *Magisterium,* p. 155.
    4.    Practice—e.g., teaching of Pius XII on membership in the church —is changed.

5. Vatican II decree on Ecumenism vs. Pius XI, *Mortalium Animos.*

6. Vatican II on Religious Freedom and teaching of Leo XIII and other popes on obligation of Catholic rulers to suppress Protestant evangelism.

7. Deepest divisions of Vatican II were over changing papal teaching.

8. "To say that an issue is settled and not a subject for dialogue is to assert that the Roman position enjoys the prerogative of 'infallibility.' If it does not, at the very least, there must exist the possibility of its being reversed. And as long as that possibility is a viable one, dialogue in the church must go on" (Wm. H. Shannon, *America,* October 12, 1991).

9. ". . . It belongs to the Holy See to support and guide the discussion (which may lead to authentic—or even definitive, therefore infallible teaching), which may issue in a definitive statement of faith. It does not belong to the Petrine office to cut short this discussion prematurely and impose a uniformity that does not actually exist. Attempts at such unilateral decision-making in the past have often been notably unsuccessful" (John A. Wright, S.J., *Theological Studies,* , March 1987, pp. 42–43).

## 20. Jews

A.  1. For centuries on Good Friday Catholics prayed for the "perfidious Jews." The Jews at the time of Christ and the Jewish people were accused of being responsible for killing Christ, justifying it from scripture passages. Many popes through the centuries issued encyclicals expressing anti-Semitism. For example: Benedict XIV in 1751, *A quo Primum*; Alexander III, 1159–1181; Innocent III, 1198–1216; Innocent IV, 1243–1254.

2. In 1555 Pope Paul IV, who set up the Inquisition in Rome, issued an edict imposing humiliating restrictions on Jews because "It is absurd and improper that Jews who have fallen into eternal servitude by their own guilt should presume . . . to make so bold as to live intermingled with Christians, to wear no distinguishing mark, to employ Christian servants, even to purchase houses."

3. The Council of Florence taught that Jews and schismatics were definitely damned.

4. Pius X wrote to Theodor Herzl, founder of political Zionism, "We cannot prevent the Jews from going to Jerusalem, but we could never sanction it. The ground of Jerusalem, already sacred,

has been sanctified by the life of Christ. As head of the Church I can give no other answer. The Jews have not recognized our Lord; therefore we cannot recognize the Jewish people."

**B.**  1.  Pope John XXIII wanted Vatican Council II to make a statement on the Jews. He dropped the prayers of Good Friday referring to the perfidious Jews.
  2.  The Vatican II declaration on the relationship of the church to non-Christian religions contains a section on the Jews.
  3.  Powerful members of the Roman Curia opposed the document prepared by Cardinal Bea. They publicly insisted that Bea's draft contradicted the biblical account of the crucifixion and refused to admit that the Jews as a people were not guilty of deicide. The declaration states that the Church "deplores the hatred, persecutions, and displays of anti-semitism directed against the Jews at any time and from any source." In effect, a condemnation of the behavior of many popes down the centuries.

## 21. Justice in the Church

**A.**  1.  Salaries and benefits of lay employees.
  2.  Stipends and retirement of religious.
  3.  Racism in the Church.
  4.  Sexism in the Church.
  5.  Due process.
  6.  Ordination of women.

**B.**  1.  Synod of Bishops, 1971: "Anyone who ventures to speak to people about justice must first be just in their eyes."
  2.  NCCB pastoral letter "Economic Justice for All": in paragraphs 347–358 of the pastoral the bishops speak of "the Church as an economic actor" and they reiterate the Synod's teaching that the Church's own life and action must reflect the justice it preaches. The bishops stressed that "all the moral principles that govern the just operation of any economic endeavor apply to the Church and its agencies and institutions; indeed the Church should be exemplary."

## 22. Laity—Participation in the Church

**A.**  1.  Catholic Action or the Lay Apostolate was described as the "participation of the laity in the apostolate of the hierarchy."

2. Pius X in *Pascendi* 1907 stated, "Note here venerable brethren the appearance of that most pernicious doctrine which would make the laity a factor of progression in the Church."

3. Bishop Kenrick said, "It is about time we teach the laity not to interfere in the affairs of the Church."

**B.** 1. Second Vatican Council spoke of the people of God, clergy and laity, regarded in their radical equality as baptized members of the church. All people are called to participate in the life and mission of the church, not by permission of the bishop but by their baptism and confirmation.

2. All members of the church are called to teach as well as to learn. All are called to participate in worship. All are called to be witnesses and disciples.

3. All are members of the Body of Christ, gifted by the Spirit and called to participate in the mission of the church.

## 23. Local Church

**A.** 1. During the 18th and 19th centuries there was a great stress on the church as a perfect society. It stressed the importance of the universal Church and the authority of the Holy Father. "Perfect-society ecclesiology fostered a universalist ecclesiology that left little room for theology of the local Church, stressing as it did papal power and the privileged role of the universal Church. Dioceses are not perfect societies because they do not possess the fullness of legislative, judicial, and coercive power. This universalist view resulted in other ecclesiological formulations: the universal Church is the source of the local Churches; Bishops receive their authority from the Pope; uniformity is the ideal and diversity the exception. Centralization and monarchical governance became normative, and the entire Church was looked upon as one large diocese with the Pope as Bishop" (Patrick Granfield, *The Limits of the Papacy*, p. 110).

**B.** 1. Second Vatican Council rediscovered the importance of the local Church. The universal Church is the sum and communion of the local Churches.

2. Vatican II said: "The Church of Christ is truly present in all legitimate congregations of the faithful, which, united with their pastors are themselves called churches in the New Testament." Bishops, said the council fathers, are not to be regarded as "vic-

ars of the Roman pontiff" for they exercise an authority which is proper to them . . . "their power, therefore, is not destroyed by papal power. On the contrary, it is affirmed, strengthened, and vindicated thereby."

## 24. Marriage—Definition of

**A.** 1.  "Marriage is essentially a contract . . . in which the spouses gave rights over their bodies to each other at the wedding and sealed the union indissolubly with the first act of sexual intercourse" (cited by Jack Dominion, *The Tablet*, 16 January 1988).
  2.  Pius IX

**B.** 1.  "The intimate partnership of married life and love has been established by the creator and qualified by His laws. It is rooted in the conjugal covenant of irrevocable personal consent. Hence, by that human act whereby spouses mutually bestow and accept each other, a relationship arises which by divine will and in the eyes of society too is a lasting one" (*GS* 48).

## 25. Membership in the Church

**A.** 1.  Pius XII, *Mystici Corporis,* 1943: "Those who are divided in faith (Protestant) or government (Orthodox) cannot be living in the one body such as this, and cannot be living the life of its one divine spirit" (Denzinger-Schönmetzer, 3802) He excluded from unity of the Body of Christ both Protestant and Eastern Churches—but discussion continued.
  2.  Pius XII referred to this in *Humani Generis,* n. 27, reproving those who still thought this an open question.

**B.** 1.  Vatican II Decree on Ecumenism (*UR* 3).
  2.  "subsists": Church of Christ subsists in the Catholic Church (*LG* 8).
  3.  First draft of *Catechism*—"Church of Jesus Christ is the Catholic Church" (par. 1736; changed translations).
  4.  Feeney excommunicated for holding literally to "outside the church no salvation."

## 26. Modernism

**A.** 1.  Pius X condemned modernism in 1907, *Lamentabili* and *Pascendi.* Modernism was an effort to adapt Catholic doctrine to the intellectual, moral, and social needs of the new century.

The condemnation of modernism affected the American Church for over fifty years, stifling Catholic intellectual life.

2.  Modernism was described as "all systems of thought by whatever name which expounded an evolutionary theory of religion or suggested that the Church had reshaped eternal truths in every period of history according to its understanding or otherwise threatened the validity and stability of dogma."

3.  *Pascendi* specifically forbade meetings of priests, for these had been "among the means used by the modernists to propagate their opinions." The encyclical also commanded bishops to establish vigilance committees.

**B.** 1.  Benedict XV made it clear from his first encyclical, *Ad Beatissimi*, that his main aim was to put a stop to the anti-modernist campaign his predecessor Pius X had encouraged.

2.  Most of the condemnations of the modernist period were dropped during Vatican Council II.

## 27. Moses—Author of the Pentateuch

**A.** 1.  Multiple authorship condemned in 1907 by Pius X, *Pascendi*, n. 34.

2.  Fr. Henry A. Poels—Dutch Old Testament scholar at Catholic University—removed for doubting it.

3.  Biblical Commission—in early decades of 20th century—unduly restrictive.

**B.** 1.  Pius XII eased the restrictions.

2.  John Paul II spoke of the Yahwist in a recent talk. If he had said that in 1910 he would have been removed.

## 28. Religious Freedom

**A.** 1.  At time of Augustine, it is considered virtuous for bishops to invoke imperial force to compel heretics to return to the church.

2.  St. Thomas—It is a doctrine that a relapsed heretic will be judged by the ecclesiastical authorities and remanded to the secular authorities for execution (*Summa Theologiae* II-II. 11. 4, ad 1).

   a)  Universally taught (Lucius III, *Ad abolendum* and Gregory IX, *Decretales* Greg IX 5.7.9). The duty of a good ruler was to extirpate not only heresy but heretics.

   b)  Thesis—ideal—state should be the physical guarantor of

orthodoxy; hypothesis—tolerance for the lesser evil—it is
for the common good to refrain from religious persecution.

3. For over 1200 years, popes, bishops, theologians regularly and
unanimously denied religious liberty to heretics.

4. Gregory XVI in 1832 condemned the "absurd and erroneous
opinion or rather madness claiming that freedom of conscience
is to be asserted and vindicated for everyone."

**B.** 1. Leo XIII—obligations binding on Catholic rulers of Catholic
nations to suppress Protestant evangelism; condemned it as
"contrary to Sacred Scripture and tradition."

2. John XXIII, *Pacem in Terris.*

3. Vatican II's Declaration on Religious Liberty (October 25,
1965, voted; December 7 promulgated) claims freedom to believe is a sacred human right.

a) It is founded on the rights of the human person.

b) It is taught by revelation.

c) Each human being is the possessor of a precious human
right to believe and to practice in accordance to belief.

d) State's interference with conscience is denounced.

e) The act of faith is a free act.

f) Archbishop Lefebvre denounced this.

g) The Council reversed the teaching of the ordinary papal
magisterium.

## 29. Revelation

**A.** 1. *Humani Generis* adopted the opinion of J. B. Franzelin that revelation was given to the apostles and to the bishops rather than
to the church.

2. The first draft of Vatican II's document on divine revelation was
called "The Double Source of Revelation." The text said, "Tradition preserved in the Church in continuous succession by the
Holy Spirit contains all those matters of faith and morals which
the apostles received either from the lips of Christ or at the
suggestion of the Holy Spirit, and which they passed on as it
were from hand to hand so that they might be transmitted by
the teaching of the Church."

**B.** 1. The notion that revelation was given to the apostles and to the
bishops rather than to the church was dropped in *Dei Verbum* of
Vatican II.

2.  *DV* speaks of revelation as the acts and words that God uses to reveal the hidden mysteries of the divinity. *The Catechism of the Catholic Church* (quoting *DV*) says that the divine plan of revelation is realized simultaneously "by deeds and words which are intrinsically bound up with each other" and shed light on each other. God communicates himself to man gradually. He prepares him to welcome by stages the supernatural revelation that is to culminate in the person and mission of the incarnate word, Jesus Christ (*Catechism*, par. 53).

## 30. Sacramental Theology

**A.** 1.  There was no agreement on the number of sacraments until the 13th century when the church set the number at seven.

**B.** 1.  "There are also many other questions which must be regarded today as open in sacramental theology and which have no prospect of finding a real and convincing answer, if we only appeal to 'Denzinger' or other explicit declarations of the magisterium in the past. On the one hand, we must form a truly historically convincing idea of the meaning of the statement that (or how?) the sacraments have their origin from Jesus (instituted by him) and on the other hand we must consider what is the connection of the individual sacraments with the nature of the church as 'basic sacrament' of salvation. Only in this way can we hope at the present time to find a plain answer, for example to the question of who can be a recipient of the sacrament of Holy Orders (a woman?), what sacramental signs may perhaps be sufficient in extraordinary cases, how the one sacrament of Holy Orders may possibly be differentiated into individual sacramental functions (differing in character and grade), etc." (Rahner, *Theological Investigations,* vol. 18, p. 19).

## 31. Salvation

**A.** 1  Anselm explained the salvific work of Christ looking solely at his death, interpreting the crucifixion as satisfaction vicariously offered to God for human sin.

**B.** 1.  "Those also can attain salvation who through no fault of their own do not know the Gospel of Christ or His Church, yet sincerely seek God and, moved by grace, strive by their deeds to do his will as it is known to them through the dictates of conscience" (Vatican II, *LG* 16).

## 32. Sexuality

**A.** 1. Husbands and wives should refrain from sexual relations before going to Holy Communion—*Roman Catechism.*
   2. Unclean.
   3. No light matter in sexual sins. All thoughts, desires, words, actions are mortally sinful.
   4. Catechism of Council of Trent speaks of "the value of occasional abstinence from the marital act": "Following the pious traditions of our fathers, married persons could observe this abstinence, particularly for three days prior to their receiving Holy Communion, and also for the duration of the Lenten fast" *Roman Catechism*, Part 2, the Sacraments, 7 Matrimony, no. 34).

**B.** 1. Sexual pleasure is a good: *Catechism of the Catholic Church* (par. 2362).
   2. Vatican II, *GS* 49: marital actions are noble and worthy ones—signify and promote that mutual self-giving by which spouses enrich each other with a joyful and thankful will.

## 33. Slavery

**A.** 1. "It was Catholic moral teaching that slaves should be treated humanely and that it was good to give slaves freedom . . . but Catholic moral doctrine considered the institution of slavery acceptable" (Noonan, "Development in Moral Theology," *Theological Studies*, 1993, 665).
   2. Paul accepted it—Philemon 11-19.
   3. Popes Alexander III, Innocent III, Leo X, Paul III, and the Third Lateran Council accepted it.
   4. 1839 Gregory XVI condemned the slave trade (Noonan, 666).
   5. 1849 Pius IX—The Catholic Church "teaches slaves to remain true to their masters, not as much from the compulsion of their state as from delight in duty" (quoting St. Augustine).
   6. 1866 Holy Office—"Slavery itself, considered in its essential nature, is not at all contrary to the natural and divine law, and there can be several just titles of slavery."

**B.**  1.  "Whatever is opposed to life itself . . . whatever insults human dignity such as . . . slavery . . . all these things and others of their like are infamies indeed" (*GS* 27; see also *GS* 19).

## 34. Social Teaching

**A.**  1.  From the 6th century onward popes were temporal as well as spiritual rulers. The Papal States came into existence to fill the power vacuum in the West. They lasted for more than a thousand years. At the height of the medieval period in the 1320s Pope John XXII was the richest monarch in Europe. He grew rich on the sale of benefices. He condemned the Franciscan view that "Jesus and his disciples held everything in common." Any talk of social doctrine in such a period would have been laughable.

   2.  Pius IX, the last temporal ruler of the Papal States, dismissed socialism, communism, democracy and all other forms of modernity as a threat to the Church.

**B.**  1.  After the loss of the Papal States, the popes began to address social problems. The first social encyclical, *Rerum Novarum,* appeared in 1891. It defended private property and the rights of workers to form unions.

   2.  Catholic social teaching has expanded and progressed during the 100 years since 1891.

   3.  John XXIII stressed the defense of human rights.

   4.  Paul VI in *Populorum Progressio* in 1967 said that the north-south divide was more threatening than the east-west divide. He spoke of development as the new name for peace.

## 35. Teaching Role of Bishops

**A.**  1.  Jesus revealed the hidden mysteries to the Church: Jesus gave the teachings to the Apostles who handed them on to the Bishops (Deposit).

   2.  Propositions—static.

**B.**  1.  Vatican II: Teaching office of the shepherds, like that of the whole church, stands under the word of God (*Dei Verbum*).

   2.  Jesus gave the teachings to the disciples and to the whole church—the apostles and bishops have a special role within the church.

   3.  *Communio fidelium* is not just a passive role.

## 36. Women

**A.**  1.  Temptress
    2.  Inferior
    3.  Unclean
    4.  Out of the sanctuary
    5.  Acceptance of sexism

**B.**  1.  Vatican II—discrimination based on sex is to be condemned—all are equal.
    2.  Bishops—sexism is a sin.

## 37. Worship—Changes

**A.**  1.  There was a centuries-long ban on missals for the laity.
    2.  The Chinese were forced to have only the Latin language and also Western rites and customs as a condition for Catholicity.

**B.**  1.  The ban on the use of missals for the laity was removed by Leo XIII in 1897.

## II. TEACHINGS THAT COULD CHANGE

1. Anglican Orders
2. Birth Control
3. Capital Punishment
4. Celibacy of the Clergy
5. Communion for Divorced and Remarried
6. Deterrence—Nuclear Weapons
7. General Absolution
8. Homosexuality
9. Intercommunion
10. Internal Forum Solution for People in Second Marriages
11. Just War
12. Mandate (canonical) for Theologians
13. Ordination of Women to the Diaconate
14. Orthodox—Reunion with
15. Patriarchy

*Key*:
**Teaching**
**A.**  Description and Source
**B.**  Teaching as changed, developed, expressed differently, or denied

### 1. Anglican Orders

**A.**  1.  *Apostolicae Curae,* 1896—Leo XIII—"on our authority and initiative with certain knowledge" that "ordinations performed with the Anglican rite have been and are absolutely null and utterly void." The letter "is and shall be always valued and in force."
   a)  intention
   b)  succession

**B.**  1.  Ordination services currently in use should be reexamined. Use of "Old Catholic" bishops as consecrators.
   2.  Some are now re-ordained conditionally.

### 2. Birth Control

**A.**  1.  "Any use whatsoever of matrimony exercised in such a way that the act is deliberately frustrated in its natural power to generate life is an offense against the law of God and of nature and those who indulge in such are branded with the guilt of grave sin." Pius XI, 1930, *Casti Connubii*.

2. "This prescription [of Pius XI] holds good today just as much as it did yesterday. It will hold tomorrow and always, for it is not a mere precept of human right but the expression of a natural and divine law." *Allocution to Midwives*, Pius XII, 1951. However, rhythm is acceptable.

3. "The Church, calling men back to the observance of the norms of natural law as interpreted by their constant doctrine, teaches that each and every marriage act must remain open to the transmission of life." *Humanae Vitae*.

**B.** 1. The Birth Control Commission established by Pope Paul VI overwhelmingly suggested reversing the decision of his predecessors.

2. Suenens: not another Galileo case.

3. Numerous bishops' conferences around the world accepted the encyclical of Paul VI as authoritative teaching. However, many of these conferences drew attention to the primacy of conscience. For example, the American Bishops said, "The encyclical does not undertake to judge the consciences of individuals but to set forth the authentic teaching of the Church which Catholics believe interprets the divine law to which conscience should be conformed . . . married couples faced with conflicting duties are often caught in agonizing crises of conscience. For example, at times it proves difficult to harmonize the sexual expression of conjugal love with respect for the life-giving power of sexual union and the demands of responsible parenthood. Pope Paul's encyclical and the commentaries of the international episcopates on it are sensitive as are we to these painful situations." NCCB, "Human Life in Our Day," 1968, pp. 41, 43.

## 3. Capital Punishment

**A.** 1. For many centuries the church has taught that it is lawful for the state to take the life of a criminal in certain instances.

**B.** 1. There is a growing consensus that the death penalty is not just. It fuels vengeance, diverts from forgiveness, greatly diminishes respect for all life, and is an affront to human dignity.

2. The *Catechism of the Catholic Church* states that since the taking of a life must be the last and only available way to carry out a legitimate need of the state, the death penalty can rarely, if ever, be morally justified.

3. Capital Punishment—"The nature and extent of the punishment must be carefully evaluated and decided upon, and not to go to the extreme of executing the offender except in cases of absolute necessity... today, however... such cases are very rare, if not practically nonexistent." Paragraph 56, *Evangelium Vitae*, John Paul II, March 25, 1995. Ratzinger said the *Catechism* would have to be revised.

## 4. Celibacy of the Clergy (practice)

**A.** 1. Early church priests married.
2. Fourth and fifth centuries—daily Mass—sexual intercourse considered unholy and defiling.
3. Benedict VIII (1012–1024)—11th century—celibacy as a discipline without exception—Gregory VII
4. Lateran Council (1123).

**B.** 1. Married priests in Czech Republic.
2. Could be changed by papal directives.
3. More concern about celibacy than about Eucharist.

## 5. Communion for Divorced and Remarried

**A.** 1. Forbidden by Ratzinger—"Universal magisterium"—indissolubility of marriage: receiving communion while objectively in a state of sin—not able to image union of bishop and the church.

**B.** 1. Three bishops of Germany—Karl Lehmann, Oskar Saier, Walter Kasper—invited people in second marriages to receive; three conditions (1) time of sorrow and healing; (2) confessor or spiritual director involved; (3) their conscience is clear. Bishop Spital of Trier gave his priests permission to do it.

## 6. Deterrence—Nuclear Weapons

**A.** 1. Accepted as part of the right of a nation to self-defense.

**B.** 1. 1982, John Paul II to UN "in current conditions 'deterrence' based on balance certainly not as an end in itself but as a stage on the way towards a progressive disarmament, may still be morally acceptable" (Consequentialism or proportionalism).

2. 1983 NCCB Pastoral on Peace: accepted it—as long as progress was being made

3. Others—wrong to destroy cities—wrong to threaten to destroy —possession and manufacture is wrong.

## 7. General Absolution

**A.** 1. Rome against its use.

**B.** 1. Allowed in extraordinary circumstances—war, ship sinking.
2. New Rite of Penance gives three forms. Form three (general absolution) has conditions.
3. There are many ways to be reconciled with God.

## 8. Homosexuality

**A.** 1. "Objectively disordered"—1986 Congregation for the Doctrine of the Faith
2. Okay to discriminate.

**B.** 1. Gumbleton—conscience.
2. Evidence that people are born disposed to homosexuality. What does God expect?
3. Seminary—crisis of faith.

## 9. Intercommunion

**A.** 1. Forbidden—except in rare cases and with conditions.

**B.** 1. Vatican II Decree on Ecumenism called for prayer together.
2. Communion as a sign and as a cause of unity. Faith in the Eucharist, not just social acceptance, reward, or food.

## 10. Internal Forum Solution for People in Second Marriages

**A.** 1. Forbidden.

**B.** 1. Possible (a) evidence that first marriage is invalid, but cannot be proved; (b) first marriage is broken; (c) repentance; (d) stable and enduring now; (e) scandal.
2. Follow authors.

## 11. Just War

**A.** 1.  Conditions necessary for just war.

**B.** 1.  With total war: proportionate and discriminate not possible; no such thing as just war possible today. Modern war is always immoral except in strict case of self-defense.

## 12. Mandate (canonical) for Theologians

**A.** 1.  Canon law—efforts being made to make it tougher "Ex Corde Ecclesiae."

**B.** 1.  Discussion by U.S. bishops and university leaders to work out a *modus operandi*.

## 13. Ordination of Women to the Diaconate

**A.** 1.  Not allowed.

**B.** 1.  Possibility that it was done in the past.
2.  Women deacons mentioned in New Testament.
3.  Every year I asked for its study—six years 1973–1979—told to shut up.

## 14. Orthodox—Reunion with

**A.** 1.  Divided since 1054—political causes.

**B.** 1.  No real doctrinal differences—except for role of papacy.
2.  Can we go back to first millennium?
3.  Can we tolerate differences?

## 15. Patriarchy

**A.** 1.  Looked upon by Roman Curia as essential.

**B.** 1.  It is sinful.

# Bishop Raymond A. Lucker:
# Some markers of a life

February 24, 1927

Born in St. Paul, Minn., the third in a family of six children

June 7, 1952

Ordained a priest of the Archdiocese of St. Paul

1952–1958

Assistant director of the Archdiocesan Office of the Confraternity of Christian Doctrine (1958–1964—director of the same office)

1957–1968

Professor of Catechetics at the St. Paul Seminary

1964–1966

Doctoral student in theology at the University of St. Thomas in Rome. (He arrived in Rome on September 11, 1964. Vatican II's Dogmatic Constitution on the Church was promulgated on November 21, 1964.)

1966

Received a Doctorate of Sacred Theology from the University of St. Thomas of Rome

1966–1969

Assistant superintendent and then superintendent of schools for the Archdiocese of St. Paul and Minneapolis

1969

Received a Ph.D. in education from the University of Minnesota

1969–1971

Director of the Department of Christian Formation of the United States Catholic Conference

September 5, 1971
>
> Ordained auxiliary bishop of the Archdiocese of St. Paul and Minneapolis

1971–1974
>
> Auxiliary bishop and pastor of St. Austin's Church, Minneapolis

1974–1976
>
> Auxiliary bishop and pastor of the Church of the Assumption of Mary, St. Paul; during this time he also served as director of the Liturgy Office for the archdiocese

December 30, 1975
>
> Appointed Bishop of the Diocese of New Ulm, Minnesota

February 19, 1976
>
> Installed as Bishop of New Ulm, where he served the diocese for twenty-five years

May 23, 1993
>
> Honorary Doctorate of Humane Letters, *Honoris Causa,* College of St. Catherine, St. Paul, Minn.

November 17, 2000
>
> Retired as Bishop of New Ulm upon being diagnosed with malignant melanoma

September 19, 2001
>
> Died at Our Lady of Good Counsel Cancer Home, St. Paul, Minn., in the care of the Hawthorne Dominican Sisters and their staff of nurses and care-givers

Bishop Lucker's episcopal motto:
*"Lord, I do believe. But help my lack of trust"(Mk 9:24).*

# A view into the life of Bishop Raymond A. Lucker

JOHN M. MALONE

Raymond A. Lucker, one of six children, was born February 24, 1927, to Josephine Schiltgen, a farm girl, and Alphonse Lucker, a railroad worker. Together they raised their family in a working-class neighborhood. Farm issues and rights of workers would always be important to Ray Lucker.

As a young priest, ordained on June 7, 1952, to serve the St. Paul-Minneapolis area, Fr. Lucker was the assistant director and later director of the archdiocesan office of the Confraternity of Christian Doctrine. He later was also superintendent of schools for the archdiocese.

Graduate studies brought Fr. Lucker to Rome during the Second Vatican Council. Not only the content of the conciliar deliberations, but equally the spirit of the Council filled his being. In addition to earning an S.T.D. from the University of St. Thomas in Rome (the "Angelicum"), Fr. Lucker received a Ph.D. in Education from the University of Minnesota. These degrees equipped him to serve as director of the Department of Christian Formation of the United States Catholic Conference from 1969 to 1971.

Raymond Lucker, ordained auxiliary bishop of the Archdiocese of St. Paul and Minneapolis, served as pastor of St. Austin's Church, Minneapolis, and later as pastor of Assumption Church, in St. Paul.

Pope Paul VI appointed Raymond Lucker Bishop of the Diocese of New Ulm, Minnesota, on December 30, 1975. While serving this rural diocese, Bishop Lucker was an advocate for the family farm and for stewardship of the environment. He preached the gospel in its pristine simplicity.

Following his retirement in November of 2000, after having been diagnosed with malignant melanoma, Bishop Lucker was recognized for his contributions by two groups. First, the Catholic Theological Society honored him for a life dedicated to bridging the realms of academic

theology and pastoral practice. Bishop Lucker had been a regular at-
tendee and a frequent presenter at Society meetings over three decades.
Pax Christi USA awarded its highest honor, the Ambassador of Peace
Award, to Bishop Lucker two months before his death.

That award was given in a small ceremony at Our Lady of Good
Counsel Cancer Home in St. Paul, Minn. Bishop Lucker had moved to
the cancer home from the retirement home for priests, also in St. Paul,
in July, 2001. He was cared for there by the "Hawthorne" Dominican
Sisters. These nuns, whose motherhouse is in Hawthorne, New York,
have as their full name: "The Servants of Relief for Incurable Cancer."
They, along with their lay nurse and care associates, cared for Bishop
Lucker up to his death on the morning of September 19, 2001. While
Bishop Lucker was at Our Lady of Good Counsel he often observed,
"I'm just lying here enjoying how much God loves me."

Bishop Lucker served his church best as a good shepherd, one who
understood himself to be an educator into the marvel of the simplicity
of the mystery of God living among his people.

# List of contributors

J. Michael Byron is assistant professor of dogmatic/systematic theology at the St. Paul Seminary School of Divinity, University of St. Thomas. He is a priest of the Archdiocese of St. Paul and Minneapolis.

Russell B. Connors, Jr., is associate professor of theology and chair of the theology department at the College of St. Catherine.

Catherine Cory is assistant professor of theology and director of the masters of arts in theology program at the University of St. Thomas.

Paul Feela is director of worship and instructor in sacraments and liturgy, St. Paul Seminary School of Divinity, University of St. Thomas. He is a priest of the Archdiocese of St. Paul and Minneapolis.

Chris A. Franke is professor of theology at the College of St. Catherine.

J. Michael Joncas is associate professor of theology and of Catholic Studies at the University of St. Thomas. He is a priest of the Archdiocese of St. Paul and Minneapolis.

Shawn Madigan, C.S.J., is professor of theology and director of the masters of arts in theology program at the College of St. Catherine.

John M. Malone is a priest of the Archdiocese of St. Paul and Minneapolis and pastor of Assumption Catholic Church in St. Paul.

William McDonough is assistant professor of theology at the College of St. Catherine.

Catherine Michaud, C.S.J., is assistant professor of theology at the College of St. Catherine.

Amata Miller, I.H.M., is visiting professor of economics at the College of St. Catherine. She is also social justice scholar-in-residence there.

Terence Nichols is associate professor of theology and chair of the undergraduate theology department at the University of St. Thomas.

Corrine Patton is associate professor of theology at the University of St. Thomas.

Vincent T. M. Skemp is assistant professor of theology at the College of St. Catherine.

Paul J. Wojda is assistant professor of theology at the University of St. Thomas.

Susan K. Wood, S.C.L., is professor of theology and associate dean of the School of Theology.Seminary, St. John's University, Collegeville, Minnesota.

# Index